ORANGE TAILS
& VAPOUR TRAILS

WIND IN THE WIRES TO GLASS COCKPITS, A PILOT REMEMBERS

PAUL LIEBRECHT

First published by Paul Liebrecht, 2020
Copyright © 2020 by Paul Liebrecht

978-0-620-90003-4(print)
978-0-620-90004-1(e-pub)
978-0-620-90005-8(mobi)

Illustration, Cover Design and Typesetting: Gregg Davies Media
(www.greggdavies.com)

All rights reserved. The moral right of the author has been asserted. No part of this publication may be reproduced, distributed, or transmitted in any form or by any means, including photocopying, recording, or other electronic or mechanical methods, without the prior written permission of the author, except in the case of brief quotations embodied in critical reviews and certain other non-commercial uses permitted by copyright law.

CONTENTS

Introduction	ix
Wind in the Wires to Glass Cockpits, a Pilot Remembers	1
1. The Early Years	3
2. LEARNING TO FLY	6
Frank Lister's Flying School	7
The Red Baron Syndrome	8
The Forced Landing	9
Mealies and Mayhem	12
The Okavango Swamps and Crocodile Camp	16
Willie, Wheels Ups and Pretty Girls	20
3. SOUTH WEST AFRICA	23
(Namibia)	
The Namib Desert Mines	25
Otjiwarongo	28
Outjo	29
Gobabis and the Love of my Life	29
Illicit Diamonds and Entrapment	31
Down in the Atlantic and Locked Up	33
The Sewage Farm	35
Mercy Flights, Body Bags and Vocal Corpses	36
4. ALL GOOD THINGS COME TO AN END	39
SAA acceptance testing	39
Chief Cook and Bottle Washer	41
The Kavango	42
5. THE BOY PILOT	46
Captain Mumbles	47
Lost in Lisbon	48
The Aural Invisibility Syndrome (1)	49

6. VISCOUNT DAYS	53
Ground Controlled Approaches	54
The Dying Fleet	55
7. The Hijack	59
8. LIFE AS A FLUFFY COPILOT	77
The Spoories Sick Fund	77
Jokes Aside	80
The Well Done Steak	83
The Wonderful old 'Queen of the Skies'	87
9. RIO	91
The Perils of the Copacabana	93
Crooks with Hooks	95
Creeping Liquor and Other Delights	97
Corcovado Experience	98
Pretty Hostesses and Scary Rats	100
Breaking the Casino	103
The Aural Invisibility Syndrome (2)	105
10. Robert, Blackie and Ava	107
11. SANCTIONS BUSTING 707 OPERATIONS	112
Paris	113
Instant Justice	115
Pissing off the French	116
12. THE JUMBO JET	120
Big Mary and the Baby	121
The Breakfast Lights	122
Sal Island	124
13. AT LAST! FOUR GOLD BARS AND A COMMAND	127
The 'Captains Course' and 'VIP lunch'	128
14. THE DECENTRALISATION SAGA	131
The Rebel Tours	132
The Move	133
A Couple, Seven Dogs and a Mini	135
Mickey	136
The Hunt	138

The Cape to Rio Yacht Race	142
The Sword of Damocles	145
15. OPERATION RESCUE	147
The Small Misunderstanding	149
The 'Cape Doctor' Arrives Unexpectedly	150
A Cascade of Technicolour Yawns	152
Rescued at Last, but no Lobster Lunch	156
16. BLOWN AWAY	158
BMP	160
Camaro	162
The Hurricane	164
Damp Squib	168
The Flight Home	169
Smoke and Mirrors	171
17. SECURITY?	175
The Tall Poppy Syndrome	176
The 3 : 1 : 1 Rule	179
The Hijack that Ended in a Fatal Ditching	180
9/11 and Political Correctness	182
Perth Irony	183
Who's Protection is Prioritised?	184
18. LOVE, LUST AND FLOATING TROPHIES	186
The Lotharios	186
Senior Captains and their Late Midlife Crises	187
The Floating Trophys	188
19. Glass Cockpits and Other Delights	190
20. DANGEROUS TIMES	193
The downing of the Air Rhodesia Viscounts	193
The Deafening Silence	194
Anti Missile Manoeuvres	195
Luanda and the Brigadier	196
Tramp Operations	198
The Hell Run	198
Deaf Ears	201
A Brutal Tragedy	203

21. THE SLIPPERY SLOPE	206
The Start of the Rot	207
To Hell with SAA's Proud History!	209
SAA's New History as seen by Andrews	210
The American Invasion	210
The Andrews's Wild West Show	211
Andrews and the Pilots	213
From First Officer to Vice President in One Giant Leap	215
The Hamburger Man, The Gambler and The Schoolmarm	217
R232,000,000 Down Jackson Hole	220
The Ever Steepening Slippery Slope	223
22. Career's End	226

INTRODUCTION

I think that a sure indication that one is aging is the realisation that one spends less time thinking of the future and more time thinking about the past. Of late this is something I find myself guilty of, possibly due to the fact that during a long career involved in aviation, I experienced some quite colourful, interesting, unusual and sometimes terrifying events.

I am sure that most old pilots have amazing stories to tell but, surprisingly, very few commit their stories to paper. Of the many hundreds of pilots that have flown for South African Airways since its inauguration in 1934, I am aware of only one that has attempted a book and that was a rather simplistic regurgitation of oft repeated stories that could be described as 'airline urban legends'.

As such, with much encouragement from SAA colleagues, I decided to attempt to write of the kaleidoscope of amusing, colourful, sometimes terrifying but always interesting incidents and stories that speckled my forty year career in aviation.

After much thought I decided to use Orange Tails in the title for the simple reason that seventy five percent of my time with SAA was spent in the shadow of the orange tail livery. These orange tails were so distinctive that any South African arriving at a foreign airport and catching sight of them would feel a tug on his heartstrings, knowing that little part of South Africa would be the chariot soon to carry them home.

As beautiful as the new livery is, it tends to blend in with all the other modern liveries and worse, I cannot help but associate the beginning of the demise of SAA with its introduction. On a lighter note, it was hard to resist the word play on 'tales'.

WIND IN THE WIRES TO GLASS COCKPITS, A PILOT REMEMBERS

The approach was into Johannesburg, Highveld thunderstorms were all around the airfield. Rain and hail were pelting the aircraft, it sounded like being inside a kettle drum, in addition visibility was marginal. We had earlier in the flight suffered an hydraulic failure and the controls were heavy and unresponsive under my hands. Lightning flashed, further reducing visibility, and air traffic control warned of wind shear below five hundred feet and poor braking action on the runway due to standing water.

I glanced across the cockpit at my co-pilot who was gazing frozenly through the haze with perspiration visibly beading on his forehead when, as we encountered the predicted violent wind shear, the number one engine flamed out and died.

Now under normal circumstances this chain of events would have had any pilot's heart racing and adrenalin surging through their veins but for the first time in my flying career none of these symptoms of stress were present. Why? Well for starters we were in a simulator but that by no means explains why I was free of the stress that my co-pilot was obviously feeling. Failing to cope with the situation in an aircraft would threaten life, in a simulator it could initiate a chain of events that would threaten a pilot's livelihood.

It was the stress generated by the knowledge of this that caused pilots to hate the bi- annual simulator rating renewals. Many pilots suffered from the equivalent of 'exam nerves' which did nothing to enhance their performances. Despite having gone through over sixty of these 'simulator torture sessions' without ever failing one I was, in the normal course of events, not immune to these stresses.

This session, however, did not fall into the category of the normal course of events, as it was my last licence renewal prior to retirement and, even if I had completely mucked it up, there would have been no repercussions. The airline would not have been willing to spend money on additional training for someone about to retire and time would not allow the procedures for any other line of action to be carried out. Thus my last simulator session was the first stress free and the most enjoyable of my career.

For a while after my retirement I would have a recurring dream of this session and I think this dream sparked my looking back through the years to the start of my passion for flying and flying machines.

1

THE EARLY YEARS

My mother Millicent, brother Tony and I lived in then little village of Somerset West on the edge of the Cape Winelands. Our home was under the flight path from the approach beacon at Sir Lowrys Pass (Sierra Papa) to the then DF Malan Airport which was Cape Town's main airport. I knew the time of every SAA arrival and departure that would fly via Sierra Papa and when not at school would lie on my back in the long grass of the huge empty field that our home backed onto and wait for the DC4 Skymasters with their four thundering Pratt & Whitney fourteen cylinder radial engines to pass over. Later it was the Viscount 813 with its screaming Rolls Royce Dart turbines and a rare treat, the occasional DC7B or, better still, a Lockheed Constellation with its beautiful dolphin shaped fuselage and triple rudders.

Back then there were many more airfields scattered around the area. The airfield at Eerste Rivier doubled as a motor racing track several times a year and with friends I would hitch-hike there for the double treat of seeing racing cars and aeroplanes. A De Havilland Dragon Rapide biplane would be taking people for flips between races and although we never had money to pay for one, just watching the take-offs and landings were more than enough for us. On one occasion a wealthy businessman arrived in a twin engined Piper Aztec. Despite it being rather ugly by today's standards, we thought it was the pinnacle of streamlined beauty and aviation technology, which I guess it was alongside the Rapide.

On the odd occasion when Mom would brave the trip to Cape Town in our old Citroën Traction Avant, much begging and pleading would eventually result in her routing via Youngsfield air force base where we could watch the South African Air Force pilots practising take-offs and landings in the Harvard trainers. There was even an airstrip between Strand and Gordon's Bay which, while not very active, was within easy range of our bicycles. Sadly none of these airfields exist today.

I suppose it was pretty natural that as I approached the end of my school years I would apply to the South African Air Force for pilot training. Unfortunately for me things went horribly awry when I had a motorcycle accident and injured my knee so badly that at one stage amputation was discussed. Thanks to the dedication of local medics at the Hottentots Holland Hospital and their 'let's give it a go attitude', I was spared this fate. During the six months I spent in the hospital the SAAF contacted my mother and she had to inform them of my situation.

A few weeks later a SAAF appointed orthopaedic specialist by the name of Dr Hayward arrived at the hospital to examine me. He was a rather taciturn individual and offered me no comment on his conclusions but a month later a letter from the SAAF arrived informing me that on the grounds of a medical disability that they considered permanent, my pilot training application was rejected. My time in hospital was, however, not wasted as I was able to write my matric exam with an invigilator, kindly supplied by the Education Department, by my bedside.

Oddly I also learned to knit, as the sweetest of old ladies would regularly visit and supply balls of salvaged wool and knitting needles to enable the patients to knit squares for quilts. The squares would later be collected, sewn together and distributed in Somerset West's poorer communities. The old dears would patiently teach anyone who volunteered for this activity to knit. As I was the only occupant of the male ward to volunteer, I also learned how to handle the resultant good natured mockery from my fellow patients who dubbed me 'Granny Paul'.

After leaving hospital I was fortunate to obtain a position as a guide on the famous Highgate Ostrich Show Farm in Oudtshoorn. On my days off I often stood in as a guide at the Cango Caves taking parties of tourists through the world renowned caves. Due to this I was privileged to see Cango II which even now is not open to the public despite Cango III, IV and V having been discovered. It was a wonderful experience and to this day the Little Karoo remains my favourite place in all the world.

What with the outdoor activities and healthy air of the Karoo, my leg soon recovered and gained strength. Enjoyable as it was, I could see no real future in what I was doing and aviation had by no means lost its fascination for me, so always having had a technical bent, I decided to do the next best thing to flying and apply to SAA for an apprenticeship in aircraft engineering. My application was successful and, with a heavy heart, I left home and the beautiful Cape to board the train for Johannesburg.

My introduction to the apprenticeship was spending six months in Sam Small's filing school which occupied a vast area inside SAA's Technical School. These six months were spent with a file in one's hands shaping pieces of steel into all manner of tools and shapes designed to instil precision and working to fine tolerances into us. It also had the effect of causing those amongst us not super keen to become Aircraft Technicians to drop out. To this day, thanks to Sam Small's indoctrination, I am a demon with a file!

Fortunately, after six months of this penance, the course became infinitely more interesting as we learned to rig airframes, disassemble and reassemble the great rotary piston and jet aircraft engines. We also learned about the myriad systems that make up an airliner. These included electrical, hydraulic, air conditioning and pressurisation, flight controls, landing gear, braking, fire protection and instrument systems. We also learned aerodynamics, safety, redundancy and good workshop practice.

2

LEARNING TO FLY

Despite this, it did not take me long to realise that, although I loved the technical aspects of aircraft, my true passion would always be flying them. I think the major factor that brought about this epiphany was the fact that in the hanger adjacent to the Technical School or apprentice training hanger housed three retired SAA Lockheed Constellations. Every lunch break I would sneak into the hanger, eat my sandwiches and dream in the eerily quite atmosphere of the Connie's cockpit. I soon began to investigate the possibility of learning to fly, and to this end joined the Transvaal Aviation Club at Rand Airport in Germiston.

It did not take me long to come to the conclusion that the Club was not an ideal place for a cash-strapped apprentice, who wished to make a career out of flying, to pursue his goals. There were simply too many distractions. Too many members who were wealthy, flew as a hobby, or belonged to the Club solely for the cheap bar prices and the social side. It was simply too easy to get sucked into the Club social life and a night or two at the bar could cost one the price of an hour's flying.

FRANK LISTER'S FLYING SCHOOL

Rand Airport was a fascinating place back in the sixties. It was a general aviation airport and had more aircraft movements than any other airport in South Africa. It had a small terminal, a control tower and there were also aircraft sales organisations, maintenance companies, charter and aerial survey firms. Even regional airlines like Comair, now a major SA airline, were based there. Rand was like a box of chocolates to a young aviation enthusiast.

As I spent more time wandering around and exploring the wonders of Rand, I became aware of a small flying school, by the grand name of 'SA School of Flying'. It was operated from the Mobil fuel depot which was a little building painted, fairly subtlely by today's standards, in the Mobile corporate colours. Frank and Cecily Lister had the Mobile aviation fuel franchise at Rand and Frank operated his 'shoe string' flying school from the building.

Frank was the most generous and laid back character you could ever hope to meet, and he was a very experienced flying instructor, having been a Squadron Leader and A1 instructor in the RAF. During the war he had been sent out to take up duties training South African Air Force pilots, prior to them joining active squadrons overseas. After the war Frank and his family returned to England, but Africa had woven its spell and it was not long before they returned. After several visits to Frank's school , I knew this was so much more to my liking than the Transvaal Aviation Club. In May 1964 I had my first lesson with Frank in a Tiger Moth.

All the students were young and keen to make a career of flying. Practically all were short of cash, many were far from home. Mrs Lister was very motherly and treated all the students like family. We all affectionately called her Ma Lister, being all roughly the same age as the her son Mike.

Frank too treated his students like family. He was a friendly fellow who invariably wore a wide smile on his broad face.

He cared little about money, for him it was all about the love of flying. So many times I heard him say "Don't worry, just pay me when you can!" Many professional pilots, including airline pilots, went through Frank's generous 'fly now, pay later' operation. No interest was ever levied on the deferred payments and, to my knowledge, none of the student pilots ever abused Frank's generosity by not eventually settling his account. Frank would even give me flying credits in return for cleaning and performing servicing and minor maintenance on his aircraft. I would also perform duties refuelling the aircraft of his Mobil customers.

Frank had two Piper Cubs, which were later joined by a third, a Bolkow Junior and a Piper Cherokee 180. The school also had the use of a Tiger Moth, a Piper Cruiser and, of all things, a Persival Gull which was a British aircraft designed in 1932. The Cubs could be flown at R2.50 an hour, the Cruiser at R3.50 and the Cherokee was R4.50. R1 had to be added for dual instruction. At the time the exchange rate was R2 to the British pound. Seems awfully cheap by today's standards but as an apprentice aircraft technician at SAA, I was grossing the princely sum of R60 per month. The option of replacing a worn out pair of shoes or buying an hour or two of flying had to be weighed up very carefully.

THE RED BARON SYNDROME

Frank was the Chief Flying Instructor and his permanent instructor was a Hollander by the name of Keith. For the busier weekend periods Frank employed a number of part timers borrowed from the air force. These were all youngsters and great fun. As they were of similar age to the students, there was an extremely good rapport between them and ourselves. Unfortunately the same could not be said of our relationship with Keith who tended to be a bit impatient and grumpy so he was not terribly popular with the students.

One day Keith and I proceeded to the General Flying Area in a Tiger Moth with the intention of practising stall and spin recovery. Keith had a little affectation whereby, whenever he flew in the Tiger, he would wear a, much treasured, WW1 leather flying helmet and goggles. We would refer to this habit, but never in his presence, as 'Keith's Red Baron syndrome'.

It was a beautifully clear Highveld winter day and as we headed towards the prescribed training or GFA we commenced a slow climb to a safe height from which to practise our manoeuvres. Once having reached this safe altitude we performed the required safety checks involving three hundred and sixty degree turns left and right. I then closed the throttle and pulled the nose up, applying full left rudder as she stalled. This initiated a spin, but as the Tiger started to spin the change in the direction of the airflow lifted Keith's Red Baron outfit off his head and overboard. Keith immediately grabbed the controls, stopped the spin almost before it began, and dived the Tiger after his free falling helmet and goggles. Amazingly he managed to catch sight of them and was able to position them just off the lower left wing.

I was at a loss to imagine what his next move would be and it soon became patently obvious that Keith had no idea either. The ground was looming closer and now I began to fear that Keith would obsessively follow the Red Baron outfit, just off our left wing, into the ground. Losing my nerve, I shouted "pull up!" over the intercom and simultaneously started to pull back on my stick. This had the effect of breaking the spell and, amid much cursing, level flight was resumed.

The training session was immediately cancelled and we returned to Rand with no further communication between us. After landing Keith stumped off in high dungeon and was to be avoided by all for at least a week, during which he borrowed a Land Rover and tried to find his helmet in the area he thought it had landed. Unfortunately, he never did find it and it was months before anyone was brave enough to suggest it was probably adorning the head of some local farmhand as he operated his tractor.

THE FORCED LANDING

Learning to fly was far less complicated then. The Cub had three flight instruments, three engine instruments and an exterior fuel gauge. Our aircraft were not even required to carry radios. For take off we lined up at the holding point, did our checks and waited for a green light from the tower. For landing, one joined the circuit and similarly waited for a green light.

After going solo, I served the required number of hours doing circuits and bumps (take-offs and landings) until I was eventually let loose, signed out and told to proceed to the GFA where I was to practice steep turns and stalls. I was assigned a Piper Cub ZS-BAF which had just left the workshops after a major engine overhaul. She had flown on one quick test flight which had consisted of a circuit and landing and had certainly not included stalls. A stall is when an aircraft, flown too slowly, loses lift, stops flying and falls from the sky. All pilots must be trained to recover from an inadvertent stall.

This was a wonderful moment for me. At last being able to leave the circuit and, unsupervised, enjoy the euphoria of flight. Reaching the GFA and the safe altitude for practising stalls, I diligently performed my safety checks and, closing the throttle, began to ease the nose up to the required stall attitude. As the nose came up, the speed dropped and the wings stalled, unexpectedly the engine stopped and suddenly I was falling out of the sky while staring at a stationary wooden propeller.

The Cub had no electric starter and starting was normally accomplished by means of swinging the prop by hand, patently impossible when airborne. I had been briefed that the procedure for an airborne restart was to dive the aircraft until the airflow over the propeller would cause it to turn and restart the engine. This I duly did and even though I must have come close to the Cub's 'never exceed velocity', the prop stubbornly refused to budge, as the newly overhauled engine had not yet loosened up and was simply too stiff to be turned in this manner.

By the time I had pulled out of the dive I had lost quite a bit of altitude and was now only about 1200 feet above the ground desperately looking for a place to land. Not that there was that much choice, for as far as the eye could see there were only vast areas of mealie (corn) fields bisected only by the busy road between the Reef and Vereeniging, with the railway line running parallel to it. The only sign of human activity were three of those typical little red brick railway workers cottages alongside the tracks. So a mealie field it would have to be!

I had driven down the road and through those mealie fields, with a friend, only a few days before. It was a drought year and no rain had fallen since the fields had been planted. I remembered having commented to him that the mealie plants were very stunted and straggly only having reached a height of between three and four feet.

I was now getting pretty close to the ground and had competed the checks including cutting the electrics and fuel. Missing my chosen field was not an issue as it was vast. I planned to level the Cub with the undercarriage brushing the tops of the mealie stalks, and holding her there until the speed bled off and she would stall and drop, through the mealie stalks, the three feet to the ground. Just before levelling off I glanced at the railway cottages and noted that it would be a fairly short walk to reach them after the Cub had come to a stop.

As planned, I levelled off with the wheels brushing the tops of the mealies until the Cub stalled. I was expecting a three foot drop to hard dry ground through scraggly mealie plants but at that point things began to go badly wrong. The Cub just kept dropping through thick, lush and tall mealie stalks that seemed to be moving upward past the side windows for aeons. Eventually the thick mealie stalks halted the forward progress of the main wheels, the nose pitched into the ground and the tail inscribed a graceful arc over the nose and came to rest amid the tops of the stalks. I was now hanging upside down by my seat belt while the smell of aviation fuel leaking from the fuel tank was becoming stronger with each passing moment.

In haste, I released the belt, fell on my head, crawled out from under the upside down Cub and took off into the mealies in an attempt to put as much distance as possible between myself and the avgas soaked environs of the aircraft. When I eventually came to an exhausted halt I faced a new complication. The mealies were eight feet high and very dense, I had become totally disorientated and had no clue as to which direction to walk in to extricate myself from the field and find help. It was noon and the sun was directly overhead so there was no help from that quarter. Noticing the tops of the mealies were bent over in a gentle breeze. Hoping that the wind was blowing from the same direction as it was when I took off at Rand, and knowing that the railway line lay to the west of my field I guesstimated west and started walking through the mealies.

More by luck than judgement, after ten minutes walking, I emerged from the field and, there before me lay the railway line, with the three red brick cottages not far away. I was able to phone Frank from one of the cottages and an hour later the rescue crew arrived. We were soon able to locate and right the Cub discovering that the only damage was that one of the tips of the the propeller blades had snapped off. In fact, if the propeller had came to a stop in the horizontal, rather than the vertical position there would have, most likely, been no damage at all.

We also discovered that had I initially run in the opposite direction, I would have emerged on a wide access track for large agricultural machinery within fifty metres of the aircraft. Thus by flattening a small area of mealies, we were able to push the Cub out of the field and up to the three cottages.

By the next day, we had obtained permission from the Directorate of Civil Aviation (DCA) to fly the Cub out from the passing road and fitted a replacement propeller. We were able to push her over the railway line at the crossing for the cottages and on to the side of the road. The police were kind enough to stop the traffic and as regulations required a commercial pilot to perform the take off, one of Frank's part time SAAF instructors, Piet Nel, flew her back to Rand.

Shuttling by road from Rand to the scene of the forced landing and back, it became apparent that the field I had chosen was the only one in the whole area with mealies strong and healthy and above four feet tall. The mystery was solved upon our discovering that the field was owned by the Rand Water Board and somehow they had managed a plentiful water supply to irrigate their mealies in the midst of a drought.

Murphy had struck once again!

MEALIES AND MAYHEM

Strangely enough another rather embarrassing incident from my time at Frank's SA School of Flying also involved Piet Nel, a Cub and mealies. Just prior to taking your Private Pilots Licence (PPL), you were required to demonstrate that you were capable of navigating a triangular cross country flight without getting lost or have some other disaster befall you. Due to time constraints this did not form part of your exam by the DCA testing officer but was conducted by your flying instructor. He was basically there as an observer and was not supposed to offer any help but merely to fill in the assessment form that would pass or fail you. This, however, did not prevent him from interrogating you with questions such as "Give me five reasons why you say that the dorp (little village) on the left is Waboomskraal".

Piet and I knew each other well, and had often flown together. I think he viewed the test as pretty much a formality. I noticed as we walked out to the aircraft that Piet had a Zane Grey western paperback novel jammed into his shirt pocket. The Cub that had been assigned to us was ZS-AYT which Frank had acquired only a few days previously. Neither Piet nor I had flown her before, She had been modified so as to incorporate a second fuel tank in the right wing. I am pretty sure this was not an approved factory modification but, nevertheless, there it was. Inside the cockpit, where the wing joined the fuselage above your head, was a bright red valve marked 'FUEL – ON – OFF. No reference to this modification was to be found amongst the Cub's paperwork.

The standard Cub had one fuel tank mounted between the engine and the cockpit. In fact, the occupant of the front seat practically sat with the fuel tank in his or her lap. The fuel cap sat on top of the cowling a few centimetres from the windscreen. The fuel gauge was a wonderful piece of sophisticated engineering. It consisted of three centimetres of thin tube soldered into the top of the fuel cap. Through this tube passed a straight piece of wire with a cork attached to the bottom and the top bent over to prevent it disappearing into the fuel tank. Thus, peering through the windscreen, the greater the length of wire seen protruding from the fuel cap, the more fuel was in the tank.

The routing for the triangular cross country was to be from Rand to Ventersdorp in the Western Transvaal then on to Vereeniging and back to Rand. True to the maxim of 'Never do anything in the air that you could have done on the ground' I was very well prepared for the exercise with all winds, distances, ground speeds, times, headings and checkpoints carefully laid out in my flight plan.

The flight to Ventersdorp was uneventful although an annoying facet of the new Cub began to manifest itself. Between the bottom of the windscreen and the cowling there was, a previously unnoticed, gap of about ten millimetres. Through this a cold wind whistled making it difficult to maintain orderly paperwork. The landscape to the west was relatively featureless and I was concentrating on getting everything spot on, while Piet, seemingly disinterested, was deeply immersed in his Zane Grey paperback.

In those days the airfield at Ventersdorp was merely a runway cut out through, you guessed it, a mealie field. It had a windsock and a small hut that housed fuel drums, and that was about it. We duly landed, shut down and walked about to stretch our legs. While we were doing this an old farm bakkie (pick up) appeared followed by a tractor pulling a high sided trailer which carried half a dozen farmhands and a pile of sacks. The farmer dispersed his farmhands to harvest mealies while he strolled over to inspect the Cub and chat to us. He was a friendly fellow and we enjoyed chatting with him. As we prepared to leave, he called to one of the farmhands to bring over a sack of the freshly picked mealies which, with old fashioned courtesy, he presented to us.

This created a problem for us. It would have been churlish to refuse his gift and besides they were very nice mealies but, where on earth, would one stow a sack of mealies in a Piper Cub? The Cub had an interesting access door arrangement in that it only had a door on one side. This door ran the length of the cockpit and served the occupant of both the single front and single rear seat. The door was a horizontally split arrangement by which, when opened, the upper half swung upward to the overhead wing, where it was held in place by a spring clip, similar to those that kept kitchen cupboard doors closed. The lower half just swung down and hung above the undercarriage.

We solved the problem by Piet climbing into the rear seat and closing the lower half of the door. I removed the mealies from the sack and just piled them in until Piet was practically sitting in a bath of mealies. Piet set the throttle and magnetos for start. I swung the prop and hopped into the front seat over the closed bottom half of the door.

As I taxied to the end of the runway I began to perform the before take off checks, one of which was 'Full and free movement of controls' in which the stick is moved fully forward and back and left to right and the rudders fully left and right. The rudders moved fine but the stick could hardly be moved at all. It did not take us very long to realise that Piet's stick, which was directly connected to mine was being severely impeded by the mealies. Nothing daunted, Piet burrowed down through the mealies, by feel, pulled the pin securing his stick in its socket, and laid the stick down beside him, on top of the mealies.

I now had full and free movement but the Cub no longer had dual controls. We took off and slowly ambled along into a strong headwind to Vereeniging. Having landed there we came to the conclusion that shutting down the engine and leaving the cockpit, would involve too much hassle with the mealies, so we did a full stop landing without shutting down the engine. We then taxied back to the runway for take off and were soon airborne.

About halfway back to Rand there were only a few centimetres of wire protruding from the fuel cap so we decided to switch the wing tank selector to ON so that both fuel tanks would now be feeding the engine, or so we thought. Soon it was time to start descending for our landing at Rand. As I started the descent, I noticed that our track would take us over the Germiston race track and that, as it was a Saturday afternoon the track was buzzing with activity.

Coming up to the track I recall a sudden fountain of fuel spurting out from fuel cap and entering the cockpit through that annoying gap below the windscreen. I remembered it hitting me in the face and nothing further until we were on final approach for a landing at Rand with Piet flying from the rear seat.

After landing Piet filled me in on what had happened. Apparently after receiving a face, eye and lung full of avgas, I had passed out and collapsed over the stick, putting the Cub into a dive. Piet's stick was still lying on top of the mealies, and realising that there was no way in which time would allow him to relocate it in the same way as he had removed it, he flung open the door. With arms flailing like a runaway windmill, he managed to eject enough of the mealies to reveal the socket, into which he was able to locate his stick. It was a near thing, but he just managed to reach over, haul me back and pull the Cub out of its dive.

We refuelled the Cub realising that the wing tank did not feed the engine but rather just bled its fuel, by gravity, into the main tank when its valve was opened. This Heath Robinson system did not cater for overflow protection and neither of us had noticed the piece of wire, that was the fuel gauge, growing to its maximum length. We had parked the Cub in its hanger and were busy giving it a clean when Frank ambled in, his face like a thundercloud.

The racetrack stewards had read the registration ZS-AYT painted under the Cub's wing, phoned the Rand tower and been given Frank's number. I am sure their lurid account of events was rather exaggerated as they described a Stuka like attack, raining bombs in the form of mealies upon them. They spoke of a disrupted race, bolting horses and punters baying for blood. By the grace of God they were not able to claim any injuries.

Frank was halfway through his bollocking when he was unable to hold his pose any longer and the three of us ended up rolling around the hanger floor convulsed with laughter. My only punishment was that three weeks later I could still taste avgas. Piet's was that he was well into his Zane Grey western which, with the mealies, was pitched out over the Germiston race track and he never did get to find out how it ended.

With this exercise completed the paperwork was signed and submitted and in March 1966 I became the proud holder of a Private Pilot Licence. Now the long slog to build up hours from 40 to the 200 required for a Commercial Pilot licence, with very little money, began. This was achieved by organising fly away weekends with friends who would share the cost of the flying hours, hitch-hiking all over the country to fetch and deliver aircraft but mainly by just hanging around Rand and offering to do anything that could lead to some free airtime that could be logged.

THE OKAVANGO SWAMPS AND CROCODILE CAMP

It was during this period in 1967 that Frank became involved with Bobby Wilmot who was of an old Botswana family . Bobby had been granted the crocodile hunting concession in the Okavango Swamps by the Botswana Government and, if memory serves me, his quota was two thousand crocodiles per year, for their skins. Bobby was very keen to move away from the crocodile hunting and into the, then non existent, photographic safari business. He and Frank had been discussing an arrangement whereby Frank would fly six clients from Johannesburg to Maun on a weekly rotational basis. Frank had negotiated the use of an Aero Commander and as I was on the cusp of gaining my Commercial Pilots Licence he was keen to have me come in on the project.

During the planning stage, Frank and I were invited up to Maun so that we could gain some insight into what Bobby had in mind to offer the clients on photographic safaris. Frank and I set off in a Cherokee 180 and five and a half hours later landed in Maun where Bobby collected us in an old series I Land Rover and drove us through Maun to Crocodile Camp on the banks of the Okavango River. The main road of Maun was just a dirt track. There was a police post, a General dealer, two shooting safari companies, KDS and South Safaris, the District Commissioner's residence, a small hotel, hospital and a smattering of European style houses. The rest of the village was made up by the dwellings of the local tribe. I was told that the population of Maun was about 5000. The atmosphere of Maun was pretty like that of the Wild West what with the cattle ranchers and white hunters as they were then known.

Crocodile Camp was a 'boma' style construction on the river bank with loads of character. There were two tame Civet Cats that lived at Crocodile Camp and their antics were very entertaining. Bobby intended building two other camps, on islands in the swamps, which would facilitate his six day photographic safaris.

His crocodile hunters were young South African lads of about my age. They worked, played and drank hard and I got on very well with them. I witnessed an incident where, as a joke, they tipped one of their colleagues out of the boat and into crocodile infested waters so they could observe how quickly he could get back into the boat.

Frank and I were taken into the swamps by boat and shown the wondrous game that was so abundant on the islands of the Okavango Delta. This included Africa's 'big five' although rhino were very scarce as a result of years of hunting. The water was crystal clear and the scenery was amazing. A wonderful experience.

One evening while we were sitting around the camp fire a rather gaunt elderly hunter arrived. He was very dusty and stripped down to have a wash at the wash table, with its jug and basin, that had been provided for the purpose. I could not help noticing that the front of his body, from neck to knee, was one mass of scar tissue. Upon asking about him later, I was told that he had been attacked by a leopard and had managed to keep its jaws from his throat and kill it by strangling it with his bare hands. In the process the leopard had clawed him savagely and he had been extremely fortunate to have survived. He was but one of a variety of unusual characters that wandered into Crocodile camp during our stay.

On the day before we were due to leave we witnessed an interesting event. The previous night a young Botswana Government Extension Officer and his local assistant had arrived, in a Land Rover, and pitched camp fifty metres down river from Crocodile Camp. That night he joined us for drinks around the camp fire. He was a pleasant chap, fresh out from England, with the typical ruddy complexion of one whose skin has not regularly been exposed to the African sun. He informed us that his mission was to teach members of the local tribe to fish on a larger scale than traditional methods allowed for. A study had revealed a lack of protein in the local diet, and in the swamps there was more than sufficient Bream, that could be easily caught, to correct this deficiency.

In the morning a fishing net was taken out of the Land Rover, and a boat borrowed from Bobby. One end of the net was attached to a tree on the near bank and the other end taken across by boat to be attached to a tree on the far bank. The empty net being light, all this was accomplished, by the young officer, his assistant and with one of Bobby's crocodile hunters operating the boat.

By now a large crowd, of several hundred noisy local tribe members, had gathered to watch the fun. The boat returned from the far bank and amid much merriment everyone sat down to await developments. By noon it became obvious that the net was full of Bream and that, if left much longer, was in danger of breaking.

And now a problem arose, the net full of fish was simply too heavy for the officer, his assistant and the few of us still at Crocodile Camp to pull in. Nor could the Land Rover be utilised as the low section of bank on which we were gathered was inaccessible and boggy. Well, how could this conceivably be a problem? There were, after all hundreds of local tribe members present and the fish in the net were destined for them, as was the net, when the exercise was completed.

It soon became apparent that no willing hands were going near the net and that the tribal headman and elders were engaged in a animated indaba. (debate, conference, powwow) After an hour or so of this, the headman approached the officer and informed him that they would not assist in pulling in the net unless they were paid to do so. One can only imagine how this information was received and reconciled in the mind of a British civil servant only recently arrived from Blighty and with little understanding of the African psychic.

The officer had not been supplied with any means with which to pay anyone anything and so the net result was, that the boat travelled back to the far bank and the ropes securing the net to the tree were cut, thus releasing tons of fish. The boat returned and the, now light, empty net was hauled in and bundled into the back of the Land Rover.

That night, around the camp fire, and with abundant alcoholic lubrication, I quietly listened, with great amusement, to the old Africa hands explaining to, a very puzzled Extension Officer, that if 'a few backsides had been soundly kicked', this very night, hundreds of the local tribe would have been happily sitting around fires enjoying a, protein rich, meal of Okavango Bream with a regular supply to follow.

In the morning the Land rover departed for Gaberones and I never did hear whether, or not, further government initiatives on this 'protein from the swamps' project were followed up upon.

That day we too had to leave the swamps and return to Johannesburg. I was sorry to leave, as in the short time we were there I had made interesting new friends and my life had been enriched by the whole experience. Even sadder was the fact that our planned enterprise never got off the ground. Before Bobby had completed the camps, he was out hunting crocodiles when he was bitten by a Boomslang. (A deadly African tree snake) They were deep in the swamps and had insufficient anti snakebite serum. Poor Bobby died a painful death in the bottom of his boat with just two of his crocodile hunters to keep him company and try to ease his pain.

Shortly thereafter I became a qualified aircraft engineer and obtained my Commercial Pilots licence and Instructors Rating. I visited the hallowed halls of SAA Flight Operations and was able to arrange an interview with the then Chief Pilot, Captain Pine Pienaar. At the time there was a regulation stating that no one was to be appointed from outside the organisation if someone, meeting the minimum requirements, applied from within the organisation. This was, however a bit of a grey area where pilots were concerned.

Pine seemed to me to be a rather fatherly figure and when I asked for his advice on the way forward, I think it came out of genuine empathy and from the heart. He advised me not to pursue the in-house avenue but to resign from SAA, go out into the general aviation world, get a few thousand flying hours under the belt and then reapply to SAA as a pilot.

Following this advice turned out to be a very fortuitous decision as two years later when I reapplied to SAA, who should be the head of the selection board, but Captain Pine Pienaar. Each SAA advertisement for pilots resulted in hundreds of applicants and only a handful being accepted. Having no delusions regarding my suitability to be one of the chosen few, I can only assume that, having followed his advice to the letter, he could not find it in his heart to knock me back, and I found myself accepted for the next SAA pilot intake.

WILLIE, WHEELS UPS AND PRETTY GIRLS

After having resigned as an aircraft engineer from SAA, I soon found a job, as a flying instructor, with a small Company based at Wonderboom Airfield which is situated to the north of Pretoria. I found lodgings in one of those residential hotels that were so popular back then. It was situated in Sunnyside, a suburb of Pretoria. Due to the University and the collages situated nearby it really was a swinging place. Apart from myself, the residents at the hotel were almost exclusively students. By a happy coincidence eighty percent of them were very pretty young women and the social life at the hotel was amazing.

The company that employed me as a flying instructor was owned by two brothers whose main business was a large panel beating firm in Pretoria.

They also built the most fantastic beach buggies at a time when they had only just come onto the market in the form of kits. At quiet times we would performance test them down the length of the main runway. I was very tempted to trade in my old Citroen ID19 on one of them. Fortunately sense prevailed as it would have been a totally impractical vehicle for the path my life was to follow.

The company had managed to acquire the South African franchise for Siai Marchetti which was a range of Italian manufactured light aircraft. Unfortunately they came with teething troubles and soon gained a bad reputation for wheels up landings. Not surprisingly, as I was doing plenty of flying in Siai Marchettis, my turn came. On the roll out, after landing at Wonderboom, the left landing gear of the Siai S205 I was flying collapsed causing the tip of the wing to strike the runway and slew the aircraft around and onto the grass beside the runway. There I sat, at an interesting angle, staring at the, still illuminated, three green lights that indicated that the gear was down and locked.

These wheels up landings were doing the reputation and, as a consequence, the sales of Siai Marchetti no good at all. The brother who oversaw the flying side, Willie, would dearly have liked to blame me, but the three green lights that would illuminate whenever the master switch was in the on position, despite the collapsed gear, made this an impossibly hard sell. His attitude did, however, lead to a deterioration in our relationship.

A flying instructor's busiest periods during the week are early in the morning and late afternoon. This is because some pupils like to get in an hours flying prior to work and others after work. The periods in between, for the most part tend, to be fairly slack.

On this particular day, I had been giving instruction for two hours starting at first light. I also had bookings for two sessions in the late afternoon, the last ending just before last light. Having no bookings for the interim period, I had nipped up the road to a local supermarket to purchase a few, much needed items and it was then that Willie had decided to visit the flight office and found that I was not there. Upon my return a blazing row followed despite my explaining that I had been at the airfield since before first light, and that my later bookings would mean that I would still be there after last light.

Now, given enough stimulation, I can be as Bolshie as the best of them. I could see he was in a blind rage and not thinking straight, so I meekly asked him if from now on he wanted me to work office hours. To my utmost surprise he said yes, so I pushed it still further by asking him to define 'office hours', write them down and sign the paper. This, to my even greater surprise, he did and I thus started arriving at the airfield just before eight and departing just after five. This meant taking no early or late bookings, a ridiculous situation for a flight school and huge underutilisation of a flying instructor. I never did get around to pointing out to him, that 'office hours' generally did not include weekends, as then I would hardly be doing any flying at all.

I was of course hoping that he would come to his senses and rescind his ridiculous edict, bringing an end to this nonsense, but I underestimated his capacity for stubbornness. I was getting paid for doing very little work, and not only did I love to fly and needed to build up hours, but felt that I was letting my pupils down and felt very uncomfortable in this regard. Thus when I saw an advertisement from a company based in Windhoek, I decided to apply.

Two weeks later I was interviewed in Johannesburg by Frank, the aircraft sales manager for Air Oasis in Windhoek. I immediately took to Frank's engaging personality and, to my great surprise, was offered the job there and then. I was working out my notice month at Wonderboom when the news reached me that Frank Lister had died. He had acquired the agency for a four seater aircraft built by Partenavia, an Italian company, and badged as an RSA Falcon 200 for the South African market. It looked like, but had little of the sophistication of a Cessna 172.

Frank was demonstrating the Falcon 200 at an air show on the South Coast near Durban when the aircraft hit trees and Frank did not survive the ensuing crash. Frank never made much money out of aviation, but he helped so many youngsters fulfil their dreams of becoming professional pilots, that any list of South African aviation legends would be incomplete if it omitted the name of Frank Lister.

3

SOUTH WEST AFRICA

(NAMIBIA)

Having said my, not too tearful, goodbyes to Willie and his Siai Marchetti operation and my, far more tearful, goodbyes to all my friends and the lovely ladies of the Sunnyside residential hotel, I packed all my worldly possessions into the Citroen ID 19 and set off for faraway Windhoek, the capital of South West Africa, now Namibia.

Back then it was a long trek from Pretoria to Windhoek as the Kalahari Desert had to be skirted via Kuruman and Upington. There were long stretches of bumpy and extremely dusty dirt roads and I was very glad that I had not traded in my comfortable and relatively dust proof ID 19 for one of Willie's beach buggys.

Frank had acquired a one bedroom flat for me above the butcher shop in Klein Windhoek, a nearby suburb separated from Windhoek by a range of hills. After settling in, I was shown the Air Oasis flight office at Eros airfield and introduced to the Chief Flying Instructor, Gus Uys, who was a very nice man and one of the popular and colourful Windhoek characters. I was also introduced to my new boss, the owner of Air Oasis, one Derek Hattingh who's main business was a Windhoek company that sold paint.

The Air Oasis office and flight school was housed in a small prefab building, fairly remote from any other airfield buildings and quite close to the northern end of the main runway. Gus and I were the only instructors and our secretary was Kathy, a charming and pretty blonde lady.

Air Oasis had the Cessna agency and its core business was the sale of Cessna aircraft which the flight school merely facilitated. Our main rivals were the Piper agents who also ran a very low key flight school at Eros. Derek was a super salesman and in order to develop a market for used aircraft, traded in on new Cessna aircraft he had sold, he had managed to promote the formation of various flying clubs in remote parts of the country. These included not only remote towns but also mines such as Strathmore Tin and Brandberg West.

This was a brilliant strategy as the miners earned good money but were starved of entertainment and had very little to spend it on. A flying club not only provided them with an exciting activity, but also with the means to facilitate getaway weekends to the 'bright lights' of Windhoek and Swakopmund.

Naturally a flying club needed an aircraft, which Derek was delighted to offer on hire purchase, with easy payments, and hence a sale was made. A flying club also needed an instructor, which Derek was also only too happy to supply, in the form of myself. South West Africa was a country of great distances between centres with a very rudimentary road network so, the more people that learned to fly, the more aircraft were sold, hopefully by Air Oasis.

Thus my weekly program started bright and early on Monday morning with a flight to Strathmore Tin mine in the Namib desert where I would spend the day giving instruction, overnight there, and leave for Brandberg West mine the following morning. Wednesday would see me servicing Otjiwarongo and Outjo and Thursday Gobabis on the edge of the Kalahari desert.

Friday morning I would return to Windhoek, have the rest of the day off and be ready for the weekend pupils in Windhoek. In between all this was slotted the odd charter, emergency medivac and aircraft demonstration. I loved it!

The only dark shadow was the death of Frank, the Air Oasis salesman who had hired me, shortly after I arrived. He had been demonstrating a Robertson STOL Cessna 182, hitting a fence on take off and not surviving the ensuing crash.

THE NAMIB DESERT MINES

Young as I was, I was treated like a VIP at all the venues where I gave instruction. My money was not accepted at the Brandberg West clubhouse bar and I was even wined and dined at the mine manager's home. At the time these managers enjoyed privileges almost akin to those of old English feudal lords. I also became an unofficial courier between the mine and Windhoek when essentials were urgently required. I even carried the precious cargo of miners' children between their boarding schools in Windhoek and the mine.

There were no children at Strathmore Tin which was pretty much in the development phase and an all male affair. It lacked all the amenities which the far older and more established Brandberg West enjoyed. Brandberg West was also situated close to the Ugab River and was in an area of great scenic beauty with many trees and wonderful rock formations, whereas Strathmore Tin was situated on a flat piece of featureless sandy desert.

Finding Strathmore Tin and its airfield from the air was quite problematic if one had not been there before. Often pilots on their first trips would give up, fly on to the coast and follow it south down to Henties Bay where they would pick up the road to Strathmore and follow that to their destination. One of my pupils even managed to lose the airfield while we were practising 'circuits and bumps' (take offs and landings) in the circuit. Eventually I positioned the aircraft on a short final approach for him, and only then did he regain his orientation.

Flying over the desert in the lower levels was a bumpy affair due to thermals caused by the differing rates at which the multi coloured surface of the desert absorbs heat. On another occasion, this same pupil was suffering from airsickness obviously caused by this turbulence. He was however putting on a brave face and made no mention of this to me. This was unfortunate in the extreme, as that day the lesson was spin recovery.

A spin is occasioned when one of the aircraft's wings stalls and looses lift while effectively the other is still flying. This may occur if a pilot inadvertently flies too slowly in a turn and the result is that the aircraft practically falls out of the sky while rapidly rotating around its own axis. Unless firm corrective action is applied it will stay in this configuration until such time as it crashes into the ground. Spin recovery must be instilled in all pilots prior to sending them solo.

Being totally unaware of the state of my pupil's stomach, I proceeded to demonstrate a spin recovery which, of course, meant deliberately placing the aircraft into a spin, a rather uncomfortable manoeuvre not to be attempted on a queasy stomach. And sure enough, as we entered the spin, the stomach contents of my pupil began to fill the cockpit. As the aircraft was basically falling, this technicolour mixture remained suspended in the air within the cockpit. Therein lay a dilemma and it is strange how ones mind works in situations like this. I actually kept the aircraft in the spin while trying to think of a way of avoiding the inevitable.

Eventually, with the desert rapidly looming, I was forced to apply the spin recovery procedure and the well dispersed liquids and solids that had previously been suspended, settled on everything below the roof lining, including my pupil and myself. The story was a source of great amusement to the miners and I heard it retold endlessly in the mine pub.

Despite the best efforts of the Strathmore Flying Club members to clean and sanitise the aircraft, an aerosol room freshener had to be carried as part of that aircraft's kit for months thereafter.

There being absolutely no amenities on the mine, we would occasionally make the sixty km trip through the desert to the little village of Henties Bay where there was an excellent pub. Getting there before the light was lost was never a problem, but on the return journey, in the dark, and with the driver 'a little worse for wear' things became rather more complicated. Once one turned off the coastal salt road, there was little to distinguish the road through the desert from the desert itself. Many a carload returning to Strathmore Tin from Henties Bay became lost and spent an uncomfortable night in the desert, awaiting the sunrise and the orientation it offered.

The road to Strathmore Tin ran right past a hill that was covered in large chunks of Rose Quartz which everyone was free to collect and many garden walls in Henties Bay were constructed from this largesse. Whenever my eye is caught by a polished and mounted piece of Rose Quartz, attached to a hefty price tag, in a jeweller's window, I cannot help recalling the garden walls of Henties Bay.

Despite millions of Rands being poured into Strathmore Tin, it never produced any viable quantities of tin and was eventually shut down amid rumours of salting, fraud and tax dodges.

I was also shown many wonders of the Namib desert, the most amazing canyons, dry riverbeds, rock formations and areas where semi precious stones lay thick on the ground. The famous 'White Lady' rock painting is to be found high up on the Brandberg (Burning Mountain), in the shadow of which lay the Brandberg West tin and Wolframite mine.

On one memorable occasion I was able to get a week off and join the Brandberg West crew on an excursion all along the Skeleton Coast to Cape Fria near the Kunene River mouth where we saw the boilers of the Dunedin Star, a British ship wrecked there in 1942. Lying nearby was one of the motors of the PV1 Ventura bomber of the South African Air Force that crashed during one of the many ill fated attempts to rescue the ship's passengers who were stranded on the beach. A book 'The Skeleton Coast' by John H Marsh tells the full story and is an enthralling read.

To offer a break from life on the mine the company had built four rondavels on the beach opposite the place where the road to the mine joined the coast road, known as mile ninety five, as places on the coast road were located by the number of miles they were from Swakopmund. These rondavels were christened 'Brandberg Bungalows' and many marvellous fishing weekends were spent there. The fishing was the best I have ever experienced, and a good catch was virtually guaranteed.

The Brandberg West airstrip ran between two round hills. These had a venturi effect that substantially increased the speed of the wind as it blew between them. With a bit of practise, and the right wind, it was possible to hold the Cessna 150 stationary above the runway between the hills, then slowly backing off on the throttle, it would begin to creep backwards, stall and touch down while still moving backwards. I have, over the years, seen impressively short landings but none as short as those that could be achieved at Brandberg West.

OTJIWARONGO

From the Namib mines my next port of call would be Otjiwarongo, a small town 250km North of Windhoek, where I had several pupils. On one occasion, the training flight having been completed, I was conducting a leisurely debriefing with Mike, my pupil, the two of us being the only people on the airfield.

It was a very hot day and we were sitting on the ground in the shade afforded by the wing of the Cessna when a local business man and farmer, Barend, arrived. He was accompanied by his young son aged about five and two hefty and apprehensive looking farm workers. We later learned that Barend was taking the two farm workers for their first taste of flying as a reward for hard work and loyalty.

We watched as they pushed a Cessna 177 Cardinal out of one of the three hangers on the airfield and Barend completed his preflight checks. The Cardinal had modern laminar flow wings and this resulted in it having far less forgiving flight characteristics than the Cessna 172 it was meant to replace. It was rather underpowered with its 150 hp engine and altogether rather an unsuitable aircraft for a low time pilot in the hot and high altitude conditions at Otjiwarongo.

I had returned to the debriefing task at hand and only looked up as the Cardinal taxied past on the way to the runway. I noticed that the little boy occupied the front passenger seat while the two hefty farm workers were seated at the back. This was not ideal as far as weight distribution was concerned and I cursed myself for not noticing it in time to bring it to Barend's attention.

We watched as the Cardinal commenced its take off run , rapidly diminishing into the distance and eventually becoming airborne. It rose about 30ft into the air when the left wing suddenly stalled, rolling the aircraft through 90° and causing it to fall back onto the runway amidst a mighty cloud of red dust.

Mike and I raced to his pick up truck, which was parked nearby, and went charging down the runway to the scene of the crash. Fortunately there were no signs of fire and as we approached we could see all four occupants emerging from the wreck, none of whom, miraculously, seemed to be suffering from serious injury. The two farm workers hit the ground running. They rapidly disappeared into the thick bush that surrounded the airfield and I did not see them again.

Barend and his son only had minor cuts and bruising and were suffering from shock, as were Mike and I. Witnessing something of that nature does not leave one untouched.

OUTJO

Outjo was an even smaller town 70km to the north west of Otjiwarongo where I had two pupils. The only thing of note that I recall about Outjo was arriving there one day and seeing a Cessna 150 lying upside down on the roof of Outjo airfield's only hanger. Its owner had neglected to tie it down and it had been picked up and deposited there by a dust devil.

These dust devils were very common all over Namibia in the hot months and they could be extremely powerful. They were always something to be watched for when flying close to the ground such as when takeing off or landing. It was also a great idea to have one's aircraft tied down at all times when on the ground in these conditions.

GOBABIS AND THE LOVE OF MY LIFE

Gobabis was my last port of call before returning to Windhoek for the weekend's instruction. It was a neat little town in the Kalahari Desert lying 200km to the east of Windhoek and about 100km to the west of the Botswana border. In those days the road to Gobabis was very bad, making the trip from Windhoek a torturous affair, so being able to fly, and having access to an aircraft, was a great advantage to those living in Gobabis. My list of pupils there included the local doctor, magistrate, police chief, two businessmen and several farmers from the district.

I recall landing in Gobabis the first time and seeing a bloke in a khaki safari suit busy strapping a large dead Springbok to the top of each wing of a Piper Cherokee 180. He and his two mates had obviously been on a hunting trip and, not having room inside the aircraft, this was their way of getting the spoils home.

I strolled over for a chat with him and when I queried his methodology for conveying the Springbok, he very earnestly showed me how he had calculated that the Cherokee's load was within the weight limits shown in the manual. I had great difficulty in suppressing my laughter as I asked him what effect he thought two dead Springbok would have on the aerodynamic qualities of his aircraft's wings as far as both lift and drag were concerned?

His face was something to behold as the penny eventually dropped and the Springbok were hastily unstrapped from the wings. They managed to cram one of them into a rear seat and the other was presented to me. Fair enough, I thought as, after all, I had probably saved their lives!

Gobabis was also where I experienced a life changing advent as this was where I met my wife, Corleen, under rather unusual circumstances. I always stayed overnight in Gobabis as the guest of the local doctor, Hugo, and his lovely wife Irene and on that particular night, as fate would have it, it was my birthday.

That night there happened to be, for Gobabis, the major event of a first ever wine tasting in, of all places, the local Dutch Reformed Church hall, being the only large venue in Gobabis at the time. Hugo and Irene had been invited to attend and insisted, despite my pleas of a lack of suitable dress, that I accompany them. Thus, attired in a rather ill-fitting outfit that Hugo provided, I set off with them to the wine tasting which was being presented by the KWV, the export arm of the South African wine industry, based in Paarl. The, rather misguided in my opinion, aim of the exercise was to introduce the local population to fine wines in the hope they would be weaned from their staple beer and schnapps, thus creating a market for wine in SWA.

To this end they arranged an itinerary and dispatched a large pantechnicon, with two drivers. This truck carried all the gear that was needed to set up wine tastings in the remotest of venues, which included trestle tables, table cloths, candles for atmosphere, brochures and, of course, a great number of cases of wine. Accompanying this truck were two cars carrying six very attractive young ladies who were the KWV's public relations officers and who would be conducting the wine tastings.

As we entered the hall one of the young ladies came up and introduced herself as Corleen from the KWV and in turn Hugo introduced himself, Irene and me, adding the rider that it was my birthday. The tasting was great fun and I did notice that Corleen was, while simultaneously doing her job, paying quite a lot of, very welcome, attention to me.

When the tasting ended, several of the Gobabis younger set and I accompanied the girls to a house that had been rented to accommodate them and the party continued there.

Corleen told me how she was dreading the return journey over the road, cum riverbed, to Windhoek. When I suggested that she flew back with me and that it would only take a little over an hour, including some game spotting on the way, she readily accepted my offer. That evening we had dinner together at the Kaiser Krone Hotel but sadly their tour was over and the girls had to return home the following day.

Three days later I managed to step off the veranda of the flight school, a drop of fifty millimetres, and twist my ankle so badly that I was booked off flying duties for three weeks. Of course, I spent my three weeks R and R with my mother in Somerset West, only a forty minute drive from Paarl where Corleen lived and worked. Thus started a whirlwind romance and shortly afterwards we were married and took up residence in Windhoek.

ILLICIT DIAMONDS AND ENTRAPMENT

In the sixties Windhoek was a very exciting town to live in. It seemed to have a pioneering spirit. It was rather like village life where nothing could remain confidential for very long and everybody knew everybody's business.

The two popular newspapers were the German Allgemeine Zeitung and the Windhoek Observer with its controversial editor Smittie.

In the cafes of Windhoek, when the paper came out, the first page we would turn to would be the court reports where we could see if anyone we knew had been charged with IDB (Illicit Diamond Buying). This was rife in the territory and viewed by many as unfairly protecting wealthy monopolists rather than a crime.

Entrapment was used extensively to achieve convictions and many people that would not normally have become involved in this activity were tempted by these entrapment practices. Pilots by the very nature of the mobility their professions afforded them, were often suspected and targeted by the entrapment teams. We were all extremely wary of the many invitations extended to us to purchase or deliver uncut diamonds.

One of our friends, a local businessman, became a Windhoek legend for managing to get away with snatching the bait from a police trap. He had been approached by a local offering him a large uncut diamond and was pretty sure that this was a police entrapment operation. He refused to even look at the diamond but made arrangements to meet the seller at an abandoned farm airstrip, between Windhoek and Gobabis, that Saturday.

He had a private pilot licence so instead of driving to the rendezvous he flew there, and on arrival noted the seller standing on the runway as well as two police vehicles hidden in the nearby bush. Landing quickly he taxied back to the end of the strip and, without killing the engine of the Cessna 172, opened the passenger door and beckoned the supposed seller over. The police used rather unsophisticated locals, often convicted criminals in these traps, for authenticity, and this worthy taken by surprise and not briefed for this eventuality duly went over to the aircraft and handed the large and tempting diamond to our friend for examination.

At that point, had the diamond and price been satisfactory, money would have been handed over and the trap would have been sprung. That, however is not what happened. With the diamond in his hand, our friend banged open the throttle and released the brakes. The seller who was standing on the ground but leaning into the aircraft over the passenger seat, leapt for his life, there being no way he was going to be dragged into the air by an infernal machine that he was deathly scared of.

Looking back our friend noted that the police vehicles had emerged from the bushes and were chasing him down the strip, alas for them, far too late. Of course, a police alert for the aircraft went out immediately and one can imagine police patrols rushing out to airstrips all over the territory.

Forty minutes later, when our friend landed at Eros Airport in Windhoek, the Cessna was surrounded by policemen who immediately arrested him. However, a thorough search of both his person and the aircraft revealed no trace of either the diamond or any money. He was duly taken into custody and hauled off to the local goal where he spent the weekend before his case was summarily dismissed on Monday for lack of evidence, the only witness, to what the police alleged had occurred, being a convicted criminal.

Why was the diamond not found? Well our friend had, after getting airborne, placed the diamond in a Dayglo bag, made a small deviation on route back to Eros and tossed the bag out over the farm of a friend of his, recovering it months later, when the heat was off.

There would have ended the story had our friend not decided to entertain the inmates, he had met during his weekend in goal, by doing a low level shoot up of the prison, in his Cessna, during exercise hour the following week. The local aviation authority 'threw the book at him' and his flying licence was suspended for six months.

DOWN IN THE ATLANTIC AND LOCKED UP

It was at about this time that our Chief Flying Instructor, Gus Uys, acquired the agency for Bellanca aircraft and arranged to fly to the United States to ferry back a brand new Bellanca Viking. This was a very fast, sleek four seater with single 300hp engine. The Viking that Gus was to ferry had been prepared by the factory and extra fuel tanks were fitted inside the cabin to ensure the required range for a transatlantic flight.

Gus had just passed the halfway mark on his transatlantic leg when he ran into turbulence so heavy that the landing flap on the left wing deployed and jammed in the down position. All Gus's efforts to retract it were of no avail and the aircraft was now seriously out of balance with Gus having to hold the control wheel over to the right to keep the aircraft flying straight and level. The extra drag caused by all this meant a large reduction in airspeed and an increase in power just to maintain level flight.

Naturally the range suffered and it was not long before Gus came to the realisation that he would fall far short of reaching Africa.

Knowing that a transatlantic shipping route lay a short distance to the north he took up a northerly heading and shortly noticed several ships beneath him. Knowing he was now over a busy shipping lane he decided to fly on in the direction of Africa until he found what he thought was a suitable ship to ditch the aircraft beside.

Eventually, with less the an hour's fuel in his tanks and the light fading he buzzed a small ship until they, realising his attentions to ditch, brought the ship to a stop and launched a lifeboat. Gus was able to ditch close to the lifeboat and step out onto the wing before the aircraft sank. The crew of the lifeboat were so efficient and arrived so quickly that Gus was able to step from the wing into the boat, barely getting his feet wet in the process.

Up to then everything had gone exceedingly well, but as Gus stood in the boat watching the beautiful Bellanca sink beneath the waves, the realisation struck him, that in the panic of trying to survive the ditching, he had not even taken his papers, including his passport, with him into the boat.

The ship turned out to be a large Spanish trawler and their next port of call was the island of Sao Tome where they disembarked Gus, a man with no papers whatsoever.

At the time Sao Tome was locked in a political struggle with Portugal over their independence and the authorities could not preclude the possibility that Gus was a spy so they detained him. Fortunately he was treated very well, not locked in a cell during the day, when he had the run of the jail.

In the end poor Gus spent over three months in jail on the Island, which was how long it took the International Red Cross to extract him.

Gus was a bit of a legend in South West and thus another story was added to the many.

Another character of note was my boss Derrick Hattingh, the only living person I ever knew who caused a common use expression, using his name, to enter the local vernacular. Derrick was the original 'Promises Pete' and would promise the world in order to close a deal. The trouble was that very few of his promises ever came to fruition and hence the expression " You're not doing a Derrick Hattingh on me, are you?" became commonly used in the territory whenever someone was sceptical of promises being made to them.

THE SEWAGE FARM

In 2005 I was watching the news on Australian TV when a politician came on and was spruiking a newly built plant, that could convert sewage water into potable (drinkable) water, as an 'Australian world first'. Hang on a minute, I thought, as my mind went back to 1969 and South West Africa.

One of the flying crowd, often to be seen at Air Oasis, was the then Mayor of Windhoek, Con Katzke, a jovial fellow and a very keen private pilot. I had flown with Con when he required a conversion onto another type of aircraft or an annual licence renewal test.

The Windhoek City Council had just built a sewage plant that produced potable water and Con had invited us all to attend the opening ceremony. Boring I know, but young bachelors, as I then was, very seldom turn down invitations that involve free food and booze.

The reason that this occasion is so indelibly etched on my mind is, that as part of his opening speech, Con had to drink a glass of newly purified sewage water that the plant had just produced. The idea was supposedly to reassure the highly sceptical population of Windhoek that the resultant brew was fit for human consumption.

I shall never forget the look on Con's face as he fought a magnificent battle to suppress his gag reflex and get that glass of water down. Having accomplished this feat, he was rather green around the gills and his smile was frozen as he assured the audience how good the water had tasted. I did notice at the party afterwards that no one was drinking their usual whiskey or brandy with water, but instead opting for fizzy mixers that came in bottles.

Another occasion that the Windhoek Sewage Farm featured in my life was, at the time, not quite so amusing. A friend of the owner of Air Oasis had died and had written in his will that his ashes were to be scattered over his game farm on the edge of the Khomas Hochland, a very rugged hilly territory adjoining the western side of the valley in which Windhoek nestles.

Some bright spark had come up with the idea that, due to the ruggedness of the terrain, the most effective way to scatter the ashes would be from an aircraft. Liking the idea, the widow then contacted Derrick and asked him to make arrangements. Of course, Derrick then hastily delegated the duty to me.

On the appointed day the gentleman's two sons arrived at the airport with their father's ashes in an urn. There had been delays and by now it was mid afternoon on a summer day, and thunderstorms were already beginning to form over the hills surrounding the city. The wind was fairly light from the North so we taxied out to runway 01 for take off. Climbing to a height that would clear the hills, I asked the tower for the latest surface wind, and then turned and headed to position the aircraft over the northern side of the farm, figuring that the wind would then scatter the ashes towards the south and over the farm.

The window of the Cessna was opened and the ashes released but within two minutes the wind had swung completely, as happens in the proximity of thunderstorms, and was now blowing from the south west. With abject horror we watched as the cloud of ash drifted away from the game farm only to settle over the open tanks of the aerators at the sewage farm.

Prior to landing, the two brothers and I swore a vow of silence and assured anyone who asked, that the operation had been carried out in the most flawless and dignified manner.

MERCY FLIGHTS, BODY BAGS AND VOCAL CORPSES

On the odd occasion we were asked to fly out injured and seriously ill people from remote locations, which were often farms in the 'back of beyond'. At the time there was no Red Cross aircraft based in Windhoek. For these flights we would normally use a Cessna 206 as it had many desirable characteristics for this kind of operation. It had good short field performance, its high wings could clear low bushes on either side of a narrow track and it had a type of landing gear that could handle rough terrain. The high wings also gave an unobstructed view of the ground which helped when trying to locate a small strip hacked out of the bush.

Carrying out these operations during the daylight hours was quite manageable but when the request was received in the late afternoon and darkness fell before reaching the destination, it would become a far more frightening prospect. The technique was to fly to the town or village nearest to the destination and then set a course that hopefully took me to the lonely farm strip where the casualty would be waiting.

On a moonless night this could often mean flying for a long time over absolute blackness and then hoping to find the lights of a bonfire and the vehicle headlights that would mark the farm landing strip. Once the strip had been found, a landing had to be made using those vehicle headlights and the aircraft's own landing lights, neither of which gave one the perspective of proper runway lights, to judge one's height on approach.

This kind of operation really got the adrenalin pumping but not nearly as much as the time I was asked to fly to Grootfontein in the north in order to collect a body for burial in Windhoek. To facilitate this, the front passenger seat and both rear seats were removed from the 206 and I set off for Grootfontein. After landing there was a long delay but eventually the body arrived. If I had thought about it at all, I would have assumed that the body would be in a coffin but was rather unsettled to find that it was in a sort of home made body bag, that looked as if it had been made from ordinary bed sheets. This was duly loaded into the 206 with the feet to the rear and the head and torso on the floor where the front passenger seat had been, right next to me. I insisted that the body be strapped down, to ensure it could not slide forward and obstruct the rudder pedals and brakes. This was accomplished by lashing it, with ordinary washing line, to the metal frame upon which my seat was mounted, thus moving it that much closer to me.

By the time I was able to get airborne for Windhoek, it was well into mid afternoon and the thermals, that make flying in that part of the world so bumpy, were, by that time, well formed. Already feeling quite uneasy about the corpse next to me, I decided to climb to a cruising level of 10,500 ft where I hoped the air would be smoother. My gaze was fixated between the instrument panel and the view from the windows (anything to avoid looking at the body!), when passing through 9,000 ft, the corpse beside me let out one tremendously loud belch.

If I had been able to force the door open against the airstream, I would have been hanging from the wing strut outside the cabin! As it was, I think my heart just stopped and I froze, for what seemed like several minutes. I smoked back then and when I eventually was able to move, I lit a cigarette with trembling hands. The explanation was, of course, quite simple. As we climbed, the air pressure decreased and a differential between the ambient air and the air in the corpse's lungs was created. The belch was just air being expelled from the lungs to equalise the pressure. This lofty rationalisation did, however, not prevent me from having nightmares for weeks afterwards.

4

ALL GOOD THINGS COME TO AN END

SAA ACCEPTANCE TESTING

It was around this time that my pilot application to SAA had resulted in an invitation to travel to Johannesburg and attend the selection board. This would also involve a flight test, medicals and a battery of psychological tests.

The selection board was rather daunting, consisting of the Chief Pilot, a group of several very senior Captains including the Chief Training Captain, and a Captain representing the pilots union. The Flight Operations Administrative section also sat at the long table facing the lone chair upon which the applicant was invited to sit.

Fortunately a few lucky breaks came my way. Firstly, as I mentioned previously, the Chief Pilot, Pine Pienaar, had two years earlier advised me to resign my engineering position with SAA, and reapply as a pilot when I had a few thousand hours in my logbook, and here he was heading up the selection board.

Secondly, from reading my name, the Chief Training Captain, who initiated the interview, assumed that I came from an Afrikaans background and asked if I could speak English. When I hesitantly replied that I could, the whole interview was conducted from thereon in English which unbeknown to them was my home language. They must have thought that I was exceptionally bilingual.

Thirdly, most of the questions were designed to see if the applicant had been keen enough to familiarise himself with many of the aspects of SAA's operations. As I had previously spent four years with SAA these questions presented no problem whatsoever.

The flying test was conducted by a Training Captain on a Dakota and was very much a formality. The medicals were pretty much what any commercial pilot with an instrument rating goes through every six months.

The psychological testing was a different matter altogether. The tests lasted a full day and we were all bussed through to Railway headquarters in Johannesburg where the testing was to take place.

Corleen had studied psychology at university and one of her textbooks was 'White's Industrial Psychology' which at the time was the standard book used by industrial psychologists. I had read the book which explained in great detail exactly how these tests worked and what they supposedly told the examining psychologist about one's personality. It also revealed the salient fact that between tests the subjects would gather in a venue where their interactions with the other subjects would would be closely observed by the psychologists. These interactions supposedly allowed the psychologists to gauge potential leadership qualities.

Forearmed with this knowledge I had learned a variety of new jokes and made up some juicy rumours concerning our chances of being accepted into the airline. Exactly as White's had described it, between tests we all gathered in the centre of a large room where around the walls desks had been placed facing inwards. At these desks the psychologists sat and pretended to be absorbed in paperwork. To a careful observer it soon became clear that they were actually watching us and that the paperwork was a mere cover. I immediately went into my repertoire of jokes and rumours speaking too quietly for my voice to carry to the edges of the room. Before too long everybody had gathered around me and the watching psychologists must have thought that I had exceptional leadership qualities.

My response to the Rorschach ink blot tests must have frustrated them somewhat as all I could see in their inkblots were Persian carpet patterns and undersea scenes of coral heads and the like. But then I had figured that exaggerated emotions and imagination were probably not characteristics that they were looking for in a pilot.

After a long day of tests, and having people messing with our heads, we were all glad when it came to an end and we were bussed back to Flight Operations where we all met up for a drink at a nearby pub before heading for the airport and, where applicable, our flights home.

A month later a letter arrived from SAA informing me that I had been accepted as a Second Officer or 'Boy Pilot' and was to attend an intake course starting at the beginning of January. I handed in my months notice to Air Oasis and helped Gus find a replacement flying instructor. My replacement had scarcely been appointed when another letter from SAA arrived, informing me that the January intake course had been cancelled and my new date would be the 4th of April 1970.

CHIEF COOK AND BOTTLE WASHER

Fortunately I did not remain jobless. A friend, Bushy Coltman, had just been appointed to set up a Windhoek branch of a Johannesburg based company E C Lennings. This was a company that sold heavy mining and construction machinery. They also sold a wide range of stationary diesel engines. Bushy had been the Chief Mine Engineer at Brandberg West and I had taught him to fly. As I had an engineering background he immediately hired me to assist him in the project. I was given a decent salary and, best of all, had the use of a variety of company vehicles.

Lennings had sold several huge Canadian manufactured dump trucks to mines in the Namib. These would arrive by ship to the port of Walvis Bay, however, to satisfy the South African local content regulations, the rock bodies, tyres and batteries were sourced locally and had to be fitted on the dockside prior to the trucks being delivered to the mines. Fortunately the local content percentage requirements were by weight rather than value.

My first duty with Lennings was to try to locate a rock body for a large mine dump truck that somehow the South African Railways had managed to lose. The truck was on the dockside at Walvis Bay but could not be delivered to a nearby mine until the rock body had been fitted. There was also a late delivery penalty clause in the contract and the date of it coming into effect was rapidly approaching.

The rock body, which is the load carrying, tipping bed of the dump truck, had been loaded in Johannesburg but somehow never arrived in Walvis Bay. It is huge, almost the size of a small house, which begs the question 'How on earth do you lose something that big?' Only the railways would know!

I started my quest in the offices of the freight section at the Windhoek railway station where my queries met with blank stares. Giving up on the clerks, I strolled around to the shunting yards and started chatting to the workers who actually uncouple and couple the rolling stock as required. The breakthrough came when one of the wheel tappers recalled seeing the rock body at the shunting yard about two weeks previously. This was confirmed by one of the shunt masters who confirmed that it had been coupled to the Walvis Bay train two weeks previously.

The problem was now simplified, as it had passed through Windhoek and been coupled to the Walvis Bay train, it had to be somewhere between Windhoek and Walvis Bay. Deciding that the easiest way to find it would be by air, I trotted off to Air Oasis and begged the loan of a Cessna 172. Getting airborne I followed the railway line for two hundred km until Usakos, a town renowned for a wonderful range of semi precious gem stones mined in the region. There in plain view of the whole little town, on a siding, was the huge, bright yellow rock body.

THE KAVANGO

A road was being constructed along the Kavango river from Katwitwi Tuguva in the east leaving the river at Bagani and continuing on through the Caprivi Strip to Katima Mulilo in the west. At that time the SWAPO insurgency had begun and the road would facilitate counter insurgency troop movements along the Angolan border. Lennings had supplied road building machinery and Bushy and I would often be called out to repair these machines when they suffered breakdowns.

We would drive up in a truck with all the tools and spares we needed and as the road building activity had reached Nkurenkuru we would camp there under an enormous wild fig tree near the police post. This lonely post was manned by two young South African policeman, Pierre and Stony, who soon befriended us. They introduced us to the local 'night life' which centred around a small 'hotel' in the little Angolan village of Cuangar, opposite Nkurenkuru on the other side of the river.

The 'hotel' was extremely basic, consisting of a row of stable like rooms, a pub, and an outdoor area with tables and chairs. There was no plumbing and water was obtained from a well with a hand operated pump. An ancient small diesel generator provided scant lighting. Nevertheless the drinks were cheap and the Angolan Portuguese innkeeper provided the most wonderful Peri Peri Kudu steaks which we washed down with beer and Triple Sec, a strong sweet orange flavoured liqueur.

Pierre and Stony had no boat and the only means by which we could cross the river was by dugout canoe. This canoe was owned by a local fisherman, Petrus, who would for a small fee take us across the river and then return to his side and await our call to fetch us when our evening was over. Now Petrus was very happy to ferry us over to the Angolan side but extremely reluctant to fetch us after an evening of drinking. Pierre would stand on the river bank and bellow at the top of his lungs for Petrus who would express his reluctance to fetch us by shouting back "seekoei" (hippo) at equal volume. This was meant to convey to us that there were hippos in the river and to cross it was highly dangerous. There would then follow a series of dire threats shouted across as to the consequences Petrus would suffer if he did not get his dugout across post-haste.

We soon discovered the reason for this reluctance. There was a small enclosed bay on our side of the river protected by a finger of land. It was in this little bay that Petrus landed and kept his dugout. Pierre and Stony thought it was a great joke to cause the dugout to turn turtle in this little bay and swim to the bank. They had done this so often that it had become a normal operating procedure. Petrus, with good reason as it turned out, hated this and saw nothing funny about it.

This practice came to an end rather tragically. After work, one evening, Bushy and I had joined the two youngsters who were fishing in the little bay, for sundowners. Stony had a beautiful, big and affectionate, Alsatian called Wagter that was not a police dog, but his personal pet. We were chatting and enjoying our beers when Stony idly picked up a stick and tossed it into the water for Wagter to fetch. Scarcely had Wagter hit the water when there was a huge flurry as an enormous crocodile took hold of the dog and dragged it under. Stony emptied the magazine of his rifle into the spot where the crocodile had gone under to no avail.

Obviously the crocodile had been stealthily watching the activity on the river bank and awaiting its chance. It could just as easily been one of us that may have knelt at the waters edge to clean a fish or wash our hands. It was a very sobering moment when the realisation struck us that this was the exact spot where so often the dugout had been overturned leaving its occupants floundering about in the water.

We spent quite a bit of time up on the border and it was a most interesting experience. It was quite common to see sledges pulled by oxen navigating the sand tracks that took the place of roads in that area. The same oxen would be used for ploughing which seemed to be a task for wives. I often saw women, sometimes with a baby strapped to their backs, ploughing while their husbands sat under a shade tree watching and drinking beer brewed from maize.

A very attractive hardwood called Kiaat grew all along the border and deep into Angola. The Portuguese had a thriving timber industry on the Angolan side and to facilitate this a 'boat train' ploughed up and down the river connecting the little border villages. This consisted of a motor launch towing two barges with seating for passengers. These looked very much like an old world railway carriage mounted on a hull. On the South West side of the border the locals used the Kiaat to create the most amazingly artistic wood carvings that I have ever seen.

Rundu was the largest village along the border and the Commissioner for the area was based there. He had guest accommodation and we were invited to make use of this when we were working near Rundu. This accommodation was situated atop a cliff on the bank of the Kavango and afforded, particularly at sunset, the most amazing views over the river.

During one visit the police told us a truly harrowing story. The previous year an officer from the Department of Agriculture had been teaching the one or two local farmers, who were sufficiently interested to attend the course, some basics of farming such as contour ploughing, fertilisation and rotation of land usage. That year one farmer in particular who adopted this methodology had noticeably superior crops to the majority using the traditional farming methods.

A witch doctor then informed this group that the way for them improve their crops was to kill the successful farmer and sprinkle his blood over their lands. This they duly carried out and while we were in Rundu the hunt was on for the witchdoctor. The police had borrowed two Bushman trackers from the army's anti insurgency unit to assist in the hunt. We met these strange wizened little men who were childlike and friendly. Their tracking skills were almost supernatural and the policemen we chatted to were in awe of them.

They tracked the witchdoctor to the bank of the river where he had stolen a dugout and disappeared into the bush on the Angolan side. We heard months later a rumour that the Portuguese police had apparently got their hands on him, for stirring up trouble on that side of the border, and he had not survived the ensuing interrogation.

All too soon the time arrived for us to pack up and head for Johannesburg, to attend the April intake 'Boy Pilot' course at SAA. It was a well known saying in South West Africa that 'If you wear out one pair of shoes in SWA you will never want to leave'. How true that was! With very mixed feelings we took leave of all our friends and departed SWA to begin a new chapter in our lives.

5

THE BOY PILOT

I previously mentioned the term 'Boy Pilot', but allow me to expand a little on the concept of 'Boy Pilots' in SAA back in the seventies and eighties. Unlike certain other airlines, SAA had no flight training schools and only employed fully qualified pilots. The 'nursery school' for these pilots tended to be either the South African Air Force or general aviation, which back then in SA, tended to consist mainly of charter companies. Neither of these tended to be a suitable introduction to the world of airline operations. Thus SAA created the position of Second Officers who were immediately nicknamed 'Boy Pilots'. The purpose of the position was to introduce to and familiarise new recruits with an airline operation. It also meant that, by having an additional crew member, flight and duty limitations could be extended. This was very handy when, for political reasons, we could not overfly North Africa and thus took the long route around the 'bulge of Africa'.

The Boy Pilot sat in the observer's seat behind the Captain, operated the radio and was responsible for always having the correct navigation charts, ready and correctly folded, should the Captain or First Officer require them. He was further responsible for lugging around the 'Nav Bag', a very heavy satchel containing the myriad charts, airport landing plates and other necessary paperwork that an airline operation requires.

He also acted as a relief pilot on long-haul flights but may legally only occupy a pilot's seat above 20,000 feet in the cruise. Officially he is third in command of the aircraft, based on the fact that, should the Captain and First Officer become incapacitated, he is the only remaining crew-member that can actually fly the aircraft. Be that as it may, this fact would never be apparent to anyone observing an SAA crew in any situation. It would soon become clear to any such observer that he was the low man on the totem pole, often treated with contempt by all and sundry members of the crew.

The Boy Pilot further filled the roll of adjutant, general factotum and chief cook and bottle washer for the rest of the crew. On slips he was always the keeper of the kitty for the crew, and therefore responsible for paying all the bills, buying tickets and generally managing the finances. Any activity that was less then fun would be decided in terms of seniority and thus would always fall to the Boy Pilot. This could be anything from organising an outing to taking a drunken crew-member back to the hotel.

It was a very good introduction to airline life. Some of the recruits were 'Top Guns' in the Airforce and characteristically cocky. A stint as a Boy Pilot soon taught them humility and when taken to task, even unfairly, to immediately apologise and vow to do better in future, rather then to argue the point. There was one particular Captain who would not even allow his 'Boy Pilot' to adjust the volume on the radio without his say so.

It was also a very necessary introduction to the high pressure flying in the busy European and American airways and at their high traffic airports. We had learned our flying in the very relaxed skies of South Africa and thus, for us, the first time flying into Heathrow, La Guardia or Orly was a mind boggling experience.

CAPTAIN MUMBLES

As a Boy Pilot I nearly had my confidence shattered by a certain Captain. When you operated the radio and were queried by Air Traffic Control, you often needed to consult the Captain for a decision. An example of this would be "Springbok 203 would you prefer a straight in approach to runway 32?" This particular Captain was a mumbler of note, and after such a query from ATC, I would look at him for an answer and he would mutter something into his beard. Picking up only a word here and there and with ATC impatiently waiting for an answer, I would, through a process of guesstimation and what I thought was logic, give an answer. This would invariably be followed by a blast from the left hand seat and an effusive apology from myself.

This happened so often that I began to have doubts as to whether I had any command ability at all after making so many incorrect decisions.

These doubts were fortunately later dispelled when a group of us on a refresher course discussed the matter and found that we were all in the same boat. One of the wiser heads pointed out that the Captain never actually rescinded the answers we had given to ATC but merely carried out whatever procedure his Boy Pilot had informed ATC was preferred. On reflection, I think Captain Mumbler was just having a bit of fun and teaching us to think on our feet at the same time.

LOST IN LISBON

Having said that the Boy Pilot was the low man on the totem pole, this was not always true as occasionally there was one even lower and this was the Supernumerary Boy Pilot. Prior to being thrown in at the deep end the airline allowed you one familiarisation trip as an observer. You would assist the Boy Pilot and try to absorb as much as possible prior to your first trip in the 'hot seat'.

I recall my first flight as a Supernumerary Boy Pilot which was to Lisbon. As an additional crew member, accommodation was not always available at the contractual crew hotel and thus I was dropped off at a small, not very grand, hotel that was very remote from the crew hotel.

Having never previously been out of Southern Africa, I was extremely excited to be in Europe and particularly in such a different cultural environment. So excited in fact that I suffered a severe attack of 'brain fade'. Shortly after arriving early in the morning, I rushed out of the hotel and spent the day exploring Lisbon.

Towards mid afternoon fatigue began to catch up with me and I decided to return to the hotel for a much needed sleep. Only then did it slowly dawn on me that, not only had I no idea of the location of the hotel but neither did I have the faintest clue as to its name. Nor did I even remember the name of the hotel where the rest of the crew were staying.

This was really a moment for panic, totally lost and alone in a strange city where I was not even able to speak the language. I think at that stage I was too tired to sustain a panic for any length of time, and as the ability to think returned I realised that there must be an SAA sales office in Lisbon. Soon I was able to find a local taxi that knew where the SAA offices were and took me there.

There followed a period of intense embarrassment as I tried to explain my predicament to the staff that had all emerged from their various offices and formed the small crowd that surrounded me. Of course, I knew what they were thinking. 'Can this clown really be one of our pilots, one of a team that could safely navigate an airliner halfway around the world?'

Eventually I was able to convince them that this was indeed the case, and I was rescued. After that incident, I never left an unfamiliar hotel without making sure that all its details were written down and in my pocket.

At least my little incident did not come to the notice of anyone outside of the Lisbon office and there were no repercussions whatsoever.

Sadly this was not the case in later years for a Boy Pilot and his Supernumerary Boy Pilot colleague on a London trip.

THE AURAL INVISIBILITY SYNDROME (1)

Vlokkie (pronounced 'Flocky'), the Boy Pilot was on his first trip as a Boy Pilot, having only a week previously completed his Supernumerary Boy Pilot trip.

Standard practice would have been to roster a supernumerary with an experienced Boy Pilot. Either the rostering clerk was asleep, or had a more sinister motive, as a Supernumerary Boy Pilot had been rostered with Vlokkie, and it would be Vlokkie's task to 'show him the ropes'.

The supernumerary had, shortly after joining the airline, been nicknamed 'Falconetti', purely on the grounds of his physical resemblance to the actor who played the villain in a popular series 'Rich Man, Poor Man' that was showing on SA TV at he time.

These two, one on his first and the other on his second overseas trip set off for London. Arriving very early in the morning, they and the rest of the crew were taken to the Mount Royal Hotel which was our crew hotel at the time. Having been allocated rooms on one of the upper floors, they agreed that they would have a sleep prior to getting together to see what London had to offer. They had bade farewell to the rest of the crew they had arrived with, knowing that they were rostered with a different crew on the return flight to Johannesburg.

Now anyone looking at this pair would immediately know that they were trouble looking for a place to happen and, sure enough, it wasn't long before they fell victim to what I like to call 'The Aural Invisibility Syndrome'.

Afrikaans is, by global standards, not a widely spoken language. This fact gave certain of our international aircrew a false sense of security in that, as long as they spoke in Afrikaans, they could say what they liked and no one would understand. This idiotic notion has had serious consequences for several of our crew-members over the years. This, however was a classic case of idiocy as it took place in a crew hotel by two Boy Pilots who had just joined SAA and would not have known what any of the crew that they had not flown in with looked like.

At the prearranged time 'Falconetti' knocked on 'Vlokkies' door and they proceeded to the lifts.

As luck would have it, the Chief Pilot International, Meyer Botha, was roomed two floors below and also preparing to leave the hotel. Meyer was slight of build and notably had a rather long and pointy nose. He was rather an eccentric dresser and for his foray on the streets of London wore a check shirt under a little yellow waistcoat and topped it off with a flat tartan cap complete with pom-pom.

Meyer entered the lift and nodded to the two Boy Pilots who towered over him. The doors closed and the pair looked at Meyer, then at each other before 'Vlokkie' announced loudly in Afrikaans,

"Look at this little twerp, he must think he's Pinocchio".

Meyer gave no indication that he understood, and thus rude comments, in Afrikaans, continued until the lift doors opened at the lobby floor where Meyer and the two Boy Pilots went their separate ways.

Of course, Meyer, despite having never laid eyes on the pair before, knew exactly who they were. After all, it was the crew hotel and here were two hulking Afrikaans speaking youngsters with regulation haircuts. The clincher was that they were both wearing dead give-away Boy Pilot watches.

Boy Pilot watches were the subject of much mockery amongst the more seasoned crews. They were the large Breitling Navitimers, complete with aviation calculator dial, so favoured by any Boy Pilot who could afford one.

Unfortunately, I did not fall into that category, as even second-hand they are worth a small fortune today.

The next evening at 'call time' our two friends arrived in the lobby to find that 'Pinocchio', resplendent with four gold bars and the three stars of a Chief Pilot on his sleeve, was their Captain for the flight home. This flight would not have gone well for them and it was doubtful that they had any rest breaks. Meyer, despite his comical appearance, was not one to be trifled with!

If I have given the impression that being the 'low man on the totem pole' had no upside, this was totally unintentional. The large majority of the more seasoned crews were always willing to teach, assist and afford the 'Boy Pilot' the benefit of their experience. Some of the older Captains were quite paternalistic towards their Boy Pilots. I recall as a Boy Pilot being given a lecture over dinner, regarding the importance of eating my vegetables, by a well-meaning Captain.

Furthermore you bore very little responsibility, never had to make decisions and the scope for messing up was fairly limited. You stayed in five star hotels, were given generous meal allowances and had fun while visiting exotic destinations. All in all, It was a huge step up from air force life or the hard scrabble of charter, ab initio flying instruction, or crop dusting.

All of the Boy Pilots were young and most of them unmarried. Often they were mothered and spoilt by the older hostesses, and naturally were a romantic target for the younger hostesses. Oh well, another tough day in the airline!

VISCOUNT DAYS

Having spent a year, after joining SAA, as a Boy Pilot and enjoying all the excitement of being an international crew member on Boeing 707's with hardly any responsibility beyond doing what one was told to do, I was notified to report for a course to qualify as a First Officer on the Viscount 813.

This was wonderful news as operating as a Boy Pilot, actually getting to fly was very much dependant on the good will of the more empathetic Captains who would on occasion allow you to fly the aircraft during the climb and descent. Flying the aircraft manually in the thin air at cruising levels was extremely difficult and not really an option. In later years when I was a first Officer on 707s we had both autopilots fail over the Atlantic. The Captain, the 'Boy Pilot and myself flew manually, in twenty minute shifts, for six hours. It requires plenty of concentration, is very tiring and no fun at all.

A conversion course starts with aircraft technical which involves several weeks in the classroom familiarising oneself with every minute detail of how the aircraft's many systems work. This would include engines, airframes, control systems, hydraulics, electrics, fuel, pressurisation, air conditioning, propellers, landing gear, flaps, brakes and a myriad of other ancillary systems even including such things as the mechanics and electrics that allow aircraft's toilets to function. During my time as an apprentice aircraft engineer I had spent a year working on Viscounts so all this did not present too much of a problem. It was, however, quite amusing to watch the reaction of some of the less technically minded pilots on the course as they were bombarded with this avalanche of mind boggling technicalities.

The lecturers were normally drawn from the ranks of our Flight Engineers and they possessed a truly huge amount of patience as well as a great sense of humour. At the end of the course the exams were rigorous and a mark of under 90% was unacceptable. After the technical came courses on emergency procedures, flight planning and weight and balance.

Having completed these courses successfully, simulator training began and consisted of ten four hour sessions in the simulator. In these sessions handling every conceivable emergency situation, including multiple system failures, was practised. Having passed the simulator competency test, conducted by a Training Captain, the more pleasant aspect of the conversion began with flying training in the actual aircraft and ending with twenty sectors on the route with various Training Captains. Having completed all this one is finally let loose on the routes with ordinary line Captains.

GROUND CONTROLLED APPROACHES

During my route training I was fortunate to have been able to experience several Ground Controlled Approaches (GCA) in actual low cloud, low visibility instrument flying conditions. Cape Town was the only airport in the country that had the equipment to offer this service. Unlike modern Instrument Landing Systems where all the relevant data, regarding one's position and altitude in relation to an ideal electronic path to the runway, is displayed on instruments in the cockpit, the GCA is carried out by obeying instructions from a suitably qualified Air Traffic Controller. This controller will have two radar screens in front of him, one showing the aircraft's alignment with the runway and the other showing the aircraft's height in relation to an ideal approach slope superimposed on the screen. He will issue a series of verbal instructions to keep the aircraft aligned with the runway and at the correct height relative to its distance from the runway.

These procedures depended on a great deal of trust between pilots and controllers which resulted in the build up of an excellent relationship between them. On taxiing to the terminal after a successful GCA, in foul weather, the pilots would thank the controller and the spirit of camaraderie would be practically tangible. Sadly the last GCA was in early 1971, after which they were phased out and the equipment scrapped.

The Viscount was a lovely aircraft to fly, with mild manners. Being a turboprop it was quiet and smooth in flight compared with piston engined aircraft. Outside the aircraft, while running, a high pitch scream was emitted from the large engine-driven Rootes compressors that provided air for cabin pressurisation. Having spent a fair amount of time around Viscounts I am left with the memento of near deafness on the frequencies emitted by those compressors. Fortunately being deaf to those high frequencies was not a factor in flying medicals, being well out of the range of speech.

The Viscount had water methanol injection which increased the power of the engines for take off at high altitude airfields such as Johannesburg. It also had an amazing 47 degree flap setting which would always save your bacon if you misjudged your approach, or were held up by ATC and were too high. You could not land with that much drag so the flaps automatically retracted to 40 degrees when power was applied prior to touchdown.

THE DYING FLEET

By the time I took up a position of First Officer, or co-pilot on the fleet, the turboprop Viscounts were earmarked to be phased out replaced with Boeing 737 200 jets and thus had become, what I call a 'dying fleet', my course having been the last SAA Viscount course. All attention was focused on the new arrivals and the 'Cinderella' Viscount Fleet was just left to get on with it and thus enjoyed a great deal of autonomy with very little interference from the powers that be. To amplify this freedom, SAA was short on Captains and required their Viscount Captains to be converted onto the new jets. As the SAA Captains left the Fleet they were replaced by

Viscount Captains on loan from Air Rhodesia who had surplus Captains at the time.

The Air Rhodesia Captains were highly individualistic characters that really did not take easily to SAA bureaucracy and procedures that they considered to be overly fastidious. This did not mean that they were not safe and careful operators all being highly experienced pilots with loads of knowledge regarding flying in Africa, they just had a more relaxed attitude towards the operation than SAA would consider appropriate and this led to some pretty interesting flying experiences for a green young co-pilot.

The Viscounts had been taken off the main routes between Johannesburg, Durban and Cape Town and we mainly serviced South West Africa, now Namibia. One of our flights was a three day programme with both night stops in Windhoek. On the first day we would fly to Windhoek from Johannesburg via Kimberly, Upington and Keetmanshoop. The second day would take us to Alexander Bay, Cape Town and back to Windhoek again via Alexander Bay. On the third day we would return to Johannesburg via Keetmanshoop, Upington and Bloemfontein. These routes were characterised by a great deal of turbulence, due to the heat over the desert-like landscape, so the Viscounts were soon dubbed the 'Vomit Comets'. We were even seconded to fly the 'Air Sickness Tests' that in those days the poor aspirant cabin crew were subjected to.

On the Cape Town Alexander Bay sector we would often, at the Captain's discretion, fly low level up the coast all the way, then after take off at Alexander Bay would continue the low level coastal as far as Luderitz before turning inland and setting course for Windhoek. These were wonderfully scenic flights with a great deal to see including wildlife, fishing and shipping activities. The approach into Alexander Bay was often quite exciting as the low cloud caused by the juxtaposition of the cold Benguela current and the warm desert would often cover the airfield. In this case our only option was to go low level and follow the bed of the Orange River sneaking under the cloud until one, hopefully, sighted the airfield

On the sector from Windhoek to Alexander Bay we would often deviate from our planned route so we could fly down the Fish River Canyons, another wonderful scenic experience. On one memorable occasion, I was flying and the Captain was playing with a newly acquired, state of the art, video camera. He had decided that he would like to film the Fish River Canyons and so we had set a course from Windhoek that would route us that way and commenced our descent early so that we would be at low level over the canyons. Back then video cameras were not the small digital devices that they are today and when the Captain had his eye against the eyepiece, he could see very little other than what was revealed to him through the viewfinder.

Of course, everything he viewed through the viewfinder looked a lot smaller and further away. At the time I did not realise this and so, despite a certain amount of trepidation, I obeyed his repeated commands to fly lower until we were actually below the lip and well into the canyon. When the skipper eventually removed his eye from the eyepiece and saw the world as it was, I think, he came very close to heart failure. I often wonder what the sightseers at the view sites on the lip of the canyon thought, when an airliner came steaming down the canyon below the level at which they were standing and they found themselves gazing at the top of its fuselage.

Surprisingly these escapades never seemed to come to the attention of the powers that be at SAA, although I do recall one exception. On a hot day at the altitude of Johannesburg, when the aircraft was heavy, water methanol injection was needed to boost the power of the engines and thus ensure that the take off limits were not exceeded. The four switches, one for each engine, that activated the water methanol injection were situated on the co-pilots side of the cockpit and on the Captain's command he would switch them on when the aircraft was lined up with the runway prior to the engines being spooled up for take off.

This particular day there had been a number of distractions that kept the crew very busy just prior to take off and, as a water methanol assisted take off was the exception rather than the rule, somehow the take off was commenced with the injection switches in the off position. This was realised shortly after the engines had been spooled up and the take off run commenced. Switching on the water methanol when the engines were delivering take off power could seriously damage them so the Captain throttled right back before asking the co-pilot to flip the switches to on. With the switches now on, the throttles were once again advanced and the take off successfully completed.

If it had just been left at that, all would have been fine and the incident soon forgotten but unwisely the Captain decided to rationalise the incident to the passengers and, no doubt, to the attractive air hostesses, in a way that would make him look good. On the climb he picked up the public address microphone and after welcoming and giving the usual flight details to the passengers he apologised for the start-stop-start take off and explained how, just after the start of the take off roll, a little dog had run across the runway. He further explained that, not wanting to hit the little fellow, he had slowed, in order to allow it to get clear, after which he again opened the throttles and resumed the take off. This went down well with the passengers and, no doubt, scored him some brownie points with the hostesses on his Windhoek night stop.

A week later things began to unravel for him when a letter from a dear old lady arrived on the SAA Chief pilots desk. The letter sang the praises of the wonderfully kind Captain who had gone to such lengths to avoid hitting a little dog. Unfortunately our Chief Pilot, who was a crusty character at the best of times, failed to see any humour in the situation and the reaming out received by our hero was legendary.

All too soon the Viscounts were sold to British Midland Airways, the Rhodesian Captains returned to Air Rhodesia and the SAA co-pilots were placed on conversion courses, the unlucky ones to the Hawker Siddeley turboprop twin that SAA had a brief flirtation with, and the luckier ones, myself included, to the newly arrived Boeing 737-200.

THE HIJACK

The Boeing 737-200 had a nickname in America where it was known as 'Fat Albert' after a character in one of Bill Cosby's sitcoms. In SAA it was affectionately called 'Fluffy' which stood for 'fat little ugly fucker'. It was SAA's first jet that was operated by two pilots with no Flight Engineer. Despite an electronic warning system that alerted the pilots to any failure, the lack of an extra pair of hands and eyes meant a far higher workload for the pilots.

The 737-200 conversion was my toughest conversion course in SAA. It was a far more serious introduction to 'Boeing Philosophy' than was the 707 Boy Pilots course, and a new concept in ergonomics. The 737 also covered the ground a great deal faster than the Viscount meaning one had to think twice as fast to anticipate and stay ahead of the aircraft. This became very apparent on short sectors where the climb was almost immediately followed by the descent with practically no level cruising time.

Such a sector was Port Elizabeth – East London and the Captains delighted in putting new co-pilots under pressure on this sector. A factor that assisted them in this light hearted activity was the fact that the caterers in East London made the tastiest of pies. The Captains would insist that the new co-pilots took orders for these culinary delights from the whole crew and passed them on to the East London caterers on the radio via SAA traffic. This had somehow to be fitted in amongst the high workload while flying what was basically a parabola.

After having flown the 737 for a few months you would sit on the Port Elizabeth – East London sector with plenty of spare time on your hands and wonder what on earth you had been doing to have been so pressurised.

The 'Fluffy', having only two engines was also what pilots call 'a hot ship'. This may sound contradictory but, for certification by the Federal Aviation Agency in America, an aircraft must be able to fly a stipulated vertical profile after the failure of an engine. A four engined aircraft after an engine failure has lost only 25% of it's power, while a twin will have lost 50% but must still be able to fly the same profile. The upshot of this means that with both engines working a twin has an abundance of power making it a 'hot ship'.

On the afternoon of the 26th of May 1972. My standby was only a little over two hours old and already I was bored stiff.

Back then we were required to be at the airport when on standby. There was a morning and an afternoon standby crew to cover flights in the event that a crew member failed to arrive for a flight, or an extra unscheduled flight needed to be operated. I was on afternoon standby which started at noon and ended when the crew for the last flight signed on, normally at around 8 pm.

I was a very new co-pilot on Boeing 737-200s at the time and we were relaxing in the crew lounge. This was opposite the Flight Operations counter where the crews sign on, read the Notices to Airmen, check the weather and decide on the fuel to be carried. Also housed there is ZUR, call sign 'Springbok Johannesburg', the long-range company radio station that allows SAA's Flight Operation to communicate with our aircraft wherever in the world they may be.

I glanced across at Capt. Mynhardt Slabbert with whom I was partnered on this standby session. Slabbie was infamously known as 'Captain 13' and I had never flown with him but had heard all about how he had earned his nickname. He looked as bored as I felt, and he was just suggesting that we should go and find a cool-drink, when we became aware of quite a disturbance emanating from Flight Ops. It was almost as if someone had kicked over a beehive.

Strolling across the corridor to the counter we eventually found someone coherent enough to tell us what all the commotion was about. Apparently one of our aircraft had been hijacked!

SA 209, the SAA Boeing 727, ZS-SPE 'Letaba' had departed Salisbury at 12.50 and was scheduled to land at Jan Smuts Johannesburg at 14.20. The crew had earlier operated the morning Johannesburg - Durban - Johannesburg flight and were on the return leg of the Johannesburg - Salisbury - Johannesburg Flight with 76 passengers.

The cockpit crew was made up of Captain Blake Flemington, First Officer Archie Schultz and Flight Engineer Bert Cheetham. The cabin crew were Chief Steward Dirkie Nel and Stewards Lance Gwyther and Joppie Nieman. The two Air Hostesses were Thea van Rensburg and Talana Nel.

Shortly after Blake had made the descent announcement over the PA, a very flustered Tia van Rensburg came into the cockpit. She had been told by two, rather desperate and sinister looking passengers, to inform the Captain that he was to change course and fly to Khartoum, also that any attempt to land in South Africa would result in them blowing up the aircraft. Blake immediately relayed this to Air Traffic Control and, hoping it was all a joke, commenced descent. At this point Lance Gwyther came into the cockpit and told Blake that a passenger had explosives and intended setting them off. Blake then stopped the descent, requested a northerly heading from ATC and asked Lance to bring the threatening passenger to the flight deck.

Here it should be remembered that this was nearly thirty years prior to 911 and international terrorism had not yet really reared its ugly head. There were no impregnable cockpit doors fitted to aircraft. The cockpit doors had, in fact, panels designed to be kicked out easily so that in the event of an accident emergency crews would have ready access to the cockpit.

A swarthy thickset man arrived on the flight deck. He was well dressed and spoke excellent English, but despite this, there was an air of menace about him. He explained that he and his accomplice had explosives and were deadly serious in their threats. Blake then explained that they did not have enough fuel to go anywhere other than Johannesburg or Bloemfontein which was their designated alternate. The hijacker then became extremely agitated and kept repeating his threats. In the meantime the Flight Engineer, Bert Cheetham had worked out that the aircraft could just make the return to Salisbury at optimum altitude and maximum range cruise.

This was explained at great length to the hijacker and he was told that the aircraft could be refuelled there. After much persuasion the hijacker accepted this plan and the aircraft returned to Salisbury where it landed with low fuel pressure lights illuminated.

When ATC was informed of the situation they immediately passed on the information to SAA Flight Operations. Efforts were soon under way to assemble a response team ready to fly to any destination where the 727 might eventually land. At the same time a 737 was being readied to undertake such a flight. Captain Slabbie and I were designated to operate this 737 and were told not to wander too far away, as the green light could come at a moments notice. We immediately drew charts from the Navigation Office for all the obvious destinations within a 727's range and retired to the crew lounge to study them. Suddenly the boredom of our standby was replaced by a state of high excitement and trepidation.

As part of the response team we were kept abreast of the situation as details were received. Of course, we knew the crew well and were shocked by the situation in which they found themselves. It was later disclosed that the hijackers had a pistol, sticks of dynamite and a metal box which they claimed contained plastic explosive.

On the ground at Salisbury there was a period of protracted negotiation between Blake and the hijackers. During these negotiations the two men refused to make any demands known and only kept repeating their demand that they be flown to Khartoum. At this point Blake asked the leading hijacker how he wished to be addressed and was told that he was to be called 'Captain Z'. Blake then informed him that there was only one Captain on this aircraft and that was himself. Blake thereafter addressed him as 'Z'.

By this time the South African security forces, who were now at Flight Ops in great numbers, had identified the two hijackers as Fouad Abdoul Kamil and Abou Yaghi, both of Lebanese extraction.

Back on board the Letaba it was explained by the crew to Kamil, ad nauseam, that the 727 was a domestic airliner and that it lacked the range for a flight to Khartoum. It was further explained that range was a factor of weight and that the more passengers that were released, the lighter the aircraft would be, and the further it could fly. It was also suggested that women and children would only create complications and would not make good hostages. Blake also tried to talk them into considering alternative destinations, his motive being that he wanted a destination in a country friendly to South Africa. He eventually managed to talk them into accepting the Seychelles, at that time under British rule.

Strictly speaking, very little of what Blake told Kamil was true but Blake was a very cool character, extremely clever and a brilliant negotiator.

In Salisbury the aircraft was refuelled at Blake's request. Kamil and Yaghi, after checking the passengers' passports, now agreed to release all but five of them. Once the aircraft had lined up for take off, the rear air-stair was lowered and the hijackers allowed the fortunate seventy-one passengers to disembark.

That rear stairway on the 727 was a wonderful innovation. It was an hydraulically operated stair that dropped out of the fuselage at the rear of the aircraft. It was lit and made rather a grand entranceway for boarding passengers, it also made the 727 independent of ground equipment to embark and disembark passengers. Sadly this type of air-stair seems have disappeared from the more modern jets. Many is the time I have wished they had not, particularly when apologising for delays in disembarking, caused by air-stairs not arriving at the parking bay.

Blake had also managed, somehow, to negotiate the release of all but one of the cabin crew. Only the Chief Steward, Dirkie Nel, would remain with the five hostages. Both Air Hostesses, Tia and Talana, volunteered to remain with the hostages but Blake would not hear of it and ordered them off.

Blake later learned that much negotiation had been going on between the South African and Rhodesian governments during this period and that, according to a reported conversation between the head of State security, General 'Lang (tall) Hendrik' van den Bergh and the Captain of the flight carrying him from Cape Town to Johannesburg, the South African government had requested the Rhodesians to shoot down the hijacked aircraft. This was confirmed by the Captain of one of the two Canberra fighter/bomber aircraft of the Royal Rhodesian Air Force which were scrambled to fall in behind the 727 and await further orders.

This request was firmly turned down by the Rhodesian Prime Minister Ian Smith, himself an ex Royal Air Force pilot. The apparent rationale behind this request was that the South African government, with the siege mentality of the time, would not allow an SAA aircraft to be hijacked. This request was made before any of the passengers were released! As Blake later remarked "This may be a solution to a hijacking, but is a little rough on the passengers and crew! Thank God for Ian Smith!"

There were no charts or navigation data on board for routeing to the Seychelles but the crew managed to establish contact with on HF radio with the SAA Company radio station ZUR, call sign 'Springbok Johannesburg'. Archie, the First Officer, managed to copy down a flight plan for the Seychelles given to him by the SAA Chief Navigator.

At 16.10 the aircraft took off, and set course for the Seychelles with enough fuel on board to reach Athens, a fact definitely not communicated to the hijackers. Shortly after the course was set, a voice speaking Afrikaans came over the air. This came from one of the RRAF Canberras tailing the 727. It was also the first inkling that the crew had of their presence. The Canberra navigator was querying their destination and upon being told, suggested that there was an error in their desired track. The crew then found that the time and heading on the flight plan had been transposed. The correction was made and the Canberras turned back at the Rhodesian border.

Night was falling by the time the 727 over-flew Blantyre in Malawi, en-route to the Seychelles, and now the crew embarked on a psychological campaign to scare the merry hell out of the hijackers. It was pointed out to them, in no uncertain terms, that Blantyre was the last city with an acceptable airport that would be available to them before attempting a night ocean crossing without suitable navigation equipment, to an unfamiliar island in the middle of an ocean.

Eventually, through repetition and amplification, the campaign succeeded in not only putting the wind up the hijackers but, according to Blake, they managed to scare themselves as well. As a result of these tactics the hijackers were persuaded to allow the aircraft to return to Blantyre where they landed at Chileka Airport at around ten in the evening. The crew had now been on duty for over fifteen hours, but this elicited no sympathy whatsoever from Kamil.

The aircraft was directed to the end of a secondary runway, where Air Malawi ground engineers immobilised it by deflating the tyres and deactivating the nose wheel steering.

At this point Slabbie and I were given the green light. A team from the Bureau Of State Security (with the unfortunate acronym of BOSS) bundled on board with the infamous General van den Bergh, founder of BOSS, as head honcho. With the exception of the General they all seemed very young, were extremely macho and most appeared to have adopted the persona of Rambo.

To add to the confusion we also had a team from, of all things, the Railway Police on board. At the time SAA was a division of South African Railways and, as ridiculous as this may sound, they were there to 'take control' of the situation.

We got airborne and just over two hours later we were on final approach for Chileka. During the approach and landing briefing Slabbie informed me of his intention to perform a low drag, low power approach so as not to alert the hijackers of our arrival. This was a feasible plan as it was by this time dark and we had turned off all the aircraft lights. This included not making use of our landing lights. Unfortunately, ingrained habits die hard and to my great amazement, on touchdown, Slabbie took a great handful of reverse thrust. Our carefully laid plan was shot to hell as anyone within a three kilometre radius would have been alerted to our arrival. Thus another story was added to the legend of Captain 13!

We parked well away from the 727 and the security team disappeared to find a venue where they could study the airport layout and plot strategy. Slabbie went along with them, being a bit of a Rambo himself.

I made my way to the control tower where I would be in the centre of any action and have a good view over the airfield.

When I arrived at the control tower only one person was present and manning the radio. This was Ralph Casey, the Air Malawi Operations Manager. By his accent I assumed he was an Irish expatriate. He was on the radio talking to Kamil, the number one hijacker. The conversation was calm and collected and after listening for a while, it seemed to me that Ralph was doing an excellent job of negotiation. Blake later concurred with this opinion.

On board, Yaghi, the second hijacker, had placed sticks of dynamite in the overhead lockers and had strung the lot together with fuse cord.

It was at this point that Kamil made his demands known. He was demanding that Harry Oppenheimer fly up to Chileka and meet with him.

Harry Oppenheimer was the chairman of Anglo American Corporation and De Beers Consolidated Mines and, one of the world's wealthiest men.

It was later revealed that Kamil had worked for De Beers' security division, apparently in the roll of an informant or snitch, trapping illicit diamond buyers and sellers and recovering stolen diamonds for De Beers. He felt De Beers had shorted him on commissions to the tune of US$5 million and was holding Harry Oppenheimer personally responsible. Of course he was sadly deluded if he thought that Oppenheimer would hop on a plane to Chileka and negotiate commissions with him.

When Kamil's plan had been conceived, he had thought that Oppenheimer's son-in-law, Gordon Waddell, the Scottish rugby international, would be aboard. This, Kamil thought, would be the lever to force Oppenheimer's hand. Fortunately for Gordon, but unfortunately for Kamil, he was not on board, being on another SAA flight from London to Johannesburg via Salisbury.

Although, in those days, global terrorism was in its infancy, it was a great relief to the crew to know that they were dealing with criminals and not fanatical terrorists.

Then at this point General van den Bergh arrived in the tower and summarily took over the negotiations which then became rather farcical, sounding something like this." We know who you are! Now be a man and come out!"

Was I hearing right? This was real schoolboy stuff! It had in fact been tried on me, all too often, by assorted masters and headmasters.

"I want the boy who threw stones onto my tin roof last night to be a man, own up and wait for me outside the Principal's office after assembly!"

Well, I must confess, I could never understand this philosophy. I could not see how owning up demonstrated you were a man. It certainly demonstrated that you were bloody stupid or a masochist, as all it was going to get you was a very sore backside after six cuts by a headmaster with, we suspected, sadistic tendencies.

Apparently Kamil felt the same way because things went from bad to worse until he refused absolutely to have anything to do with Lang Hendrik.

Thereafter the Railway Police tried to 'take control of the situation'. They were in an unfamiliar environment with no knowledge of aviation, radio procedure or indeed any procedure. There followed a period of confusion wherein they ably demonstrated the incompetence that had earned them the nickname of 'Stasieblompotte' (Station Flower Pots).

The upshot of all this was that Blake eventually refused to speak to them and only then was order restored. All further communications were conducted through Ralph Casey.

As part of the crew's tactics to make the hijackers as uncomfortable as possible the Flight Engineer, Bert Cheetham, had turned the cabin heat up, and with the subtropical temperature prevailing at Blantyre, the heat had become unbearable. The hijackers were persuaded to allow the crew to open the emergency hatches and main cabin door. A further result of the heat, only later discovered, was that the dynamite had begun sweating and the hijackers in handling this and wiping the sweat from their brows had developed splitting headaches, a known side effect of handling nitroglycerin.

During this period the crew had quietly briefed the hostages on the use of the escape slides and over-wing exits to ensure their readiness for a quick escape when possible. They were also briefed to make their escape along the fore and aft axis of the aircraft to minimise possible blast effect in the event of an explosion.

At a little after midnight with pressure and frustration mounting, Yaghi started shouting and arguing loudly with Kamil in their home language, Lebanese. Suddenly he pulled out a length of fuse cord which he ignited. A flurry of smoke and flickering blue light ensued. Blake, thinking that he was carrying out his threat to blow up the aircraft, immediately gave the order to evacuate.

Unfortunately, the Chief Steward, had imbibed a few miniatures during the long night and fallen asleep in the forward left row of seats next to the main cabin door. When the hostages began their escape, the hijackers ran forward and tried to stop them, shouting threats and abuse. The Chief Steward awoke to this apparent chaos and saw some of the passengers trying to deploy the slide raft. Cowed by the threats of the hijackers he, in his befuddled state, decided to prevent this avenue being used and the escape slide became jammed in the door. This left the two cockpit slide windows as the only other means of escape.

These windows slide open and are designated emergency exit hatches for the cockpit crew, should they be unable to evacuate via the main cabin. Thus each sliding window has a compartment in the cockpit ceiling which houses a coil of flat rope, attached within. One is supposed to toss the loose end through the window, exit feet first and shimmy down the rope to the ground, four metres below and usually hard, being either concrete or bitumen.

This procedure is far more difficult than it sounds, and is fraught with potential for cuts, bruises, rope burns and broken bones. At best it could only be considered a semi-controlled fall.

I was watching through binoculars as the crew followed by two of the passengers tumbled out of the windows and hit the ground running in their desire to get as far away from the impending explosion as possible. The co-pilot, Archie Schultz, broke his arm in the process. He also suffered from a wrenched neck which, as Blake later jokingly remarked, would in future remind him to remove his headset prior to evacuating.

We held our collective breath as the minutes ticked by, until it became clear that the explosives had not been detonated and the aircraft was still in one piece.

When it became apparent in the moonlight that there were no other escapees, Blake ordered Archie to guide the escaped passengers to the terminal buildings and to report the circumstances of the hijack to the ground forces. Then Blake and Bert returned to the aircraft, where by this time the hijackers were again in control and had made the Chief Steward use the loudhailer to call to them. As Blake stood under the nose of the aircraft, Kamil leaned out and threatened to kill the six remaining hostages unless Blake re-boarded the aircraft. Blake asked for the return of the shoes that he had left under his seat, prior to his evacuation, and to his surprise Kamil threw them down.

Kamil demanded that Blake climb up the escape rope and re-enter the cockpit by the slide window. As this was patently impossible, Blake agreed to re-enter by the aft air-stair, which the Chief Steward would have to lower. Bert volunteered to re-board the aircraft as well but Blake vetoed that, ordering him to leave and proceed to the terminal building.

Thus began phase two of the saga!

I watched Blake's lone figure walk the length of the fuselage and board the aircraft through the rear stairway, which had now been lowered. I have often wondered how many people, myself included, would have had the courage to do what Blake did that day.

On re-entering the cabin, Blake was threatened with physical violence by Yaghi who was shouting, gesticulating and very agitated. Kamil managed to calm Yaghi somewhat and Blake returned to the flight deck to re-establish communication with the ground.

I think that by this time Kamil had realised that Hell would freeze over before Harry Oppenheimer would arrive for a chat, and decided to modify his demands to $5 million and safe passage to a country that did not have an extradition treaty with South Africa.

Negotiations now proceeded at a snail's pace with Kamil demanding money and the negotiator, Ralph Casey, doing his best to obfuscate and delay any action. During a hiatus at one point around three in the morning, the Chief Steward, Dirkie Nel, who had taken up the First Officer's seat, quietly slipped out of the slide window and made his escape too, leaving Blake as the only crew member with the three remaining hostages, a welcome reduction in responsibility. This really brought on a rush of anger and the hijackers demanded that all hatches and windows be closed despite the heat.

An interesting observation at this point is that as the hijack progressed, the hostages became more and more sycophantic towards the hijackers in a classic display of what later became to be known as the 'Stockholm syndrome', where hostages develop a psychological bond with their captors as a survival mechanism, and begin to see their would-be rescuers as a threat. It is so called after a bank robbery in Stockholm in 1973 when four hostages were held by the robbers. Another classic example was when society heiress Patty Hearst was kidnapped by the 'Symbionese Liberation Army' and aligned herself, body and soul, with her captors.

One of the hostages was a medical doctor and he was administering painkillers to Yaghi who had a splitting headache from the nitroglycerin. He even massaged Yaghi's neck from time to time.

As dawn approached, a breakthrough in negotiations allowed a supposed South African embassy official to board the aircraft in order to negotiate directly with Kamil. This was, in fact, one of Lang Hendrik's State Security boys. I listened to him being briefed. He looked so young that I wondered if Kamil would ever believe he was a senior embassy official. His task was merely to assess the onboard situation. He departed the aircraft and protracted negotiations eventually reached a point where Kamil accepted $5 million and a Britten Norman Islander aircraft to fly him and Yaghi to Mogadishu. Blake agreed to fly this as though it was something that could easily be accomplished.

While this was being digested several Malawian Ministers including the Minister of Finance arrived in the tower. Kamil was eventually convinced that there was nowhere near $5 million in US dollars in Malawi, and he agreed to accept the equivalent amount in Malawian Kwachas. The Minister of Finance turned to his aid and instructed him to inform the Reserve Bank to prepare this sum and place it in trunks ready to be sent to the airport. This immediately met with some resistance from his fellow ministers and I recall being particularly impressed with the pragmatic way in which he overrode their objections. Pulling himself up to his full height, which was considerable, he stated "Do not worry, we will just print some more!" and that, was that!

Frighteningly a plan was being considered whereby the Malawi armed forces were to pick off the hijackers as soon as they had cleared the aircraft. Bert actually accompanied them to help identify Blake. As he said afterwards, it was just as well that this plan was discarded, as the soldiers only had automatic weapons and would have killed everyone.

Knowing nothing of this ill-conceived plan, Blake had informed Ralph Casey that he would be making another attempt to escape with the remaining hostages. This he would implement when the hijackers were hopefully preoccupied with the money. On being asked what assistance he would like he answered that a cold Castle Lager would be very welcome.

At around ten in the morning two large tin trunks containing the money arrived and now, at last, there was something for Lang Hendrik's merry men to do. They were tasked with delivering the trunks to the aircraft. Four of them carried the two trunks out then withdrew, after which the air-stair was lowered to receive the trunks. While Yaghi sat in the Flight Engineer's seat to prevent any further escape attempts, and Blake, who had been awake for thirty hours, feigned sleep, Kamil went down the stairs and dragged the trunks up to the cabin. When he opened one it seemed to be full of bank notes and as he rifled through this stack it became too much for Yaghi who just had to see for himself. Thinking Blake was asleep he headed down the cabin towards Kamil and the money.

As he passed the galley about midway down the cabin, Blake threw open the two cockpit sliding windows, tossed out the escape ropes and called for the remaining hostages to come forward. Two of them sprang forward but the third refused to budge and huddled in the corner. The other two hostages climbed out through the First Officer's window and Blake through his own. They were met by Pev Peverelli (one of the SAA maintenance engineers) in a van. The hostages piled into the back whilst Blake took the front seat where he was handed a cold can of Castle Lager as they sped off down the runway.

On looking back they were in time to see the remaining hostage come diving through the First Officer's slide window, turn a half somersault and land flat on his back. Pev sped back to the aircraft and the last hostage, still dazed but unhurt, was bundled into the back. On seeing the escape attempt, the hijackers ran forward but being too late returned to the money. They had not noticed the last hostage in the corner, and no doubt loneliness overcoming fear, he decided to make his break. At this point, as far as hostages were concerned, the hijack was over.

Now Kamil and Yaghi were alone in the aircraft without any bargaining chips beyond the safe return of the aircraft.

Bert was taken out to the aircraft where he shut down the APU (Auxiliary Power Unit) from the outside, leaving the aircraft without power, in virtual darkness and increasing heat. In what had become a hold-out, the hijackers continued to attempt to negotiate through the day and night using the loud-hailer until the batteries gave out.

By now the Malawian Authorities were losing patience. After all, the international airport and gateway to their land-locked country had been closed for close on twenty- four hours. Their priority was opening the airport so that the interruption to the tourist trade could be ended. There was a busy tourist trade centred around Lake Malawi and the closure of the airport would be costing the country much needed foreign exchange.

The following day, Friday, the Malawian President, Kamuzu Hastings Banda, gave the order to end the hold-out forthwith. He had made arrangements to fly to Britain on British Airways and the airport had therefore to be operational. This was conveyed to the hijackers who asked for a priest to be called to administer to them the last rites. This was done and the soldiers of the Malawi army lined up alongside the B727 and opened fire with their automatic weapons. At the first pause in the firing, the hijackers came running out with their hands raised. Yaghi had ironically been shot in the foot.

Incredibly, although over a thousand rounds were fired, there were only twenty-seven bullet holes in the aircraft.

So ended the drama of South Africa's first hijacking.

Shortly thereafter Slabbie and I took off for Jan Smuts International carrying crew and passengers of SA 029 who had been Kamil and Yaghi's hostages during the siege at Chileka. Also on board were Lang Hendrik and his merry men as well as the Railway Police contingent. After landing there were emotional scenes as the hostages were united with family and friends.

I was rather amused when the headline of The Star newspaper of May 25th proclaimed "Hijackers Were Ice-Cold Professionals". Fortunately for all concerned this was as far from the truth as it is possible to get, even for the media! They were in fact rank amateurs and bumbling clowns who had done no homework, had no idea of the range of a 727, or any idea of navigation. Their key hostage, Gordon Waddell, with whom they hoped to lever Oppenheimer turned out not to be aboard.

They allowed the aircraft to fly for an hour and twenty minutes in a direction away from where they thought they wished to go, and then hijacked it in the final stage of descent, just thirty nautical miles from Johannesburg when only diversion to Durban and reserve fuel remained in the tanks. 'The Three Stooges' must have written their script! This is not to say that they were not highly unpredictable and dangerous, which they most certainly were.

From my point of view, the handling of the incident had been amazing. Blake had managed to negotiate the release of sixty-nine of the passengers and four of the crew in Salisbury. He had then managed to land in a country friendly to South Africa. No loss of life had taken place and the worst injury was Archie's broken arm. All this despite BOSS and the Railway Police.

It must be reiterated that Blake had exceptional negotiating skills, was clever, quick witted and had a wonderful sense of humour.

He was, in later years, the president of the SAA Pilots Association. This was at a time when SAA pilots were very poorly paid and, incredibly, cabin crew were taking home more money than a domestic co-pilot.

With a brilliant strategy, Blake managed to force a recalcitrant management into almost doubling SAA pilots salaries. This was known as 'The Flemington Revolution' and while it did not bring us anywhere near being in line with international pilots remuneration, it did keep the wolf from the door and enable us to replace the bald tyres on our cars.

A leading newspaper at the time commented as follows:

"When finally put to the test, SAA rose to the occasion magnificently. Seldom in the ten-year history of hijacking has a crisis been handled with such tact, imaginative skill and total success in outwitting the hijackers. For this, particular credit must go to Captain Blake Flemington who was the man who had to bear most of the strain and make the most delicate judgements in his dealings with two desperate and possibly unbalanced men."

A team of SAA engineers were flown to Malawi to determine the damage to the 727. After re-inflating the tyres and temporarily patching up the bullet holes in the skin with an aluminium tape we always referred to as 'GT tape', the Letaba was flown back to Jan Smuts, unpressurised at 9000 feet, on the centre and starboard engines, the port engine having been disabled by machine gun fire.

Some days after the hijack, the Malawi security forces took the explosives out to the perimeter of the airfield to detonate them. They underestimated the size of the blast and although no one was injured, a number of windows in the terminal building were blown out.

A further interesting fact was that the tin trunk of banknotes contained only 10,000 Kwatcha, the currency of Malawi. Less than half was recovered and it was rumoured that all the mess bills at the local Officers' Club were paid that month.

Strangely enough, South Africa's efforts to extradite the pair came to nothing and they were tried in Malawi.

At the subsequent trial in Blantyre, it transpired that Yaghi was a Lebanese police officer on leave-of-absence who, as a friend of Kamil, had agreed to assist in the hijacking. The reasons why he agreed to this were never made clear. I assume, however, that they were purely for monetary gain. Kamil was a South African resident, married to a South African medical doctor. He had made his living as a 'diamond trap' working for the De Beers Diamond Company. This entailed him persuading people to illegally or illicitly buy uncut diamonds from him. This practice (entrapment) was a method widely used in South Africa by the Diamond Squad to discourage trade in uncut diamonds.

The commission paid for a successful entrapment was, according to Kamil, fifty per cent of the value of the diamonds. Kamil apparently claimed that he had uncovered a scheme whereby some allegedly high-up South African government officials had smuggled US$10 million worth of diamonds to Uruguay and that this had been covered up. Whatever the veracity of his story, he was convinced that he was owed fifty per cent of that sum. When he was denied this he went to London where he made further threats against the Oppenheimer family that were ignored. As late as April 7th he had sent a letter to De Beers in which he had threatened to hijack a SAA flight. This too was ignored. Colonel Flores van Zijl, who was head of De Beers and Anglo American Security at the time, confirmed much of this some years later.

Despite Malawian President Hastings Banda's statement saying that the hijackers would be left to rot in jail, they received a sentence of eleven years jail. They were sent to the main Malawi jail at Zomba where they served two years before being released for some obscure reason. Yaghi disappeared back to the Lebanon whilst Kamil continued to appear at SAA crew hotels in Madrid and Lisbon from time to time before disappearing from the scene around 1982 at the time of the Falklands war.

Kamil ended up in Brazil where he wrote a book based on his experience claiming, amongst other things, that Oppenheimer had relented and paid a large sum of money into his account. His wife divorced him and remained with the children in South Africa.

On retiring from SAA Blake immigrated to New Zealand and now lives at Hawke's Bay.

On a more personal note our younger son, Adrian, is married to Liza the daughter of Air Hostess Talana Nel.

Fouad Kamil was a very smooth talker and was known amongst his colleges by the nickname 'Flash Fred'. It is, in my opinion, a great pity that we never got our hands on him so that he could have stood trial in South Africa. He and his cohort had endangered the lives of the passengers and crew of SA029 and terrorised them for an extended period. Some of them had suffered injuries and their loved ones had suffered great emotional trauma.

Malawi's main Airport had been closed for nearly twenty four hours, and SAA's 727 required expensive repairs that kept it out of service for months. Then there was the cost of the rescue operation, the extra hours on the 727 and our 737 to say nothing of the fuel burnt unproductively during the whole fiasco. There was also the matter of the large sum of Kwachas that they had extorted from the Malawian treasury.

For all this they spent two years in jail. I find it impossible to believe that external factors, political or otherwise, were not at work here!

The final words on the saga should, deservedly, be Blake's.

"There were certainly moments of black humour as well as high drama at times during this hijack, but the aircraft, passengers and crew were in a life-threatening situation that could well have ended differently. The only solution to terrorism is when the governments of the world agree that there will be no asylum and that all terrorists on capture will be summarily executed".

8

LIFE AS A FLUFFY COPILOT

THE SPOORIES SICK FUND

This would seemingly be a strange subject to write about. I do, however, feel that anyone who has a sense of the ridiculous would find it entertaining.

Back in the seventies, when I joined SAA as a pilot, it was part of the Government organisation - South African Airways, Railways and Harbours. Despite the airline appearing first in the title, the Railways was very much the senior service. The head of the organisation was the Minister of Transport.

The pilots could often be heard to say, "Chain an aircraft to a railway engine and it's not going anywhere!" The Railways were called, and seldom affectionately, 'Spoories' from the Afrikaans word for railway, 'spoorweg'.

Admittedly, there were certain advantages to being part of the railways, but belonging to the Railways Sick Fund, was definitely not one of them and it was compulsory to belong to the scheme. This did not allow one any choice of GP, specialist or any other medical professional. Professor Christian Barnard, famous for the first heart transplant, found this lack of choice shocking enough to give it a mention in his book 'One Heart'.

The fund set up was that the Railways would appoint a panel of Railway doctors in certain areas and this panel would be paid a monthly retainer for each railway patient assigned to them. The monthly retainer was approximately 1 USD per month per patient. It was thus necessary for the panel to have as many railway families as possible on their books in order to give them a steady base-line income. They were not precluded from having non-railway or private patients on their books, and these naturally enjoyed priority over railway patients.

If you needed to be referred to a specialist, this would be to a designated Railway Specialist. Furthermore, medicines could only be prescribed if they were on a very restricted and outdated list of Railway approved medicines.

Our designated panel was in Kempton Park, a small town adjacent to Jan Smuts Airport and about twenty five kilometres from where we lived in Halfway House, where there were doctors but none who were appointed as 'Railway doctors' and thus were off limits to us.

The panel consisted of five doctors who had over six thousand railway families registered to their practise. We could not make appointments, but were expected to go to their rooms and wait until we could be slotted in. This would often mean waiting for hours in a tatty, overcrowded waiting room, all too often filled with people suffering from infectious illnesses.

Once we had seen the doctor, we could only obtain our prescription medicine from a Railway Dispensary also situated in Kempton Park. Before one could do this, however, a 25 cent revenue stamp had to be obtained from the ticket office at the local railway station. Here one would see the same people one had seen in the doctors' waiting room, standing in a queue, with people trying to purchase train tickets. The Kempton Park station ticket office was on the platform and offered no shelter from the icy winter winds or summer rain. Parking was hard to find at the station so, all too often, a long walk in all weather conditions was required.

Having acquired the necessary stamp to affix to your prescription, you then made your weary way to the Railway Dispensary where you, again, saw the same old crowd from the doctors waiting room and the station ticket office queue. Once again the wait was a long one, but at least it was out of the wind and the rain. This procedure could take up most of your day, involve driving 50 km, finding parking three times, walking and queuing in the all weathers and spending hours in close confinement exposed to infectious illnesses.

Yes, one had to think very carefully prior to consulting a Railway doctor, as this procedure often exacerbated, rather than cured, whatever ailed you.

On our panel was one particularly infamous doctor, nicknamed by the pilots as 'Praat Maar', Afrikaans for 'Speak up'.

The procedure at the practice was that when your number eventually came up, the receptionists would hand you a large buff envelope containing your medical records and, at the same time, direct you to an allocated doctor. You then entered the inner sanctum, actually a long corridor with doctors' rooms leading off it.

Praat Maar's room was at the far end of this corridor and as one entered the corridor from the waiting room you would hear a loud disembodied voice calling "praat maar!" thus prompting you to start listing your symptoms while still navigating the corridor. (Obviously when you have six thousand patient families, time is of the essence.)

Strangely enough, Praat Maar never actually looked at you during the consultation. When you entered he would be hunched over his desk, pen in hand, presumably filling out the preliminary details on the prescription he intended to issue you with.

As you finished relating your symptoms he would simultaneously finish scribbling your prescription and still without looking up hand it to you. This action would terminate the consultation.

To bait him, I once told Praat Maar that I was experiencing severe headaches and that I suspected that the six inch nail that was still lodged in my skull after an accident, was the cause. That still did not cause him to look up, but the prescription he handed me was for painkillers. I think that only the word 'headache' penetrated his consciousness.

The system really benefited malingerers who were after a 'sick note' to excuse them from work. Scribbling a sick note for someone who just wanted a few days off was a quick and easy procedure for a Spoories doctor. Pilots definitely do not fall into the malingerer category, as they invariably love to fly.

I do not mean to infer that the majority of Railway doctors were like the one I described. Many were good and conscientious doctors who were very conflicted by being a part of such an iniquitous system, and who worked hard to bring about change from within.

I do believe that the system was eventually forced to reform by doctors withdrawing, and the Railways finding it impossible to recruit new doctors. Many doctors that I spoke with at the time told me they would have nothing to do with such archaic and unempathetic practices.

Thus the new reformed medical aid, Transmed, allowed us unrestricted choice of doctors, specialists and other medical professionals. It also allowed our prescriptions to be filled by any pharmacy.

But best of all, no more standing in the icy Highveld winter wind, on the platform of the Kempton Park railway station, while queuing to purchase a 25 cent stamp.

In my later years in SAA I often had my ear bent by co-pilots with pernickety complaints about SAA. When this happened my mind would often wander back to those days of the Spoories Sick Fund. I would, however, never remind them how comparatively good they now had it, simply because they would never believe me!

JOKES ASIDE

We had the full range of humorists in SAA. I think that the many hours of boredom whilst sitting around at airports gave the practical joke specialists amongst us plenty of time to hatch their evil, and often convoluted, plots.

I first met Jimmy when I was a Boy Pilot and he was a first officer on 707s. At the time we both lived in Kempton Park, a small town adjacent to the then Jan Smuts Airport near Johannesburg. Corleen and I became house friends with Jimmy and his lovely wife Lorna.

Jimmy was notorious as the leading SAA practical joker and was prepared to spend unlimited time thinking of ways to catch out the unwary. He was bad enough as a First Officer but when he was promoted to Captain, and freed of moderating influences, the joker in him was given free reign.

The out station ground engineers at all our domestic destinations were soft targets and Jimmy took full advantage of this.

Aircraft tend to have many little panels that give access to various service items. These panels are hinged and spring loaded to open when a little flush button is pushed. When a ground engineer meets an arriving aircraft he will pop open a small panel in the aircraft's nose. This gives him access to a jack into which he can plug his headset and microphone in order to inform the Captain that the chocks are in place and that the brakes may be released. The Captain will convey to him the amount of fuel required for the next sector and inform him of any technical snags the aircraft may have.

Many an unsuspecting engineer meeting Jimmy's flight, would push the button only to have an extremely realistic rubber Tarantula spider flung at him by the spring-loaded door.

The under-wing refuelling panel, of course, afforded a bit more scope. It was much larger and could accommodate a decent size rubber snake. As whoever opened the panel would be standing directly underneath it, the 'snake' would actually fall onto them. A further advantage of this panel was that the ground engineer who opened it would invariably be accompanied by the refueler. Two birds with one stone, so to speak. On occasion, while sitting in a nearby aircraft, I saw the chaos that ensued as engineer and refueler fell over themselves and the fuel hoses in their haste to distance themselves from the 'snake'.

Eventually Jimmy was forced to desist as the engineers started to track his movements through Flight Operations. When they knew Jimmy was the Captain of an incoming flight, they would not initially go near the aircraft. Thus Jimmy would have to send the First Officer down to chock the aircraft, go and look for an engineer to give the fuel figure to and also to open the fuelling panel himself. Only then would the refuelling and transit checks commence.

Once Jimmy swapped roles. He had some time to kill in Durban between flights and borrowed an engineers overall, baseball cap, headset and microphone. So disguised, he strolled out to meet the next incoming SAA aircraft. The Captain of this aircraft turned out to be the feisty, short tempered and assertive 'Slabbie' also known as 'Captain 13'.

Now normally, after the ground engineer opens the panel and plugs his headset and microphone into the socket, the polite dialogue would go something like this:

"Good morning Captain. Welcome to Durban! The chocks are in and you may release the brakes. Are there any snags and do you have a fuel figure for me?"

However, what Slabbie heard was the terse command: "Pull your finger out of your backside and give me a fuel figure. I am in a hurry!"

Slabbie's First Officer later related that Slabbie jumped so violently that he sprained his neck, when his head came in contact with the overhead control panel. Apparently an impression of the de-icing switches could be seen imprinted on his bald pate for days thereafter.

By the time Slabbie had stormed onto the apron with mayhem on his mind, Jimmy had disappeared and no one seemed to know which engineer had met his aircraft.

A prank that always gave Jimmy great satisfaction also took place in Durban. When one taxied out for runway 23, the taxiway ran past the South African Air Force base. There was a row of red brick bungalows with a strip of grass in front of them adjacent, and in close proximity to, the taxiway. Over weekends off duty SAAF pilots could be seen on this strip of grass, in deckchairs, relaxing and sunning themselves.

As Jimmy taxied out he would say to the passengers over the PA:

> "Ladies and Gentleman, welcome aboard! As we taxi out to our left is the Durban SAAF base. You know, for some reason the Air Force pilots hate airline pilots. If you look left you will see what I mean."

The passengers would look out of the left hand windows and, sure enough, there were rows of Air Force pilots, sitting in their deckchairs, all making rude gestures towards the aircraft.

Of course, what the passengers could not see, were Jimmy's rude gestures, from the cockpit window, which had initiated this response from the Air Force pilots.

THE WELL DONE STEAK

The 737 – 200 Fleet crew members had regular night stops in Cape Town. As Flight and Duty regulations prevented the last crew in from taking the first flight out, there were generally four 737 crews at our night-stop hotel on any given night. Add to this the 727 crews and one had all the makings for social happenings.

Our night-stop hotel at the time was the Ritz Plaza in Sea Point, dubbed the Rats Plaza by the crews. This was a very tall slab of a building, whose upper floors swayed and rattled alarmingly in the frequent Cape South Easters.

A nearby restaurant, 'The Black Angus', was a very popular dinner venue for the crews. I am not sure why, although I must admit the steaks were very good. Whether they were good enough to make putting up with the proprietor worthwhile was debatable.

It was owned and run by a big burly Greek who, for some unknown reason, admired the Scots greatly and tried to emulate them in his restaurant and with his personality. Unlike the Scots I have met, however, he was dour and unfriendly.

Apparently people were willing to tolerate this, as the small restaurant was invariably overbooked on weekends. To solve this problem he would book two sittings. In order to ensure that the first sitting did not stay too long he would play loud bagpipe music that would swiftly clear the restaurant. Neither was the second sitting immune from this treatment, as when the Greek Scot thought his clientele should push off so he could get to bed, out would come the bagpipe tapes again.

To add to this the Greek Scot was highly eccentric when it came to how you ordered your steak. If you liked your steak rare or 'bleu' you had no trouble placing your order. Medium rare was frowned upon but merely attracted a dirty look. Anything north of that resulted in a lecture designed to intimidate you into changing your order to the "proper way a steak should be consumed".

I must admit that I never really understood this. I personally like my steak rare, but if I am barbecuing, and you would like your meat incinerated, I will gladly do it that way for you, just as long as I don't have to eat it. In fact we have a friend, Norman, who likes his meat way beyond well done, and we have coined a phrase for meat done this way. Everyone in our circle now uses this terminology. "Would you like your steak/sausage/chop Normanised?"

From the tables, if you looked towards the wall fronting the street, on the left was a long counter, behind which the chef and his assistant sweated over the charcoal grill. Where this counter ended, in the right hand corner was the entrance door. This was a stable type door which allowed the top half to be open whilst the bottom half was closed. The top half was always open, as it provided the only source of fresh air to the smoke filled atmosphere within the Black Angus.

Our 737 crew and a 727 crew met in the hotel pub for drinks, and decided to have dinner at the Black Angus. There were ten of us but it was during the week and we arrived early so were able to secure two tables pushed together. The Greek Scot did very well out of the SAA crews who patronised him on weekdays and in the quiet winter season. Despite this we were hardly treated like valued clients.

The 727 co-pilot was new to the domestic scene having recently qualified on 727s after his stint as a second officer, or Boy Pilot on the overseas. Willie (pronounced Villie) was very Afrikaans and the epitome of a gentleman- softly spoken, exceptionally polite and always extremely considerate of others. These traits endeared Willie to everyone with whom he came in contact. That is with the exception of the Greek Scot who took an instant dislike to Willie. You see, Willie had a fatal flaw- he could only eat meat that had been extremely well cooked.

Willie came from a very traditional Afrikaans background and that was the way his mother had been taught to cook by her mother, who had in turn been taught to cook by her mother and so on.

This style of cooking went back to the farming days in remote rural communities where no form of refrigeration was available beyond charcoal-walled evaporative cool-rooms. It made tremendous sense to cook this way if no refrigeration was available, as it ensured any parasites in the meat were well and truly dead.

The evening started off peacefully enough with rounds of drinks, but eventually the Greek Scot came to our table to take orders for the meal. The rest of us all knew if you could not eat rare steak, to give the Black Angus a miss. Unfortunately no one had thought to enlighten Willie of this. Thus Willie ordered his steak well done and became the target of the usual bullying lecture regarding the 'proper way' a steak should be eaten. The lecture also told of the difficulty in cooking a well done steak, of the thickness of those served in the Black Angus, without the steak drying out and losing its flavour.

Now Willie, despite being a perfect gentleman, and half the size of the Greek Scot, was nobody's pushover, and was not about to be bullied by anyone. He politely listened to this diatribe and then reiterated his order for a well done steak.

Any normal person would have just sliced the steak into two thinner halves and cooked the heck out of it to oblige his customer, but remember we are now talking about a Greek who thinks he's a Scot and who clears the clientele, his bread and butter, out of his restaurant by bombarding them with loud bagpipe music.

It was 'game on'! In due course, a steak arrived for everyone at the table, with the exception of Willie. We were about halfway through our meal, when Willie's steak arrived. We all watched as he cut into it and inspected the obviously rare red centre that was revealed. Nothing daunted, Willie called the Greek Scot over and sent his steak back. This was getting interesting, as none of us had witnessed anyone daring to send a steak back at the Black Angus. It seemed that the Greek Scot was also taken by surprise, and knocked off balance, by this challenge to his authority. He took back Willie's steak to the chef. This time it was wrapped in aluminium foil and placed back on the grill over a slow flame.

By the time Willie's steak arrived for the second time, the rest of us were into the Irish Coffee stage of the evening. Once again, but this time with alcohol-induced heightened awareness, we all watched as Willie once again cut into his steak and surveyed the interior which had now changed from red to a dull pink.

Once again Willie called the Greek Scot to our table and rejected his steak. This time, however, the Greek Scot was not taken by surprise.

A signal passed between him and the chef and in an, obviously well rehearsed move, the chef leaned over the counter and opened the bottom half of the stable door. Simultaneously the Greek Scot picked up Willie by the scruff of his neck and the seat of his pants, ran him through the restaurant, and tossed him out onto the pavement.

By this time the rest of us had finished our Irish Coffees and, as the bagpipes had started, we all piled out, commiserated with Willie and took him to a nearby McDonald's where we ordered him a well done hamburger.

I had another reason to remember the Ritz Plaza Hotel. I was by this time an 'old salt' as a 737 co-pilot and flying with a brand new Captain. Jimmy was in command of his first flight after having completed the prescribed number of route checks with Training Captains.

We were relaxing at the pool and enjoying a sundowner, when due to a drop in the temperature, one of our air hostesses decided to fetch a jumper from her room. For some obscure reason, while she was away, one of the hotel staff closed the glass sliding door between the lounge and the pool deck. She came running back and straight into the glass door which exploded into sharp shards which cut her face and chest so badly that they looked like a road map. The glass in the door had no decals and apparently was not safety glass.

The hotel staff seemed at a loss, so the Captain and I wrapped a towel around her face, a blanket around her body, hailed a taxi and took off for Groote Schuur Hospital post haste. This was Cape Towns main hospital where Dr Christiaan Barnard had performed the world's first heart transplant. We arrived at casualty and were shown into a room presided over by an extremely young looking intern. As we watched, he proceeded to do an absolutely brilliant job of stitching her wounds, taking so much time in placing neat and close together stitches carefully and with great concentration that, despite arriving at at seven in the evening, we were there till one the following morning.

I saw the lady a year later and there was scarcely a scar to be seen on her face or chest thanks to the dedication of that young intern.

THE WONDERFUL OLD 'QUEEN OF THE SKIES'

Just when the B737 and its route structures had become so familiar that the operation was almost second nature, I was notified that I was due for promotion to Senior First Officer and had been placed on the next Boeing 707 course.

The progression of pilot promotion in SAA was rather strange. A pilot started off as a Boy Pilot or Second Officer on the international service, moved to a domestic fleet as a co-pilot or First Officer only to return to the international service as a Senior First Officer. Promotion to Captain meant a return to a domestic fleet and the cycle would be repeated.

The only distortion to this system was occasioned by the arrival of SAA's first wide-bodied aircraft, the A300 Airbus. This was a to be used on SAA's domestic service but, as our first wide-bodied aircraft, it was a bit of a sacred cow and the powers that be decided it required a Senior First Officer in the right hand seat. Thus, when one was due for promotion, one was either allocated a Senior First Officer position internationally on the Boeing 707 or domestically on the A300. By the luck of the draw, I was allocated a 707 slot, something for which I was eternally grateful!

The 707 conversion course was, after 737 operations, all too easy as by this time we were familiar with Boeing philosophy and, wonder of wonders, there was a Flight Engineer, a Navigator and a Boy Pilot to perform so many duties and tasks that were the lot of a 737 co-pilot. In fact there was very little for a 707 co-pilot to do apart from flying the aircraft on alternate sectors.

A strange SAA policy required a compulsory written language test to assure that one was fluent in both English and Afrikaans and unless this was passed one could not be promoted to the rank of Senior First Officer. I suspect that this was a mere formality as I never heard of anyone ever failing this test.

I soon grew to love the 707, the beautiful old Queen of the Skies. She was easy to fly and a wonderfully stable instrument flying platform. Added to this was the very social aspect of flying with a large cockpit crew. Unlike the 747 there was a far closer connection with the passengers and Cabin Crew as there was only one level and one could see all the way to the back through the open cockpit door. It was also an era when people still dressed up to fly and travelling by air was a special occasion. The very 'politically incorrect' piece, written by an unknown pilot, sums up the era of the Boeing 707 for me.

> *The Age Of The 707*
>
> *Those were the good ole days. Pilots back then were men that didn't want to be women or girly men. Pilots all knew who Jimmy Doolittle was. Pilots drank coffee, whiskey, smoked cigars and didn't wear digital watches.*
>
> *They carried their own suitcases and brain bags, like the real men they were. Pilots didn't bend over into the crash position multiple times each day in front of the passengers at security so that some Government agent could probe for tweezers or fingernail clippers or too much toothpaste.*
>
> *Pilots did not go through the terminal impersonating a caddy pulling a bunch of golf clubs, computers, guitars, and feed bags full of tofu and granola on a sissy-trailer with no hat and granny glasses hanging on a pink string around their pencil neck while talking to their personal trainer on the cell phone!!!*
>
> *Being an airline Captain was as good as being the King in a Mel Brooks movie. All the Stewardesses (aka. Flight Attendants) were young, attractive, single women that were proud to be combatants in*

the sexual revolution. They didn't have to turn sideways, grease up and suck it in to get through the cockpit door. They would blush, and say thank you, when told that they looked good, instead of filing a sexual harassment claim.

Junior Stewardesses shared a room and talked about men.... with no thoughts of substitution. Passengers wore nice clothes and were polite; they could speak AND understand English. They didn't speak gibberish or listen to loud gangster rap on their IPod's. They bathed and didn't smell like a rotting pile of garbage in a jogging suit and flip-flops.

Children didn't travel alone, commuting between trailer parks.

There were no Biggest Losers asking for a seat-belt extension or a Scotch and grapefruit juice cocktail with a twist. If the Captain wanted to throw some offensive, ranting jerk off the airplane, it was done without any worries of a lawsuit or getting fired.

Axial flow engines crackled with the sound of freedom and left an impressive black smoke trail like a locomotive burning soft coal. Jet fuel was cheap and once the throttles were pushed up they were left there. After all, it was the jet age and the idea was to go fast (run like a lizard on a hardwood floor). "Economy cruise" was something in the performance book, but no one knew why or where it was. When the clackers* went off, no one got all tight and scared because Boeing built it out of iron. Nothing was going to fall off and that sound had the same effect on real pilots then, as Viagra does now for these new age guys.

There was very little plastic and no composites on the airplanes (or the Stewardesses' pectoral regions). Airplanes and women had eye-pleasing symmetrical curves, not a bunch of ugly *vortex generators, ventral fins, wing-lets, flow diverters, tattoos, rings in their nose, tongues and eyebrows.

> *Airlines were run by men like C.R. Smith and Juan Trippe, who had built their companies virtually from scratch, knew most of their employees by name, and were lifetime airline employees themselves....not pseudo financiers and bean counters who flit from one occupation to another for a few bucks, a better parachute or a fancier title, while fervently believing that they are a class of beings unto themselves.*
>
> *And so it was back then....and never will be again!*

* Jimmy Dolittle: An American General and aviation pioneer. He pioneered early coast to coast flights in America, won many flying races, helped develop instrument flying and fighter tactics as well as planning and leading the first bomber raid of WWII on Japanese soil.

* Clackers: An aural warning making a loud 'clacking' sound as the aircraft approaches Mach 1 (The speed of sound).

* Vortex generators, ventral fins, winglets and flow diverters: All varieties of fins and fences designed to reduce drag by controlling the airflow over the aircraft's surfaces. Some can be extremely ugly and spoil the clean lines of an aircraft's design.

9

RIO

Back in the seventies there were destinations that we serviced only once a week.

A weekly service, with a same day turn around, meant that the crew bringing the aircraft in would have to remain at the destination for a full week, waiting for the next inbound aircraft which they would then fly home or on to a further destination.

On my beloved 707 we had several such destinations. One of these was Rio de Janeiro, a truly beautiful city on the Brazilian coast. Not only was Rio beautiful in an aesthetic sense, it was also truly alive, vibrant and colourful.

We were rated on the 707A, B, and C models and flew all three interchangeably.

For our South America trips that were long-range flights against the prevailing wind, we always hoped that a B model would be scheduled as it was the most fuel-efficient and an often heard phrase was "The 707B makes fuel". The B model also had the best cockpit foot warmers, very important on a long flight where cold soak was a factor.

We would fly a loose compound great circle course which would carry us quite far south over the Atlantic and bring us within VHF radio range of

Gough Island, a little dot in the South Atlantic where South Africa maintained a weather station. An all male crew manned this and their stint on Gough was a lonely twelve months with very little contact with the outside world. We would pass nearby in the middle of the night and always called them for a chat. We would describe to them, in graphic detail, how gorgeous and sexy our hostesses were and then get one of the hostesses up to the cockpit to chat with them until we flew out of radio range. We knew our weekly contact was such an event in their lonely lives that they would tumble out of bed, in the middle of the freezing night, to sit in the radio shack and wait for our calls.

We were extremely fortunate that our crew hotel was in Leme at the eastern end of the Copacabana and practically on the beach. At the western end of the Copacabana is Ipanema, so well know as a result of the song, 'The Girl from Ipanema'. And speaking of girls, watching the girls go by on the Copacabana is a rewarding experience as so many are spectacularly attractive with a wonderfully colourful sense of fashion.

The Portuguese-speaking people are very friendly, generous and outgoing. There is, however, a dark side to Rio and it pays to keep one's wits about one and avoid compromising situations.

These were the days prior to satellite navigation systems and we carried a navigator on the 707. Thus our cockpit crew compliment was rather large, consisting of the Captain, First Officer or co-pilot, Second Officer or Boy Pilot, the Flight Engineer and the Navigator. I must say that I enjoyed being part of a large crew. It meant that there were plenty of resources in the cockpit and it was also very sociable. I felt it was sad when technology phased out the Navigators, and later even the Flight Engineers.

On our 707s the Navigator's main tools were Doppler, a roof mounted bubble sextant, and a radar altimeter. Doppler worked on the principal of the shift in frequency, such as we notice with the different sounds a fast moving vehicle produces as it approaches, passes and distances itself from us. Doppler was useful in finding ground speed and drift.

The sextant fixed one's position by means of the stars and the radar altimeter could be compared with the pressure altimeters to provide information on pressure patterns and winds. The operation of all of these aids required a great deal of skill, very little of which is needed to operate modern satellite or inertial navigation systems. Many a Navigator, in blissful ignorance, checked into a crew hotel with a beautiful black eye, occasioned by the smearing of shoe polish on the eyepiece of his sextant.

THE PERILS OF THE COPACABANA

One of the more colourful characters amongst our Navigators was Al Botha, whom we suspected of having Mafia connections. He certainly looked the part and furthermore was known as 'The Godfather of Orange Grove', Orange Grove being the very old suburb of Johannesburg where Al lived. Al, to put it mildly, was also known for his love of any beverage containing alcohol.

On one of my trips to Rio, I was accompanied by Corleen, for whom it was a first visit. As luck would have it Al was our Navigator. Johannesburg to Rio is a long flight against the wind that takes at least nine and a half hours. One is also flying backwards in time so that when one lands in Rio it is actually five hours later in South Africa.

As such we were all pretty tired by the time we arrived at the hotel, except for Corleen and Al. Corleen had managed a fair amount of sleep during the flight, and Al had developed cat napping during a flight to a fine art and was well rested.

Once a Navigator had determined the aircraft's position and given the pilots a new heading there was very little for him to do until the next fix in thirty minutes time.

The rest of us agreed we would try to get some sleep and meet in the foyer in three hours time, prior to going out on the town.

Corleen, being very excited about her first time in Rio, leapt at Al's offer to 'show her the Copacabana' while the rest of us recharged our batteries. Hearing this offer, the Captain, Flight Engineer and I looked at each other with raised eyebrows. We all knew Al well and had a pretty good idea of how this would turn out. Nevertheless we retired to our respective rooms and Corleen and Al headed off to the Copacabana.

Three hours later we gathered in the foyer and set off to find Corleen and Al. Now, to the uninitiated, this would seem like an impossible task, finding two people on the Copacabana. However, knowing Al, we figured on heading straight down the Copacabana's main shopping street and looking in the first bar we came to. This we duly did but were chagrined to find no sign of Corleen and Al. The Skipper then suggested that possibly Corleen's powers of persuasion had managed to winkle Al out of the first bar, and that we should just pop into the next few bars as we strolled along. This proved to be a winning strategy as, sure enough, in the very next bar, there were Corleen and Al. Corleen had spent over three hours on the Copacabana and all she had seen were the insides of two pubs!

The main shopping street runs parallel to the beach front one street back. It is lined with bars and interesting shops selling everything from silver jewellery to shrunken heads. These gruesome shrunken head artefacts, we hoped, were fake.

Having had our fill of the shops we wandered down to the beach front for a walk along the wide, paved promenade that runs the length of Copacabana beach. The beach is very entertaining, being the venue for dozens of volleyball and soccer games, not to mention the myriad scantily dressed bikini girls.

The promenade was a favoured venue for Rio's socialites to be seen walking their dogs. This was a popular pastime and dogs were prolific on the promenade.

In the seventies their were no regulations requiring owners to remove the messes made by their dogs, and consequently, a stroll down the Copacabana was akin to navigating a minefield, made even more fraught with hazard by the obvious distractions on the beach.

There were many pavement cafes where one could have a drink and watch the passing parade, but not in peace, as one would be plagued by sundry vendors, these being too numerous for the café staff to effectively fend off. Particularly annoying were the little shoe-shine urchins. Even if you used the services of one of them, that would not prevent others from wanting to shine your shoes again. Turn one down and when your attention was elsewhere he would creep up behind your chair and smear dog excreta all over your shoes. Of this there was a plentiful supply on the Copacabana.

We soon learned not to wear leather shoes on the Copacabana. Naturally this wisdom was never conveyed to crew members unfamiliar with Rio. It was simply too much fun to observe their shocked expressions as they fell victim to this practise.

CROOKS WITH HOOKS

On one of my trips to Rio, I was caught by another less harmless little practise that none of the crew knew of.

SAA had made arrangements with all our crew hotels to, upon our arrival, pay out our meal allowances in the local currency. This allowance would be quite a substantial amount as it was based on having three meals a day at our hotels, and we were housed in pretty expensive hotels. I am sure the airline management hated this but third rate hotels, while pleasing the bean counters, would not have been good for SAA's corporate image as we checked in and departed in uniform.

Used judiciously the meal allowance would cover all one's expenses including alcohol and entertainment for the entire trip. Even gifts for the family back home.

You always faced the problem of how to keep your allowance safe for the duration of a trip. To hide it in your room was just looking for trouble. The hotel safe was an option but Murphy's Law dictated that whenever you required money, the reception staff would be busy checking in sixty passengers off a tour bus.

My previous flight had been to Buenos Aires in Argentina where I had purchased a very nice money belt, which looked just like an ordinary wide leather belt but had a zip running practically the full length down the inner side and, if the notes were carefully folded, it could hold a surprisingly large amount of money.

I had decided on the strategy of placing half my allowance in the hotel safe, and carrying the other half in my new money belt. I would then, prior to going out, transfer just as much as I thought I would need for the outing into the pockets of my jeans. A wallet was not a good idea due to the proliferation of pick-pockets on the Copacabana.

These were often extremely attractive and beautifully dressed young ladies who would 'accidentally' bump into you and remove your wallet in the process.

They would apologise profusely and flirt outrageously with their male victims, often arranging a time and place to meet with them later for a drink. The victim was so bedazzled by his good fortune, their close proximity and heady perfume, that he never thought to feel for his wallet until such time as they were long gone.

We had all decided to spend that morning on the beach, so I had just transferred ice cream and drinks money into my pockets. Six of us strolled down to the beach, found a spot to spread our towels and settled down to enjoy all the beach action that is ever present on the Copacabana. I had put my swimming costume on under my jeans, which I removed and were now lying next to me on the sand.

After an hour or so an ice cream seller came by and I reached for my jeans, only to find they were no longer there. Making my dilemma known to the rest of the crew, they all started looking around for my jeans until one of the hostesses noticed a pair of jeans, lying about twenty metres away, in an open space. These turned out to be mine. The ice cream money was missing from the pocket but the belt was still in the jeans with all the money intact. Fortunately the thieves apparently had no knowledge of the cleverly disguised Argentinean money belts.

As we knew it was extremely unlikely that anyone could have picked up my jeans without any of us noticing, we all decided to surreptitiously observe and see if we could detect any suspicious activity on the beach. Sure enough, it was not too long before the Boy Pilot, John, nudged me to draw my attention to two youths, fully dressed and slowly strolling along the beach with their heads swivelling as their eyes scanned the scene.

About five metres away from us, and on her own, was a middle-aged lady. She was tanning and appeared to have fallen asleep. Lying next to her was a large raffia handbag. The youths passed by her without breaking stride. When they were about thirty metres from her they sat down on the beach and started to watch her intently.

After about five minutes we noticed something very strange. The ladies raffia handbag was now about two metres away from her in the direction of the youths. We now all switched our attention to the handbag which slowly and seemingly of its own volition moved another metre towards the youths before coming to a stop. This was repeated until the handbag was roughly halfway between its owner and the two youths.

At this point the Flight Engineer Bert and I got up and casually walked in the direction of an ice cream cart further up the beach knowing this course would take us close to the handbag. We avoided looking at the handbag but as we passed it Bert suddenly bent down and picked it up. As he did this the two youths jumped to their feet and bolted down the beach as if their tails were on fire.

On examining the bag we found embedded in the raffia, a three pronged fish-hook that was attached to a very thin length of nylon fishing line.

Obviously they would walk past any kit that looked as if it may contain cash or valuables, and drop their fish hook onto it. They would then pay out the nearly invisible line, seat themselves a safe distance away and slowly reel in their catch when the victim was distracted or dozing. We later became aware of several of these teams working the Copacabana beach.

By a stroke of fortune my small investment in a money belt saved me a week in Rio on short rations.

CREEPING LIQUOR AND OTHER DELIGHTS

Eating and drinking in Rio was a treat. There was no such thing as a tot measure in a Brazilian bar. Order a Cuba Libre and the barman will first fill the large tumbler with ice cubes. Thereafter the rum will be "sloshed" in until all the ice was floating. Whatever space was left in the glass would be filled with Coke and a squeeze of lime.

Very generous but a drink to be treated with great respect should one wish to survive an evening out.

Another drink to be respected is the national drink of Brazil, Caipirinha. Roughly translated from Portuguese, this means "country bumpkin". It is made from Brazilian rum called Cachaca and mixed with seasonal fruits to produce a refreshing drink with quite a kick.

Dining in Rio was also a treat. Our hotel served up the most amazing buffet breakfast, which consisted of a huge variety of tropical fruits, with an equally impressive variety of cold meats and cheeses all included in the room price. For some reason this fact had escaped the bean counters in SAA, so the cost of a breakfast was included in our daily allowances. As the breakfast buffet remained open until ten thirty, it served us as a brunch. This left us with the whole daily allowance, meant for three meals, to spend on dinner, drinks and entertainment. Wonderful times!

For the evening meal, a favourite crew restaurant was the Jardim. As the name suggests, it was in an open courtyard shaded by lush tropical growth on trellises.

Large chunks of a variety of meats were grilled over open fires on long sword-like skewers. These were then brought to the tables where slices of the meats of your choice were carved to drop onto your plate. The waiters kept returning with newly charged skewers and there was no limit as to how much you could eat for the fixed price. The Brazilian beef was particularly good.

The little restaurants on the Copacabana served a variety of Tapas dishes, all delicious. Quail eggs seemed to be a standard snack, a dish of which would accompany an order of drinks. A firm favourite of mine was palm heart and tomato salad, palm hearts being something I had not seen anywhere else. Before leaving Rio, I would always visit a nearby supermarket for a few tins to take home.

CORCOVADO EXPERIENCE

Something that occurred in Rio nearly forty years ago is still so fresh in my mind that my thoughts often return to the occasion.

The night before, several of us had decided that we would visit the Corcovado, the thirty eight metre high statue of Christ that overlooks Rio from the top of Mount Corcovado. The following morning found us at the lower station of the old cog railway that runs up to the Christ statue. This railway was completed in 1884 and the train was steam driven until 1910 when it was electrified.

The railway also served as a commuter train for residents of the villages along the line.

In Rio, unlike most other places in the world, the wealthy live on the flat land while the less privileged occupy the slopes with the more spectacular views. I was told that the reason for this is, that the slopes are unstable in the rainy season and subject to mud-slides.

The train was very rickety looking and, except for a roof, the carriages were open to the elements. Apart from us there were few passengers. It seemed that most tourist preferred to utilise the more comfortable taxis that congregated in great numbers around the lower station.

The train clicked and clacked its way slowly through the most dense tropical forest on the lower slopes. On the higher slopes the forest gave way to more open ground and spectacular views.

At the top the statue was most impressive and the views even more spectacular than those from the train. Surprisingly though, for me the best was yet to come, when eventually we tore ourselves away from the awe inspiring views and boarded the train for the descent. About halfway down we entered the forest and shortly thereafter we stopped at a village halt. Here the train was boarded by a dozen young girls all of about the same age. They were very animated, laughing and chatting away amongst themselves.

The train slowly moved away and entered the tunnel formed by the dense forest vegetation. Suddenly the girls began to sing and magic happened. I do not know if it was the acoustics of that tunnel through the forest, the clicking and clacking of the train or a combination of factors that created an electrifying atmosphere. I do know that their voices, unaccompanied by any musical instruments, were like the voices of angels. Their pretty faces and sparkling eyes completed a picture that presented to me the most moving and memorable musical experience of my life.

Sadly in 1980 a Swiss built luxury train with no character replaced the old train. This whisks six hundred thousand tourist up to the Corcovado each year.

PRETTY HOSTESSES AND SCARY RATS

A later visit to another mountain top in Rio was not quite so spiritually uplifting.

On that trip we had two hostesses, Kathy and Jane, who had not previously been to Rio. They were very keen to take the cable car and visit the famous Sugarloaf Mountain. This is a 396 metre monolithic granite and quartz mountain that rises straight out of the sea above the harbour. It affords spectacular views over Rio.

As keen as they were to visit the Sugarloaf, they lacked the confidence to navigate Rio on their own and, finding no ready takers to accompany them, they decided to focus their powers of persuasion on yours truly. I had been up the Sugarloaf several times before and was not exactly champing at the bit to repeat the experience.

However, the girls were pretty and as I had nothing better to do, I agreed to accompany them.

By this time it was already mid afternoon and after several delays in getting ourselves to the lower cable station we arrived just in time to catch the last car that would take people up that day. When we arrived at the top and disembarked, I noticed that quite a number of sightseers were waiting to take the car back down. It was not until the car had departed that I realised that the three of us were alone on the summit and would be until the car arrived to take us down in thirty minutes time.

At the summit were large flat paved areas with only a handrail separating them from the steep rock faces on the sides facing Guanabara Bay and the City. The opposite sides were encroached by dense bush. There was the odd very basic stone shelter with a bench and roof but open on three sides. We enjoyed the marvellous views with the harbour activities in the foreground and a little further away the planes landing and taking off at the airport.

By now the light was fading and despite being Rio, a chill breeze had sprung up. We became aware of rustling sounds emanating from undergrowth behind us, which we at first assumed was just the breeze. These sounds became ever more insistent and when we turned around we could see that the undergrowth had become alive with movement. This was getting scary and we began to feel very, very alone. There was plenty of movement in that bush and our fevered imaginations were conjuring up a variety of unpalatable scenarios.

When the source of the noise did emerge, it was not muggers or rapists, but hundreds of enormous rats. They were at least three times the size of any rat that I had ever seen. The girls were terrified and clung to me for dear life. Under normal circumstances this might have been quite enjoyable, but these were not normal circumstances. Could these rats attack a person? There were certainly more then enough of them and they were huge. Scenes from various Indiana Jones films passed through my mind, none of them at all reassuring.

It turned out that the rats, despite showing no fear of us, had other things on their minds. They systematically combed through the plentiful amounts of litter, left by the day's visitors, for anything edible. Having swiftly consumed everything that caught their fancy, they disappeared back into the bush leaving a very sober trio to await the arrival of the car that would take them down the Sugarloaf and to a nearby pub for a much needed drink.

Another very pleasant and much favoured SAA crew activity was a day visit to Petropolis. A one and a half hour scenic bus ride would take you to this very pleasant town in a mountainous area near Rio. Due to its elevation it provided relief from the humid summer heat in the city and was thus a favoured summer retreat for the wealthier citizens of Rio, many of whom have built holiday homes there.

There were two universities in Petropolis and the town squares and parks were invariably filled with noisy, colourful and attractive youngsters.

Of particular interest to us was the home of Alberto Santos Dumont, the Brazilian aviation pioneer. It is popularly believed locally that he preceded the Wright brothers in achieving heavier than air flight. His home, a very quaint cottage built on an impossibly steep slope, is now a museum. It is stuffed full of the most fascinating gadgetry that his extremely fertile mind produced.

An alternative to the mountains was a ferry ride to Paqueta Island in Guanabara Bay. Only horse drawn carts and bicycles were permitted on Paqueta and thus it was an extremely restful and relaxing venue. Often the whole crew would spend the day on Paqueta where we would hire bicycles and cycle around the island. This was thirsty work, necessitating frequent 'pit stops' for refreshments along the route.

The combination of cycling inexperience and Caipirinhas often led to some rather amusing incidents, particularly where the road ran in close proximity to the sea.

A wonderfully friendly atmosphere prevailed on the island and by the time you had completed a circumnavigation, you had dozens of new friends.

The traffic in Rio was quite an eye opener for someone from a 'back-water' like South Africa in the seventies. My first ride in a Rio taxi was quite a scary experience although, after a while, we got used to it and realised how good their flamboyant style of driving really was. No wonder Brazil has produced so many world class racing drivers.

As 'old Rio hands' we began to use the local city buses as a cheap and convenient means of travel and this opened up a whole new world. We were told that the drivers each had a set circular route, with no timetable, and their pay was calculated at the end of each shift according to the number of kilometres they had covered on their route.

The buses had no power steering and thus, in order to give the driver leverage, the steering wheels were enormous and required many turns from lock to lock. In order to facilitate this each steering wheel was equipped with a knob that the driver could grasp with one hand and wind the wheel like a fishing reel. Unsurprisingly all the drivers had extremely muscular arms.

The drivers would sit there twirling the great steering wheels with great panache, diving through the smallest of gaps and often taking bends in a full blown four-wheel drift. They did this while keeping up a loud stream of 'back and forth' banter with the passengers.

BREAKING THE CASINO

At the time the currency in Brazil was the Cruzeiro- the present Rial was only introduced in 1994. During the time I was flying to Rio inflation was rampant and currency devaluation was taking place at a frightening rate, and thus one thousand old Cruzeiros had become one new Cruzeiro, with one new Cruzeiro being worth only about 35 South African cents if memory serves me. Although the new Cruzeiro notes had started to appear, there were still plenty of the old notes in circulation, particularly on the buses it seemed. Our meal allowances were paid by the hotel in new Cruzeiro notes and when these were offered in tender on the buses, you would receive your change in the form of a roll of old Cruzeiro notes that would choke a horse.

This phenomenon led to one of our co-pilots hatching a rather diabolical plan. To be fair, I don't think it started out with evil intent but rather just evolved that way, as these things do. Bruce was a bachelor who shared a large house in one of Johannesburg's suburbs with housemates of both sexes. The house had a room dedicated as a pub and this was badly in need of redecorating.

While travelling with some of his crew by bus, Bruce noticed that they had each received a great wad of old notes as change, all of which had big numbers followed by many noughts on their faces. Knowing they were worth practically nothing, Bruce began to ponder on the feasibility of collecting enough of them to wallpaper a feature wall of the pub, if not the whole pub.

Deciding it was feasible, he let it be known amongst the crew that he was collecting old Cruzeiro notes and by the end of the week he had such a quantity of old notes that he had to buy a cheap tog bag in order to tote them home.

It was the evening after the day that Bruce arrived home when events began to get a little out of hand. The other residents had returned from their respective work places and were relaxing in the lounge, when Bruce decided that he would have a bit of fun with them. Entering the lounge he greeted them all with the announcement that he had visited the casino in Rio, had an amazing run of luck and had broken the bank.

Naturally there followed a chorus of disbelieving sneers, jeers and remarks, whereupon Bruce fetched the tog bag and, amid a stunned silence, dumped its contents onto the coffee table.

Bruce instantly became the man of the moment and the centre of attention. Hidden bottles of liquor appeared from all corners of the house in order to celebrate Bruce's good fortune, and the party was on.

Now this would have been a prudent time to end the joke, prior to the introduction of alcohol into the scenario. Sadly, this did not happen and with the increasing consumption of alcohol things really began to go pear shaped when Bruce began to hand out huge stacks of notes to his housemates. This largesse being accompanied by Bruce's kind suggestions of how they should spend their newly acquired wealth. These suggestions included such niceties as new cars and overseas holidays.

At this stage, Bruce's popularity knew no bounds and it was even rumoured that one of the girls had rewarded Bruce's generosity with some of her own that night.

When Bruce awoke the next morning with a truly impressive hangover he found he was alone in the house. A neighbour informed Bruce that she had seen the housemates leaving, each with a bulky supermarket plastic bag.

When it dawned on Bruce that the housemates would soon be returning and seeking his blood, after being informed by their banks that the money was worthless, he realised that discretion was the better part of valour and after rapidly packing he departed to go and live with his parents for a month, while the housemates calmed down.

Eventually the pub was wallpapered with the Cruzeiro notes but they really only served as a permanent reminder of the housemates' displeasure with Bruce.

THE AURAL INVISIBILITY SYNDROME (2)

As I previously mentioned, Afrikaans is, by global standards, not a widely spoken language. This fact gave certain of our international aircrew a false sense of security in that, as long as they spoke in Afrikaans, they could say what they liked and no one would understand. This idiotic notion which I like to call "The Aural Invisibility Syndrome' has had serious consequences for several of our crew-members over the years and a classic example of this played out on the Copacabana.

A crew had been sitting and drinking Caipirinhas at one of the pavement café bars and indulging in the favoured pastime of watching the girls go by.

As the Caipirinhas began to take hold someone began remarking on the physical attributes of the passing ladies. A few more Caipirinhas and everyone joined in the fun with the comments becoming ever more lewd as the afternoon wore on.

Of course, they were fireproof as the comments were being made in Afrikaans.

Just as these comments were reaching a zenith in terms of volume and lewdity, the extremely attractive and well-endowed daughter of the South African Ambassador to Brazil came strolling past.

It is pretty easy to identify an aircrew in a foreign country and I have often puzzled friends by pointing out aircrew in South African restaurants. The clues are the ages in combination with the genders and if you can identify the language they are speaking or their accents, you will have a pretty good idea of which airline they are with. The Captain will generally be in the forty to sixty bracket, the First Officer in the late twenties to forty. The second officer in the twenties. The Flight Engineers could be any age. If the hostesses were with them they would be young and generally attractive. This is an unlikely combination for any other group, particularly if they are sitting on the Copacabana drinking Caipirinhas during office hours.

Of course, the hostesses were not with this crew, but the Ambassador's daughter was a smart lady and identified them immediately as SAA crew. She gave no indication that she had understood the comments and the first time the crew had an inkling that something was wrong was when, over the Atlantic, they received the radio message that the whole cockpit crew was to report to the Chief Pilot after landing in Johannesburg.

At one point we would operate a flight to Rio, spend a week there, operate on to New York where we spent another week prior to flying home via Sal Island. We also operated this routing in reverse. These trips were thirteen days long, but back in those days SAA generously gave you the same time that you were away, at home free of duty.

Back then there was a great connection between South Africa and Rio. We had the annual Cape to Rio Yacht Race and the cruise ship the Achille Lauro ran regular cruises between Cape Town and Rio especially over the Rio Carnival.

Some very happy memories were made in Rio and it will always feature in my mind as one of my favourite destinations.

10

ROBERT, BLACKIE AND AVA

As a youngster one of my favourite authors was Robert Ruark, an American who was totally in love with Africa and in particular Kenya. He was also an avid hunter of big game. Besides his books on hunting he wrote books describing the birth pangs of Kenyan independence.

These were great novels such as 'A Sense of Values' and 'Uhuru' that, despite being fiction were based on fact, and revolved around the Mau Mau insurrection of the 1950s against British rule. Of course his love of hunting determined the central theme of his novels.

The main character and hero of his novels was a 'White Hunter' who owned a hunting safari enterprise and whose family had lived, farmed and hunted in Kenya for generations. Another prominent character was the wealthy American safari client, who, naturally, was accompanied by his most beautiful daughter. She, with the great white hunter, provided the romantic interest.

In those colonial days the gathering place of 'anybody who was anybody' was the grand historic old Norfolk Hotel. This was a strange Tudor styled building with a huge garden courtyard, which was established in 1904. Theodore Roosevelt stayed there in 1909.

The Lord Delamere Terrace was one of the great lounge bars of the world and the social centre of Nairobi for nearly a century. It was named after Lord Delamere who once rode his horse into the Norfolk's dining room.

This was the favourite watering hole of the 'Happy Valley' set of dissolute colonial aristocrats made famous in the 1987 movie 'White Mischief'.

Other guests would have included Karen Blixen- author of 'Out of Africa', and the aviator Beryl Markham. In the fifties African safari films were very popular and a long list of Hollywood stars would grace the Norfolk guest list.

Far less distinguished guests were the SAA 707 crews flying between Johannesburg and Rome and slipping in Nairobi.

I loved Ruark's books, but being someone who aspired to a career in aviation, and SAA being the pinnacle of aviation in South Africa, I was troubled by a scene, variations of which seemed to follow a pattern in his books.

The 'White Hunter' would meet his client, accompanied by beautiful daughter, at Nairobi airport and convey them to the Norfolk. Here they would spend a night or two recovering from the flight prior to departing on their hunting safari. The first evening the client and his daughter would naturally visit the bar to enjoy a drink and absorb some of the atmosphere of the colony.

Shortly after, a slipping SAA cockpit crew would wander in and order drinks. As the evening wore on and the alcohol flowed, the SAA crew would become ever more rowdy, crude and objectionable until one of them would begin making unwanted advances towards the client's daughter. At each rejected advance, he would become more insistent and objectionable, eventually reaching the point of harassment.

It is at this juncture that, after a hard day's work preparing for the safari and having decided to drop in at the Norfolk for a well-earned drink, our hero, the White Hunter, enters the bar.

With his eagle eye and quick brain, he sums up the situation and rushes to her rescue, thus initiating a romance that inevitably results in her ending up in his safari cot. In the process, of course, the SAA villain finds himself on the wrong end of a left hook from our hero and laid out cold on the floor of the Norfolk bar.

This was to me a minor annoyance, as I had no explanation for why one of my favourite authors should demonise SAA crew in this way. I was, however, not going to let it get in the way of a good read and so, with time, the memory faded.

Fifteen years later, somewhere over mid Atlantic in an A model 707, I was again reminded of Ruark's books and the Norfolk bar.

I was the co-pilot, the Captain was in the bunk, and the boy pilot was taking a break, chatting up one of the hostesses in the forward galley. The Flight Engineer and I were quietly chatting so as not to waken the navigator who was cat-napping at his station between half hourly position fixes.

The Flight Engineer was a wonderful 'old bird' who was on the cusp of retirement. I knew him well from our common interest in vintage cars, and always called him 'Uncle Bill'. He had been around and flown on DC 4s, DC 6s, Constellations, DC 7Bs and he had been on 707s operating to Europe via Nairobi.

That night, in the eerie red glow of the old 707's instrument panel, Bill told me a fascinating story that explained the long forgotten story of Robert Ruark's obvious dislike of SAA aircrew. What triggered Bill's story was my mention of Blackie who had been the navigator on my last trip. Blackie was a slightly built, quiet, unassuming fellow with a wry sense of humour and a charming personality. He was very popular amongst the crews and liked by everybody with whom he came in contact. He was of Bill's generation and also soon due for retirement.

Bill told me that he and Blackie had been crew on a 707 flying Johannesburg to Rome. They had landed in Nairobi, where a crew change took place, and the crew proceeded to the Norfolk Hotel for their slip. As it happened several celebrities were staying at the Norfolk, in particular the actors and film crew from Hollywood who were filming Ernest Hemingway's 'The Snows of Kilimanjaro'.

One of the stars of this epic was one of the all time great Hollywood beauties, Ava Gardner. Robert Ruark was in Nairobi researching a book and also staying at the Norfolk.

That evening when Bill, the Captain and the co-pilot met in the foyer at the prearranged time, Blackie was nowhere to be seen so they made their way to the bar.

There at the far end of the bar they saw Blackie. Sitting next to him with her back towards them was a slim brunette. Their heads were close together as they engaged in quiet conversation. Not wanting to intrude, the three sat down at one of the tables in the bar and ordered drinks from one of the very attentive waiters. They occasionally glanced across at Blackie and in so doing caught the odd glimpse of his companions face. She was beautiful and somewhat familiar but it took quite a while for the penny to drop that Blackie's companion was Ava Gardner.

Blackie later told them that she was a very down to earth person who was tired of all the inflated egos and prima donna antics of the Hollywood set and just wanted a normal person to talk to. From what they could see she appeared to be very interested in Blackie and what he had to say.

At this point a rather inebriated Robert Ruark entered the bar. He spent a great deal of time in Kenya and always stayed at the Norfolk. After a few drinks his eye alighted on Ava and Blackie and he strolled across with the intention, no doubt, of chatting up Ava. He rather rudely interjected himself into their conversation. Ava would turn and listen politely to him but then, without responding, turn back to Blackie and continue their conversation.

The third time this happened, Ruark became annoyed. After all, he was a world famous author and was being spurned in favour of a nothing SAA crew-member. He became quite obnoxious, laying his hands on Ava to make his point and get her attention. When Blackie objected to this Ruark threatened him with physical violence.

It was then that the rather large co-pilot strolled across to intervene in little Blackie's defence. But Ruark would not be calmed and in the ensuing scuffle it was he who ended up stretched out cold on the floor of the Norfolk bar.

Now I understood why SAA crew ended up as minor villains in Ruark's excellent books!

Sadly the Norfolk has become the oddly named 'Fairmont The Norfolk Hotel'. I find it rather sad that egoistic corporations find it acceptable to attach their shallow, meaningless identities to sites of great historical significance. The Norfolk, is not, and will never be the same again, a shadow of its former greatness.

11

SANCTIONS BUSTING 707 OPERATIONS

During my airline career, I considered myself very fortunate to be a 'bitter ender' on two fleets that were being phased out, as newer and more modern aircraft were replacing them. The first was the Vickers Viscount 813, and the second was my all-time favourite aircraft and 'Queen of the Skies' the beautiful Boeing 707.

SAA flew three variations of 707- the A, B and C models. The As were the original 707s and the Cs the most modern versions, prior to Boeing ceasing production of the 707. Despite some significant differences we were rated to fly all three models. In certain quarters it was believed that these differences were a contributing cause to the horrific 707 crash at Windhoek (In South West Africa, now Namibia) that cost 123 lives and left only five survivors.

This crash was before my time in SAA, although, by coincidence, I was an instructor with Air Oasis at Eros Airport in Windhoek and doing night flying training with a pupil at JG Strydom Airport, now Windhoek International. Due to the proximity of the nearby mountainous terrain, the International Airport was located some 46km to the east of the city in a very thinly populated area. As was their air traffic control procedure, when the Boeing took off, we were instructed to proceed to and hold in an area south of the airfield, which would keep us well clear of the 707. A chill still runs through me when I recall hearing the shocked voices of the air traffic controllers and looking to the east of the airfield to see the increasing blooms of burning fuel on the darkened semi-desert plain.

Back to the more cheerful subject of being a 'bitter ender' on a soon to be phased-out fleet. When a new aircraft arrives, all the serious boffins in the airline immediately switch their attentions to the new arrival. They prod and push, interpret and misinterpret, develop standard operating procedures, change manufacturer's check-lists, and require the gathering of endless data, some meaningful and some meaningless. I well remember when Hans Hermann was appointed to the position of 737 Fleet Captain from a line Captain on 747s. He took one look at the situation on the 737 Fleet and, in a shocked voice, stated, "The Standard Operating Procedures and Check-lists on this fleet have crept so far away from the Boeing Standards that I want everything 'put back to Boeing' immediately!"

The phasing-out fleet is just the opposite of all this hype. The 'flink dink' (clever thinker) boys have moved on. The old fleet operates smoothly without supervision. Nobody cares about gathering data such as fuel uplifts, usage and choice of alternates. Perfect peace! Everyone has 'been there, done that, got the T-shirt' and they are left alone to get on with it.

PARIS

During the late seventies South Africa was under international sanctions and ZS-SAH, a 707c model, was stripped and reconfigured as a freighter to be used between Johannesburg and Paris in what was basically a sanctions busting operation. The French wanted uranium, and we required spares for our Alouette helicopters and Mirage fighters, as well as computer equipment. At the time I was a First Officer on the 707.

We would fly Johannesburg to Windhoek where we would load, to maximum weight, 44-gallon drums of Yellowcake, a uranium ore concentrate. Being at max weight meant we were range limited, necessitating the use of short hops. Thus we would route Windhoek, Abijan, Isle de Sol (Cape Verde), Las Palmas, Marseilles and Paris Orly. In order to keep up a pretence of complying with some sort of Flight and Duty limitations on this marathon, we carried apart from one Captain, two full crews. The trouble was that there was no crew rest area, and the only place to sleep, when off duty, was on mattresses placed on top of the drums of Yellowcake.

We had all been issued with badges that looked like 35mm movie film and, I think, were supposed to blacken on exposure to radiation. We were also reassured that the radiation from Yellowcake was extremely low. These reassurances were immediately seriously doubted when the French authorities, on our arrival, always approached the drums wearing special suits and with a Geiger counter on the end of a five metre pole.

Having only one freighter and a once a week schedule meant, of course, the incoming crew were 'stuck' in Paris for a full week until the next aircraft arrived for them to take back to Johannesburg. This was a wonderful bonus and I have very fond memories of exploring Paris, with all its unique history, architecture, character, cuisine and art.

The French were quite easy to get along with provided one never attempted to open a conversation with them in English. We would speak Afrikaans to them, they would speak French back and eventually a rather halting English would be settled on as a common language.

We stayed in the newly-built Montparnasse Sheraton, a skyscraper of a hotel with over 900 rooms. Next to the hotel was an enormous apartment block with window walls. Due to the refreshing Gallic approach to modesty and the puritanical regime of the time in SA, this apartment block became a major attraction to the odd crew-member with voyeuristic inclinations. I recall a particular flight engineer who always brought binoculars to Paris. Often the invitation to join the rest of the crew for drinks and a meal were insufficient incentive to pry him out of his room.

There was one particularly popular apartment where a rather statuesque brunette habitually ironed laundry topless and in front of her window wall.

An amusing incident at the Sheraton involved a member of our crew who was lying naked on his bed sipping a beer and watching TV when he heard the most heart-rending cries for help from just outside his door. Thinking a girl was being mugged or raped he grabbed his beer bottle and charged into the passage only to find a group of teenagers playing the fool. Having expressed his severe displeasure to them, he turned back to his room only to find the spring mechanism had closed the door. Imagine how he felt when he realised that he was locked out of his room and standing naked in the passage.

By this time the teenagers, obviously shocked and frightened, after having been suddenly confronted by a scolding naked man with a beer bottle, had fled and thus no help was coming from that quarter. The only possible cover he could see, in the rather sterile passage, was a fire extinguisher, which he removed from the wall. Of course, Murphy's law dictated that there would be no other crew on his particular floor but he did remember the co-pilot's room number, five storeys down. In his panicked state, he decided that trying to get to that haven was his best option. It was mid afternoon, a time when hotels are at their quietest, so he pushed the down button for the lifts, getting ready to bolt should the opening lift doors reveal occupants.

As luck would have it, the first lift door that opened showed that the lift was empty, so he quickly entered it and pushed the button for five floors down. Lady luck was however just setting him up, for one floor below the lift stopped, the doors opened, and there stood a half dozen members of a visiting Swedish girls gymnastic team, staring at a naked man in a corner of the lift, protecting his modesty with a fire extinguisher. Nonplussed they all bundled into his lift and it was just as well he could not understand the barrage of, no doubt lewd, comments directed at him as the lift descended the remaining four floors to his destination.

One of the first things we needed to learn in Paris was how to navigate the Metro which was fantastic back in the seventies. It seemed one could get to practically any street corner using the Metro. Airports, harbours and bus terminals were interlinked and connected via the Metro and the country with the city by the deep Metro. There was a small museum in one of the stations where we were very surprised to learn that the first Paris Metro trains were horse drawn.

INSTANT JUSTICE

I remember a satisfying case of 'instant justice' involving the Metro. Our two crews were enjoying drinks in one of our hotel rooms when eventually a decision was made to go for dinner at our favourite cheap, but nice, restaurant, involving a short Metro ride. We set off without the second co-pilot and one of the flight engineers, who had just ordered beers, which said they would finish and join us at the restaurant shortly.

On reaching Montparnasse station a train was just pulling out and we had to wait a while for the next one, which we boarded. At the time, gangs of Algerian pickpockets plagued the Paris Metro, and as we stepped onto the train, the Skipper's wallet was lifted from his pocket. Not satisfied with theft alone, when the doors closed the miscreant banged on the glass to attract the Skipper's attention and, with a huge smirk on his face, waved the wallet in the Skipper's shocked and dismayed face as the train started to pull out.

This proved to be his undoing, as the tardy co-pilot and flight engineer had just arrived on the platform in time to witness this turn of events. They immediately grabbed hold of the culprit and relieved him of his ill-gotten gains. In the struggle, somehow, the culprit's face got rammed into the side of the rapidly departing train, which did him no good at all. They afterwards claimed it was entirely accidental.

One thing is certain, it would have been a long time before he was able to smirk again. All drinks were on the Skipper that evening!

PISSING OFF THE FRENCH

Departing Paris was always, for me, a time of mixed feelings- sad to leave this wonderful city, but great to be going back home to the family and at least nine days off. In those days SAA would give you the time you were away at home prior to the commencement of your next duty cycle. Some of our 707 flights were of thirteen days duration. This generosity did not, however, endure much past their demise.

Our clandestine operation terminated and originated in a quiet backwater at Orly Airport, well away from the public gaze. We would park right in front of a hangar that had been converted to a freight store. On either side of a cleared access space down the centre at the front of the hanger were three or four drywall and glass open topped offices where all the paperwork was handled. At the back of the hanger, away from prying eyes, was kept the freight.

I think we were fairly unpopular with the French, probably occasioned by two incidents that I had the misfortune to be involved in. On departure the tug would be connected and we would start the engines during the push-back. This was standard operating procedure. We would be pushed straight back and then turned through ninety degrees to align us with the taxiway.

The first incident was on push-back when number two engine blow-torched. This is occasioned when, on start, there is no ignition and unburned fuel puddles in the engine. Suddenly ignition kicks in, ignites this fuel, and there is a big bang plus a column of flame many metres long, and very reminiscent of of a giant blowtorch, leaping from the back of the engine.

This would not normally cause too much consternation, as the ground engineer and tug driver would at this point be a alone with the aircraft and quite familiar with the phenomenon. Somehow though there were always plenty of observers around our operation and often far too close to the aircraft. I suspect that they were mainly security and civil servants from various concerned departments. One got a strong feeling that they just wanted us out of there before anyone found out what was going on. We sometimes had whole Mirage jet fighters or Alouette helicopters on board, in blatant breach of international sanctions.

Well, when number two blow-torched, this crowed of observers, understandably, nearly died of fright! Some, in fact, falling off the vehicles upon which they were perched. There followed much Gallic emotion, jumping up and down and shaking of fists towards the cockpit, as if all of it was our fault. We just stabilised the engine and carried on, leaving much French fury behind.

The second incident was far more serious. It was winter and the apron outside the hanger had snow on it with, unbeknown to us, an underlying layer of ice. The tug was connected, we were ready to push back and the engineer cleared us to start the engines. Nobody extraneous to the operation was around, but whether this was due to the above mentioned incident or the weather I could not tell.

We had released the brakes, started the first engine and were busy starting the second. As the second engine came up to idle power and we were about to start the third, we realised we had started to move, but forwards rather then backwards. What was happening was that the tug could not get traction on the ice and the residual idle thrust of the two running engines was pushing the tug rapidly backwards through the open hanger doors of the freight store.

Our concentration had been inside the cockpit on the engine start and events had escalated rapidly, prior to our becoming aware that anything was wrong.

By the time we realised what was happening the tug was already entering the hanger with the aircraft soon to follow. Shutting down the engines would not have helped as by now the momentum would have just carried us in.

As no one else in the cockpit seemed to be reacting, there was only one thing I could think of to do, and that was to grab a great handful of reverse thrust. This I did and it brought the whole rig to a stop and, in fact, pulled the tug back out of the hanger.

Very successful outcome I thought! It was, however, not without a downside. The effect of two engines in reverse, blowing directly into a freight store, had some interesting consequences. For starters, the drywall offices were blown over and the flying paperwork resembled a heavy snowstorm. Several clerks were blown off their chairs. Miraculously no injuries beyond cuts, grazes and bruises occurred. Discounting, of course, massive damage to bureaucratic dignity! Once again we faced some spectacular Gallic wrath. In all fairness, when the consequences of the aircraft entering the freight store were realised, I think we were viewed in a more positive light.

The Paris freighters were hard work. Being banned from flying over most of Africa, we island hopped around the bulge of Africa due to the weight of the cargo limiting the fuel we could carry and thus our range. The consequences of having to route in this fashion were extremely long flights, with six consecutive legs and no crew rest facilities. It was often impossible to sleep on the mattresses resting on drums of Yellowcake, particularly with the extreme weather associated with the Inter-tropical Convergence Zone through which we flew. Double crew mostly meant twice the number of tired crew.

Rightly or wrongly, however, our country was under siege. We were young, and it was an exciting operation, which we were forbidden to talk about. I suppose we all felt a certain unspoken pride regarding our involvement in these clandestine activities.

Sadly it was not long afterwards that the 707 Fleet was phased out and the aircraft sold. Once again I found myself in the classroom, the simulator and in the hands of the Training Captains but this time on the Boeing 747 conversion course.

THE JUMBO JET

The 747 is a classic and a milestone in aviation history but I never really came to love her, as I loved the 707 and I am not sure why. Maybe it was due to the lack of interconnect between the Cockpit, the Cabin crew and the passengers, occasioned by the fact that the cockpit was rather remote from the cabin being on a deck above it. At the time I was on 747s, no passengers were carried on the upper deck it being devoted to the 'Sky Lounge' which was available only to the first class passengers. It had a club like atmosphere with small circular tables, each surrounded by four comfortable swivelling chairs. There was a real bar counter with barstools and this was manned by a dedicated cabin crew-member. The bar was accessed from the lower deck via a most impressive spiral staircase.

The most awe inspiring aspect of the 747 was the sheer size that earned it the 'Jumbo' nickname. I remember how in November 1971 all the pilots, who were not flying, went to the Airport to see the arrival of our first 747, named Lebombo. On final approach it hardly seemed to be moving which was an optical illusion caused by its great size. Someone immediately dubbed it 'The Aluminium Overcast' which I thought was very descriptive. When we all gathered around it, after it was parked in the Technical Section, we just marvelled at the shear size of its components and its cavernous interior.

When I came to fly the aircraft it flew pretty much like the other jets I had flown and was, in fact, very mild mannered. I have always said that a pilot really 'flies the cockpit' and whatever is behind that is not of great consequence. However, the landing technique in the 747 was something new to be learned due to the great height of the cockpit above the ground. When the 747 is parked the pilots eye level is 32 feet, or 9.75 metres above the ground. In the nose up landing attitude, when the wheels touch the runway the eye level is far higher. I recall my training Captain Flippie Looch telling me, "Don't look at the runway, look at the horizon when landing the 747". A great help was the radio altimeter which called out the height of the wheels above the runway every 10ft below 50ft.

BIG MARY AND THE BABY

We had some wonderfully memorable characters in SAA, not least of which was a cabin steward known to all the crews as Big Mary. As the name suggests he was a very flamboyant character, with an extremely camp demeanour. His rank was Senior Steward and he normally worked in the first class cabin of the Boeing 747.

Many stories were told about Big Mary, who was liked by all, due to his effusive and entertaining personality. Of the many, this one in particular always comes to my mind and never seems to grow stale with the telling.

The 747 had taken off in the evening from JF Kennedy, New York. Earlier a jewel and fur bedecked lady, with a baby in arms, had boarded and been seated in Big Mary's section of the first class cabin.

During the climb the cabin crew were very busy preparing for the dinner service when this lady beckoned big Mary over and thrust her baby into his arms with the terse instruction "My good man, kindly change the baby." For once in his life Big Mary was at a total loss for words and, by the time he had recovered his composure, she had disappeared into one of the toilets and he had, literally, been left holding the baby!

Some time later she emerged from the toilet to find no sign of Big Mary or her baby in the first class cabin. She took her seat and one of the hostesses brought her a drink.

About ten minutes later Big Mary came flouncing into the first class from economy cabin with a little black baby which he unceremoniously dumped on her lap, while loudly announcing before flouncing away again,

"Madam I've changed the baby. I'm sorry it's not the same colour, but it's the best I could do!"

On another occasion Big Mary, was being given an undeserved right bollocking by one of the VIP passengers, who was displeased with some aspect of the first class service. The passenger happened to be a South African politician who, of course, was on a 'freebie'. This worthy ended the bollocking with the words

"and do you know who I am?"

At this Big Mary looked over his shoulder at one of the stewards and called loudly

"Charles please bring me the passenger list, we have a passenger here who has forgotten who he is!"

THE BREAKFAST LIGHTS

Airlines operate in their own time zones when it comes to determining which meals will be served on a flight. Often the times they choose to serve meals bear no resemblance to reality. This is particularly noticeable on east - west / west - east flights that involve time change. An example of this is SAA's daily flight from Perth to Johannesburg. The scheduled departure time is ten minutes to midnight. After take-off the poor cabin crew have to prepare for the dinner service. Even the exhausted would have trouble sleeping under the bright service lights and the clatter of cutlery and crockery.

By the time dinner is served, the cabin cleared and the lights dimmed, one is well into the wee hours. What management nut-case determined that after midnight was an appropriate time to serve dinner?

Having provided a little background, my story took place on a 747 operating between Johannesburg and New York after the intermediate refuelling and crew change stop at Isle de Sal in the Cape Verde Islands.

The relieving cabin crew were warned about a particularly difficult and demanding first class passenger, and It was not very long before he demonstrated the validity of this warning. Nevertheless, after the customary snack was served and after a few drinks too many, the cabin lights were dimmed and he fell asleep.

The 747 trudged on through the night which was, as they were flying to an earlier time zone, fairly short. Thus it was not that long before the cabin crew had to start their preparations for the breakfast service. The senior hostess, Robyn, had just brought a glass of water for a passenger across the isle from our difficult passenger, when the bright cabin lights were switched on. This woke our friend with a start and in a bad tempered voice he shouted,

> "Who put the fucking lights on!!!!"

Robyn turned around, smiled sweetly at him, and in a voice that carried across the first class cabin stated,

> "Sir, these are the breakfast lights. The lights to which you refer are much dimmer, and you slept right through them!"

SAL ISLAND

At this stage we were still flying to Europe via the long route around the bulge of Africa, Thus, as with the 707s, we would stop at Isle de Sal to refuel and change crews. This little island in the Cabo Verde group had long facilitated this routeing and also served as a handy stop on the New York route.

The island is very small, about thirty kilometres long and twelve kilometres wide. At the time it was almost completely devoid of vegetation and the main industries were fishing and the production of salt from which the island gets its name. The island also seemed to be overrun by dogs and donkeys. Prior to landings vehicles had to be sent out to insure the runway was clear. Despite this precaution an SAA 747 did hit a donkey while landing at night.

The dogs were all mongrels and the locals seemed to have a great deal of tolerance for them. The SAA crew less so, as it was very difficult to achieve a decent sleep, prior to one's flight, due to the continual barking, howling and frequent dog fights.

Our hotel was in the small town of Santa Maria on the southern tip of the island. Called the Morabeza, it was the first resort hotel built on the island and was owned and run by a Belgian couple. Back then Sal Island was practically unknown as a holiday destination and SAA's custom was highly valued. Although the accommodation was very rudimentary, consisting of a row of stable-like rooms that fronted on to a stretch of bare sand, we were very well treated and looked after by both staff and management.

The island's fresh water supply came from a crude solar still and tasted vile. As such we were permitted to take cans of soda water off the aircraft for use on Sal. This was before the bottling of plain water water became popular and, unlike today, none was carried on the aircraft. Be assured that brushing ones teeth in soda water can be quite problematic due to the release of gas.

Today, thanks to the beautiful white sandy beaches and the 350 days of sunshine, Sal has become a popular holiday destination.To cater for this trade many fancy resort hotels have been built and shops and restaurants opened. Plenty of planting has taken place and Santa Maria has become considerably greener than it was in the seventies.

Once one had visited the Pedra de Lume, a dormant volcanic crater which was used to produce huge quantities of salt, the live rock lobster plant, the tuna canning factory and a swimming place in a cleft between rocks, unkindly named 'Dina se Gat' (Dina's Hole) after SAA's Chief Hostess, there was very little left to do except for drinking and socialising. Bored aircrew and alcohol is not a very good mix but surprisingly incidents were few and far between.

The flight from Johannesburg was a fairly long haul through the night but even after that, one of our Captains, Robin, was a keen runner and while the rest of his crew went by the crew bus, Robin would run the 17km from the airport to the hotel. This at 01.00 hours and through what was practically a desert. He would invariably arrive when we were on our second round of drinks and join the party.

In contrast, another of our Captains would spend the whole cruise in the bunk, thus denying anyone else bunk time, and on arrival at the hotel, when asked if he would be joining the rest of the crew for a drink, would announce loudly "Thanks guys, I would have liked to but I am so tired that I think I will go straight to bed."

The Russians were using Sal as a crew stop over on their flights between Moscow and Cuba and their crews were also accommodated at the Morabeza. As South Africa was engaged in the Angolan civil war in support of the anti communism UNITA and Russia was supporting Cuban troops fighting on the side of the communism supporting MPLA, one would have thought of this as a possible source of conflict. But no, the Russian crews were under the tight control of a Communist Party Commissar who would for the most part discourage any crew socialising.

On the odd occasion, when the Commissar could not refuse the offer of a free glass of top South African brandy, some very good drinking sessions resulted.

During these, despite the circumstances, we all got on very well as we had a common interest in aviation and there seemed to be an unwritten rule to leave politics to the politicians. The mutual strategy was always to pour such heavy handed tots for the Commissar that, either he would pass out or lose all interest in what went on.

As with the 707, we flew three models of 747. There was the Super B Classic Jumbo, the SP, and the Kombi which combined freight and passengers on the same deck. They were used on routes with high cargo and low passenger demand. These were done away with after the horrific cargo fire that caused the 747 Helderberg to crash into the sea off the Island of Mauritius in 1987.

The SP was a very long range 747 and this had been achieved mainly by lightening the aircraft substantially. The process of removing 47 feet of fuselage from the classic 747 had made this possible. Being so light the SP was an incredible performer on short sectors with a relatively light fuel load. On the delivery flight from Seattle to Cape Town our first SP set a record for distance flown, without refuelling, by a commercial airliner.

The airline was experiencing a period of expansion and thus I did not spend very long on the 747. The time I did spend was most enjoyable as we still flew to many of the great European cities and several destinations in the Americas as well as the Indian Ocean islands, Hong Kong and Australia.

Before I really became used to the 747 I found myself on a domestic Captains course.

13

AT LAST! FOUR GOLD BARS AND A COMMAND

Becoming a Captain is an absolute landmark occasion for any airline pilot. It marks the end of a very long period of being a co-pilot.

A co-pilot requires all the skills of a born diplomat, an aide-de-camp and occasionally an arbitrator. When criticised by his Captain he must unquestionably and immediately admit guilt, promise to correct his faults and do better in future. Any form of argument is unthinkable. An unreasonable Captain can make life very unpleasant for a co-pilot.

Originally in SAA there was the iniquitous negative 'confidential report' that a Captain could make and which could have a huge influence on a co-pilot's career. The report, being confidential, meant that the co-pilot would never even see it nor be able to defend himself against it. Yet there it was, irrevocably in his file, for the promotions review board to examine when the co-pilot came up for a promotion to another fleet or even for Captaincy. There were cases where a negative confidential report stemmed from something as trivial as competing for the affections of a hostess on a night stop.

Fortunately, under more enlightened Flight Operations CEO's the confidential report was abolished. Equally fortunate the Captains who utilised confidential reports were a tiny minority who were too cowardly to face those whose careers they jeopardised. Far and away, the vast majority of Captains I flew with as a copilot were wonderful human beings and team players, always willing to share the benefit of their experience with their co-pilots.

Nevertheless, moving to the left-hand seat is a great occasion as at last the Captaincy that one has all those years been groomed for arrives.

Once again luck was with me just as it had been when I had become a Senior First Officer and was allocated the international Boeing 707 rather than the domestic Airbus A300. At the time on becoming a Captain one was either sent to the Boeing 737s or to the Hawker Siddeley 748. The HS 748 was a twin engined turboprop designed to replace the DC3 Dakota and it carried up to 50 passengers. It was a bit like a smaller twin engined version of the Viscount. To my delight, I was placed on the 737 course.

The course was mostly the same as the 737 copilot course except in the simulator where you moved to the left hand seat, took the decision making role and a much higher standard was expected of you.

THE 'CAPTAINS COURSE' AND 'VIP LUNCH'

On completion of training, and before being released onto the routes you were required to attend a 'Captain's Course'. This mainly consisted of being shepherded round to all the SAA departments to meet their heads and become familiar with their operations.

This would have been fascinating had it been an ab initio course on first joining SAA but my colleagues and I had all been pilots with SAA for over a decade and were pretty familiar with all its departments, thus it was all a big joke and not taken seriously by any of us apart from the poor soul who had been appointed by management to 'sheepdog' the rest of us. This was a very serious young co-pilot who had applied for and been accepted as a training Captain.

Gaining a position as a training Captain in SAA was a shortcut to the four bars of command and thus a domestic co-pilot, successfully gaining a training position, immediately became a Captain. Without this incentive it would have been extremely difficult and costly to recruit Training Captains from the ranks of line Captains. For this reason our 'sheepdog' was not only the most serious fellow amongst us but also the youngest. On occasion I felt very sorry for him trying valiantly to organise a bunch of older, more experienced and irreverent pilots. Incidentally any pilot leaving the training section would automatically revert to their line seniority which in many cases would mean becoming a co-pilot once more.

The traditional highlight of the Captains course was a lunch in the Blue Room restaurant hosted by the CEO of SAA. The Blue Room was situated within the Johannesburg station and tied in with the famous Blue Train premium service of the South African Railways. This lunch was something we were all looking forward to and would go a long way to mitigating the boredom of the rest of the course, or so we thought.

The CEO at the time was Frans Swarts of "That's the price you have to pay if you want to live under the South African sun" fame, when justifying the very low salaries paid to SAA pilots who, due to sanctions, were precluded from applying for overseas positions at the time. That worthy wished to demonstrate the money saving drive he had instigated so, in place of the Blue Room, we were shown into an opulent boardroom in the SA Railway headquarters building.

The boardroom table was so long it seemed with perspective to almost vanish into the distance. Three crystal chandeliers hung above the table which was richly decorated with a silver centrepiece under each chandelier, silver place settings and lead crystal wine goblets. Seeing this we thought, 'Well no Blue Room, but this could be something special too'. Unfortunately we were soon disabused of this ridiculous notion.

After the CEO's speech, which had less to do with welcoming his new Captains, and more to do with blowing his own trumpet, a door at the far end of the boardroom opened and two aircraft galley trolleys were wheeled in by the most smartly dressed Cabin Attendants any of us had ever seen. We were given the choice of red or white wine but restricted to only one glass. The big surprise came when the meal trolley was opened and we were served bog standard domestic economy class aircraft meals in the strange blue plastic dishes with vertical sides that were in economy class use at the time.

These were the meals we ate almost every working day of our lives, when operating over mealtimes, on domestic fleets. To make matters worse we had all, with the exception of our 'sheepdog', come from international fleets where far superior food was served to the cockpit from the First Class galleys. While maybe serving as an introduction to the meals we would be eating on our domestic fleets, none of us felt that it was a fitting tribute from the CEO to celebrate the culmination of all the effort and dedication required, over the many years, to become an SAA Captain.

Neither did it take us long to figure out, that the expense involved in acquiring those meals from the caterers, transporting them all the way from the airport to Johannesburg and returning the trolleys after the meal, would have been more costly than multi course Blue Room lunches . Added to this was the cost of the Cabin Attendants that provided the service making the whole thing just an intelligence insulting, hollow paper exercise.

We were all so let down and disgusted that, on leaving, we made paper aeroplanes from the unframed certificates the CEO had presented us with. These littered the steps of the grand entrance and we all hoped the CEO would see them on leaving the building.

14

THE DECENTRALISATION SAGA

Up until 1986 all SAA's domestic fleets were based in Johannesburg and thus all its domestic pilots had no choice but to live in the Transvaal within easy range of Jan Smuts Airport as it was then named. This never sat very well with those of us who had grown up in South Africa's coastal towns and who missed the aesthetic aspects and more relaxed lifestyles that these areas offered in contrast to Johannesburg and the Reef towns that formed the busy commercial hubs of South Africa.

It was thus that several of us from the 737 Fleet formed a committee in 1983. We would hold our meetings at my home in Halfway House. Corleen volunteered to be our secretary responsible for all the paperwork and typing. The committee's sole task was to motivate to SAA the idea of decentralising 737 crews in Cape Town and Durban. This was not by any means an original idea as many airlines worldwide had established decentralised crew bases away from their home base. This is a very successful cost saving strategy as, due to safety regulations governing crew rest.

To illustrate this, assume that the last flight of the day from Johannesburg to Cape Town arrives at 10.00pm. There is no later flight from Cape Town back to Johannesburg so the crew must spend the night in a Cape Town hotel and by the time they arrived at the hotel it would be after 11.00pm. This 'night stop' would not only involve, ever increasing, accommodation costs but also transport costs and the cost of supplying each crew member with two days of Sustenance and Travel allowance based on the cost of meals at the hotel.

Due to the Flight and Duty Regulations any late arriving crew would be unable to operate the first flights out of Cape Town as the 'pick up' time at the hotel for these would be before 06.00am. Thus crews off earlier flights into Cape Town would have to 'night stop' in order to operate the early morning flights out the following day.

Of course, the same is true of Durban and thus large numbers of aircrew are being accommodated in hotels on any given night and incurring all the associated costs. However if crews were based in Cape Town and Durban they would travel, at their own expense, to and from their own homes and thus eliminate most of the costs associated with night stops.

There were many other positive aspects of basing flight crews in Cape Town and Durban which were of great advantage to SAA yet we came up against an incredibly strong resistance to change factor and it took three years of back and forth before we succeeded in getting the powers that be to accept crews based away from Johannesburg. Particularly frustrating was the fact that interested Cabin Crew members had spoken with us at length, adopted our motivations, had them accepted by their management and had established and crewed a Cape Town base, while we, a year later, had still not gained management's acceptance despite it being on then off a dozen times.

THE REBEL TOURS

In the end the frustration reached such a level that we planned, what we called the 'Rebel Tours' after the Australian cricket tours to South Africa in the eighties after tours to SA were banned by the international bodies. We drew up a block of flights out of Cape Town and Durban that could be operated by crews based there and which would tie in with the flights operated by Johannesburg crews. This was handed to management, along with a list of six crews that would be available to operate them, all of whom were already positioned at the bases. At the same time as announcing this, I made myself extremely unpopular at a meeting with the CEO of Flight Operations by accusing him and his team of economic sabotage against SAA by their failure to make a final decision regarding the cost savings inherent in the concept of decentralisation.

I have always identified this as the moment the CEO's resistance finally collapsed. He rose to his feet, turned red then blue, and I began to panic thinking he was about to have a heart attack and that I had caused it. However, he recovered and cursing me roundly, he shouted "You've got it! Now just go! Get out of my sight! His Deputy began to protest this decision and was unceremoniously told to "Shut up!"

With that, after three long years, of motivations, meetings, lobbying, endless resistance and setbacks, we had achieved a way to live at the coast and fly for SAA, a win, win situation!

The CEO, at the time, was a fellow pilot and a good chap who in the normal course of events would never curse. Years later when he was in retirement the message was passed on to me that he had for years felt bad about cursing me and that he sincerely apologised. Now I felt bad that it had plagued his conscience for years, as it really meant nothing at all to me. After all I had often, probably well deservedly, been roundly cursed and seldom received an apology. In any case anything negative that had passed between us was totally overshadowed and forgotten in the triumph of achieving decentralisation.

THE MOVE

We had determined that the most efficient strength for the new crew bases would be thirteen crews each, and as decentralisation was now official, we were all entitled to a transfer at the airlines expense. Probably being the first SAA pilots to ever be officially transferred we were now introduced to the weird and wonderful world of our senior service, the South African Railways or 'Spoories' transfer system.

The SAR transferred staff all over the country and so regularly that they had their own department dedicated to this duty. In fact it was unkindly rumoured that large staff transfers often took place merely to swing the vote in marginal seats at election time. At the time we needed to be transferred this department was overloaded and had insufficient removal trucks to handle our transfers. This was fortunate for us as they were then forced to contract private companies to handle our moves. Less fortunately, the contracts with the private companies exactly followed the SAR policy concerning moves. No SAR transfer included packing but a department van turned up and offloaded a stack of empty cardboard cartons at our homes for us to pack.

It soon became apparent that a railways transfer seemed to have been designed to move a family living in one of those lonely and remote red brick cottages that one sees alongside railway lines in the middle of nowhere. Strangely there was no provision for family pets such as dogs and cats. There was, however, provision made for one bullock and fifty chickens. One assumes that at the time the provisions were drawn up, most railway workers were fattening up a bullock and kept chickens for fresh eggs.

The fact that these regulations had never been updated came as no surprise as many of us had benefited from a regulation from the days of Paul Kruger stating that all railway employees were entitled to five scrap sleepers for firewood should these be available. Most of the sleepers were of beautiful Jarrah imported from Australia, but where the railway line passed through indigenous forests much sought after Yellowwood and Stinkwood were utilised for sleepers.

Those who imagined that surely a bullock could be replaced by a spaniel or the fifty chickens by a budgie were soon disabused of that silly notion.

Another rather incredible clause in the regulation ruled out loading any form of gardening equipment into a road transport pantechnicon. For the transportation of these items a 'rommel trok' or 'rubble truck' was provided. This was a full sized piece of rolling stock in the form of a covered goods truck. Many a 'rommel trok' was hauled the 1400km from Johannesburg to Cape Town with only a lawn mower, spade, fork and hedge clipper strapped into a corner of its cavernous maw. On the other hand these trucks provided a wonderful opportunity for those of us who had bulky objects such as disassembled collectors cars, boats under construction or great quantities of materials and hobby machinery. As such there were convenient transfers of the ownership of goods between decentralising pilots who had the need for capacity and those who did not.

We were also provided with transport for our motor vehicles in the form of open rolling stock. Tarpaulins were provided to cover the vehicles. Apparently when the regulations were drawn up, it was inconceivable that any railway worker would have more than one motor car and thus no limit was placed on the number of vehicles one could transport. This was extremely fortunate for those of us who had vintage or classic car collections.

What also made everything a lot easier was the fact that back then SAA was a big family, there was generally goodwill all round and staff would go to great lengths to assist one another. Thus by speaking nicely to the operations manager of freight section we were able to get our three enormous Saint Bernard dogs flown down to Cape Town.

A COUPLE, SEVEN DOGS AND A MINI

One who did not follow this route was Ricky who, in all probability, felt that seven dogs was probably pushing the envelope a bit. Ricky decided that the best way to move his dogs to Cape Town was to drive them down by car. Ricky's car was a Mini Minor and not the big BMW version of today, but the tiny original Alec Issigonis design.

Ricky, his girlfriend Jane and the seven dogs set off in the mini to undertake the long drive to Cape Town. On hearing of this we all assumed that the dogs would all be of a size described as 'handbag' or 'teacup'. Disbelief was rife when we were informed that they ranged in size from a Great Dane down to a Yorkie. Now I know that the Guinness Book of Records tells us that twenty seven people have managed to pack themselves into a Mini and close the doors, but two adults and seven dogs undertaking a 1400km drive must be bordering on insanity.

Most people seem to consider driving through the Great Karoo as a rather monotonous exercise as the road runs straight for many kilometres through vast flat areas vegetated only with low shrubs and bushes. It was nearing midnight and somewhere between Laingsburg and Richmond when Ricky, who was driving, fell asleep at the wheel. The Mini careened off the road and rolled several times before ending up on its roof in the veld.

Ricky was not injured, but unfortunately Jane had gone through the windscreen and had been quite badly cut about the face. The dogs were not injured but, no doubt in a state of shock, took off into the veldt. These were the days when few people had mobile phones and coverage in SA was still sketchy. However passing motorists stopped to help and alerted emergency services in both Laingsburg and Richmond. This resulted in a long delay as bureaucratic arguments ensued as to whether the accident had taken place in the Laingsburg or Richmond area of coverage.

Eventually the police and an ambulance arrived and Jane was taken to hospital. The dogs were rounded up and they and Ricky spent the few hours left till daylight in the charge office of the Laingsburg police station.

Fortunately for the rest of us, our relocations were mostly devoid of such dramatic events and it was not long before all were settled into their new homes mainly in the Southern Suburbs and Somerset West.

The Fleet's first 'office' was little more than a broom cupboard under a flight of stairs and we had no administrative support but despite this the morale was high and all the flights allocated to us were seamlessly operated.

MICKEY

Shortly thereafter the CEO retired and Captain Mickey Mitchell was appointed as his replacement. Mickey was a very different CEO and his appointment was not a particularly popular one as he was considered by many to have a 'Napoleon complex'. I had flown as Mickey's co-pilot for many years and we got on very well as our views in most aspects were pretty much in alignment.

Mickey was an innovator and when he took over Flight Operations the biggest innovation at the time was the newly decentralised 737 fleets. This was grist to Mickey's mill and immediately our status was elevated from 'Pain in the butt' to 'The greatest thing since sliced bread'. For playing a leading roll in initiating and driving the concept of this innovation, to my embarrassment, I became very much Mickey's 'blue eyed boy'.

There were many advantages to this as with Mickey's backing we were able to acquire a decent Crew Room with an attached office, hire full time administrative support and expand the fleet, allowing more pilots and their families to live in the Cape. Mickey also had a healthy discretionary budget which he was not shy to spend and he financed some pretty grand parties when we annually celebrated the anniversary of the Cape Fleet. Mickey would always attend these functions with great enthusiasm.

There was, for me, a downside to being favoured by Mickey. He had introduced a variety of consultants to assist him in his innovative approach to running Flight Operations. It seemed to us that he was never seen without one of these consultants, on his right hand, and as such the phrase 'Mickey and the Witchdoctors' was coined. These consultants invariably recommended to Mickey that his managers all attend courses that, of course, they presented for a hefty fee.

Thus I attended Dale Carnegie courses, a Visionary Leadership course and several other courses that made so little impact on me that I have forgotten what they were called. They lasted several days and I had to travel up from Cape Town to attend. The silver lining was that they were held at interesting venues, normally game parks or safari lodges. Activities that these venues offered were included in the program and, of course, the social life that occurred around the bars in the evenings was great fun.

Meanwhile life settled down on the Cape Fleet as everyone became used to their new lifestyles and activities. There were many amusing incidents involving boats and landlubbers. There was the time when a party was held on boats at the layup basin of Cape Town harbour and the 737 Fleet Captain from Johannesburg, Flippie Vermeulen, somehow managed to end up in the harbour between Ren Colyn's boat and the quay. This was not a good place to be as the concrete of the quay was covered in sharp barnacles and he was fairly badly abraded by the time we managed to haul him out. The next day it was discovered that he had also cracked two ribs.

At another boat party, this time at Hout Bay, Mickey Mitchell managed to get himself into a boat to shore slanging match with a local urchin. Mickey, handicapped by a goodly quantity of alcohol and an even greater quantity of ego, seemed utterly incapable of extricating himself, gracefully or otherwise, from the situation and the stream of cheek continued to fly thick and fast from the quay. This was very demeaning to Mickey as it was occurring in front of more than a dozen of his pilots, to whom his word was law. Eventually Ren took pity on him and told the urchin to clear off, a command which was immediately and silently obeyed. This was an enormous blow to Mickey's ego as he failed to comprehend that to an urchin at a harbour he meant nothing, while the skipper of a boat was the highest authority he knew and was to be instantly obeyed.

THE HUNT

A particular incident, not involving boats or landlubbers, but involving a member of the Cape Fleet occurred around this time and it is one that rather sticks in my memory. One of our First Officers, Pine, was a keen hunter and had organised a hunting trip with three friends. The venue for this trip was to be on a farm in Namibia, owned by one of Pine's contacts, and the four of them had arranged to fly from Cape Town to Windhoek on SAA.

In those days it was fairly common to have sporting guns amongst the baggage that SAA carried and the procedure was to hand them over to the police at the airport. They would convey them to the aircraft where they would be loaded and secured on top of the diplomatic locker. At the arrival airport this procedure was reversed and the guns could be reclaimed from the police upon presentation of the receipts issued by the police at the departure airport.

Our four friends duly arrived in Windhoek, collected their rifles from the airport police and strolled over to the car hire desk to collect the Volkswagen Kombi they had booked for the duration of their trip. This was where they immediately ran into difficulties as the young lady behind the counter, observing a motley crew all dressed in khaki and camouflage hunting gear and holding rifles, baulked and loudly announced that "No way were her company's vehicles going to be used for hunting" and indicated to them, in no uncertain way, that they should 'take a hike'.

Now here was a serious threat to their plans, stuck at the airport, which is nearly fifty kilometres from the city, with no transport. Despite their best efforts to convince the young lady that the Kombi would be utilised only for transport to and from the farm and not as a hunting vehicle, sensible girl that she was, she was not buying their story and refused to release the Kombi to them. By now the activities at the car hire counter had began to attract onlookers and an urgent call was made to the car hire HQ in Windhoek for assistance to resolve the situation.

Forty five minutes later the car hire company's manager arrived after having driven from Windhoek to the airport. In due course Pine was able to convince him that it was their genuine intention to utilise the hire Kombi solely for transportation on roads, as a hunting vehicle was available on the farm. A factor that swung the manager's decision in Pines favour was that he was able to show the manager that he was an SAA pilot and thus, supposedly, a responsible citizen. Thus the Kombi was released and the group were able to proceed if a good two hours behind their intended schedule.

An interesting fact about car hire in Namibia back then, was that the insurance offered by the car hire companies only covered incidents that occurred while the vehicle was travelling on a bituminised road. This was rather anomalous as, city roads aside, there were really only two such roads in Namibia. They formed the north-south and east-west axes and turning off these spine roads one would invariably be on a dirt road.

Once on the road the four had made good time, only stopping at a bottle store in Windhoek to purchase a few crates of the, extremely good local brew and a gun shop to purchase ammunition but despite this, with the delay at the airport, it seemed unlikely that they would make the farm before sunset. The farm lay to the west of Otjiwarongo and shortly after passing through the little town they turned off the bituminised road and onto a dirt road now heading west into the setting sun and leaving in their wake a long cloud of red dust hanging in the still, hot air. The case of beers had long since been pillaged and by now the woes at the airport had been forgotten and all were feeling quite mellow.

Unexpectedly a farm bakkie came barrelling past and suddenly visibility was reduced to zero in its dust trail. As they slowed to counter this development, there was an almighty bang and, beers and all, everybody was thrown onto the floor in front of their seats as, of course, none of them had been wearing seat belts. After the impact the Kombi came to an abrupt stop and it took a good few minutes before the dust cleared and the occupants managed to disentangle themselves from the debris on the floor of the Kombi and raise their heads to window height in order to locate the cause of all the chaos.

Looking back it soon became apparent that the large kudu lying in the middle of the road must have been responsible for the collision back there in the dust. A kudu is a large and powerful antelope with long thick corkscrew like horns. The bulls can weigh up to 300Kgs and have horns in excess of a metre in length.

Gathering their wits and clambering out to inspect the damage, they discovered that the front was badly stove in and the headlamps broken. Once they had pulled the distorted wheel-arches clear of the wheels, the Kombi, having a rear engine, seemed quite capable of still being driven.

Their attention then turned to the dead kudu as patently it could not be left lying in the middle of the road creating a hazard to navigation. It was, as they were contemplating the corpse, that someone came up with the bright idea that 'It would be a crying shame to waste all that biltong, so why don't we take it with us and butcher it when we get to the farm?'. It should be noted that later they would all deny being the originator of that idea. Nevertheless, at the time the idea was well received, the Kombi was reversed up to the kudu, the rear row of seats folded flat and, with great difficulty, the kudu was crammed into the available space.

Setting off once again, more beers were cracked, to calm nerves. By this time the sun had set and the Kombi, without headlights, was crawling along at a much reduced pace when its occupants became aware of strange sounds coming from the rear. These rapidly increased in volume and intensity until the whole vehicle was physically shaking. At this point the realisation struck, that the dead kudu they loaded into the back was, in fact, not dead at all but had merely been knocked unconscious, was recovering rapidly and in the process kicking the Kombi to pieces.

A panic stop ensued and all baled out with great haste. Having retreated to a safe distance on the opposite side of the road, the four stood in a line and watched in torchlight, the extraordinary scene unfolding before their eyes. The Kombi seemed to be growing huge lumps in its bodywork as the powerful beast tried to escape confinement. Soon the tail lights shattered, having been kicked out from the inside but the crowning glory was the huge horns that emerged through the roof of the Kombi, only to be withdrawn, and repeatedly re-emerge in other locations.

The realisation soon struck that something had to be done as the situation was unlikely to resolve itself, the question being what action to take. It was obvious that going near the rear of the vehicle was highly dangerous and even if they could get the doors open it was unlikely that the kudu, not being able to get to its feet, would be able to exit the vehicle. Thus to shoot the kudu in situ seemed like the only possible solution. A brave volunteer managed to creep up, open the front passenger door and extract one of the rifles from under the front seats where it had been stowed. He also managed to recover a box of bullets from the cubbyhole.

In the end dispatching the poor old kudu proved to be easier than they had first thought. A torch was shone through a closed window in the side of the Kombi followed by a fusillade of shots and the job was done. It was only later they discovered that some of the shots had missed the kudu and gone through the bodywork on the opposite side.

Eventually they reached the farm where the kudu was extracted from the Kombi and the mess cleaned up to the best of their ability. The hunting trip went along as planned but I am not sure if they really enjoyed it, what with the thought of having to return the wreck to the car hire company preying on their minds.

Inevitably the day of their return dawned and they set off for Windhoek airport collecting a few traffic tickets on the way. The fact that their vehicle was not taken off the road can only lead to the conclusion that a few palms must have been well greased along the way. Arriving at the airport they parked in the hire companies parking lot and soon attracted quite a large crowd marvelling at the state of the Kombi. After all how often does one see huge dents that bulge outwards in place of inwards, to say nothing of the crushed front, the shattered head and tail lights, broken windows, horn piercings and the bullet holes. The interior was also something to behold with smashed panelling, torn upholstery, ruined roof lining, destroyed interior lighting and traces of blood everywhere.

Making her way through the crowd was the car hire lady, with clipboard at the ready to note down any scratches or minor damage that might have occurred while the vehicle was in the hands of the client. She was soon sitting on a canvas chair and sipping sweetened tea, both provided by a kind onlooker.

The upshot of all this was that the passports of our intrepid hunters were taken from them and they were prevented from leaving Namibia until such time as guarantees were in place for the cost of repairing or replacing the Kombi. Of course nothing was covered by insurance as the damage was not incurred on a bituminised road. Not only an expensive hunting trip but Pine's flying roster had to be covered by his colleges on the Cape Fleet while he was detained in Namibia and they expected him to make it up to them on his return.

THE CAPE TO RIO YACHT RACE

The Cape fleet was very innovative and we managed to introduce many procedures that were later adopted, some in modified form, by the Johannesburg fleets, an examples of this was the 'Flight Watch' which replaced standby duties done at the airport. The benefit to the airline was that a Flight Watch flight backup was done at home and thus one pilot could cover all the flights on a day as opposed to the two pilots required to be on standby at the airport, one to cover the flights before midday and one to cover the flights after midday. We also introduced a system whereby one could bid for leave in place of having it allocated.

Deon Sachs and I once became so frustrated by the reluctance of certain departments in SAA to accept one of our income generating ideas that we decided to prove a point by 'putting our money where our mouths were' and chartering an aircraft from them to put our idea into effect. A friend, Tim

Redman who was an architect joined us in this venture. The occasion was the Cape to Rio Yacht Race, an event departing from Cape Town. We felt that if SAA would schedule a flight out of Cape Town to be the last visual South African contact with the yachts, not only would it be a financial success, but it would create a great publicity opportunity for SAA.

The three of us, all keen sailors, sat down and devised a comprehensive plan covering all aspects of the operation, but when I presented it to the relevant departments within SAA it was met with not only a total lack of enthusiasm, but also with obfuscation and difficulty stating. The message was clear 'You are making work for us, now go away and leave us to get back to our slumber please'. After all the hours of meticulous planning we had put into the presentation we were extremely reluctant to let go of our plan. Being so certain of its viability we decided that if SAA was not interested, we would charter a 737 from them and run the operation for our own account.

Now these departments became concerned that, should our operation be a success, it would not look good for them having turned a revenue earner down and placed every obstacle in the way of our chartering the aircraft so they told us no aircraft was available. We proved that there was a 737 sitting on the ground at Cape Town for three hours over the time we wanted to use it. Then they told us no crews were available, but we responded by telling them volunteer cockpit and cabin crew from the Cape Town bases had already been secured. Eventually under threat of having to explain in writing why they were turning down a revenue earning charter, their opposition collapsed and we were able to procure the aircraft at the standard charter rate.

Now we had to make it work as, apart from our heavy personal financial commitment, it would have been extremely embarrassing had it turned out to be a disaster. We decided that we would give a number of seats away and these were presented to a reporter from the Cape Times, the popular SABC TV announcers Dorianne Berry and Eon deVos, as well as an experienced yachtsman from the Royal Cape Yacht Club who had sailed in many previous Cape to Rio events and knew all the yachts extremely well.

Tim started off selling tickets from a folding table at the Royal Cape Yacht Club and was immediately doing a brisk trade, but soon the free publicity we received as the Cape Times reporter, Dorianne and Eon reciprocated for their complimentary tickets, with newspaper articles and many mentions on national TV, took effect and ticket sales went ballistic, we could easily have filled two 737s and it was saddening having to turn eager customers down once our 737 had been fully booked.

It was decided that Deon would fly the aircraft with our volunteer co-pilot who had drawn the lucky number and I would liaise and oversee the operation on board. All the airport staff were aware of our enterprise, were rooting for us and falling over themselves to ensure the operation went off smoothly. The Airports Company even gave us the prime parking bays for embarking and disembarking our passengers. I think it became a sort of Cape Town pride thing!

We had hand picked the brightest and best from the Cape Town based cabin crew to man our charter and we purchased two full bar trolleys from SAA. They would be placed in the front and rear galleys and each manned by a cabin crew member. Drinks would be free but only available at the bars. This we hoped would create a 'musical chairs' effect, allowing more people time at the windows, and it worked surprisingly well.

We took off three hours after the start of the race in Table Bay thus avoiding the gaggle of media light aircraft and helicopters that gather over the start of such events and set course up the West Coast and out to sea to where we would hopefully find the leaders. There was a brisk South Easter on the water and when we located the leaders, well out to sea and almost abeam Yzerfontein, we were quite surprised at the progress they had made. Our sailing expert now took over the PA, identifying the leaders and telling our passengers about the characteristics of each yacht and other interesting facts about them. Having spent quite some time with the leaders in order to ensure all our passengers had been able to enjoy a decent sighting we then backtracked through the fleet with our expert pointing out any yacht with a story he thought may be of interest.

As we had paid for an hour charter and, as a 737 is so much faster than a yacht, we had time to spare so we treated our passengers to a scenic tour around the beautiful Cape Peninsula. Dorianne Berry now took over the PA and our passengers received a most amazing commentary as we flew around the Peninsula at low level. Then to top it all off Eon de Vos, a great aviation enthusiast and now a Comair Captain, sat in the cockpit jump seat and gave a vivid, blow by blow description of the approach and landing in the strong South Easter.

The passengers loved it, so much so that many of them did not want the experience to end. As we had paid for the full bars we sent everything that was left to our crew room and invited the most enthusiastic of our passengers to join the whole crew there for drinks. Later the party moved to Atholl, the First Officer's home and continued until late. It was also a financial success for Deon, Tim and myself as we more than doubled the money we had invested in the charter. More satisfying, however, was the fact that we had been proved right against the negativity of SAA's Commercial Department.

THE SWORD OF DAMOCLES

Over the years many failed attempts were made by various SAA managers to shut down the Cape Town pilot base. These were motivated by control issues compounded by jealousy. Strangely enough, the most vocal management pilots opposing the Cape Town base were those who were afforded the opportunity to relocate to Cape Town but turned it down for various reasons. These ranged from, the market in which to sell their houses not being right or not wanting the children's schooling interrupted, to a reluctance to leave their friends or move away from their parents.

Thus the 'If I can't live at the coast, why should you be able to?' syndrome took hold.

Despite all this the Cape Town Pilot base has, so far, endured for thirty four years. In 2019 SAA management announced it was shutting down the Cape pilot base in the interests of savings to be made. Simultaneously a logic defying announcement that the Cape cabin crew base would not be shut down was made. It should be noted that Safair, Comair and SAA's own subsidiary Mango, airlines not drowning in bad management red ink, consider their Cape pilot bases to be economically viable.

At the time of writing SAA's Business Rescue Practitioners have granted the Cape base a reprieve until, at least, their rescue plan is formulated. It would appear to me, that reversing all unimplemented decisions made by SAA's management would be the way to go as their only proven track record over the last two decades is of losing vast sums of money.

15

OPERATION RESCUE

One of the requirements of our annual refresher courses was 'Emergency Procedures'. This course covered events basically out of the cockpit such as evacuation, fire drills and ditching procedures. So called live ditching drills were carried out biannually and these normally took place at local swimming baths that, by pre-arrangement, were closed to the public for the duration of the exercise. Life rafts would be launched and a good time would be had by all, particularly the male crew members who were delighted to see plenty of very attractive young hostesses in skimpy bathing costumes.

My Deputy Flight Operations Manager, Captain Ren Colyn, and I were both rostered to attend one of these ditching drills in Johannesburg about eighteen months after we had been decentralised to Cape Town. Both Ren and I were keen sailors, Ren owning a large game fishing boat, locally known as a Tunny Boat, and I had a blue water yacht. After our fun filled day at the swimming pool and over a beer at our hotel, we discussed how unrealistic the ditching exercise in a nice calm, warm swimming bath was, and we began to wonder how much value this training exercise actually represented.

A week later Ren approached me with a plan to convince the airline to conduct a more realistic ditching exercise in actual sea conditions off the Cape Coast. I thought this was a wonderful idea and if Ren would run with it, he would have my full support, and run with it Ren did. It required a tremendous effort to liaise with, and gain the cooperation of, all the organisations and departments that would be involved.

These would be SAA, the South African Air Force, Air Traffic Control, the Directorate for Civil Aviation, Court Helicopters, the Atlantic Boat Club and the National Sea Rescue Institute.

Within SAA the departments involved would be Flight Operations, Cabin Services, the Flight Safety Office, the Emergency Procedures lecturers, the Technical Department responsible for the maintenance of emergency equipment, the Aviation Medical Department and the Cape Fleet.

Fortunately, at the time the Flight Operations CEO was Captain Mickey Mitchell who was an innovator and out of the box thinker. He was also very well disposed towards the Cape Fleet, which fitted nicely into his ideas for innovative initiatives. Thus with his blessing all the SAA departments supported Ren's initiative with great enthusiasm. In hindsight, I think that if they had any concept of the difference between a ditching exercise in the Kempton Park Swimming Baths, and one in the open ocean, close to what was once called the Cape of Storms, they might not have been quite so enthusiastic.

Having gained the support of our CEO, Ren was now a man on a mission, and with admirable organisational skills he set about putting together an operational plan to implement the ditching exercise. I attended several liaison meetings with Ren, the most notable of which was the one with the Air Force, which took place at the Joint Ops Head Quarters shared by the Navy and Air Force.

This HQ is situated in extremely scenic Cape Peninsula mountains above Simonstown. The officers we liaised with were of flag rank and were very cooperative. This meant that instructions were passed down through several command layers and led to a small misunderstanding that later resulted in fairly serious consequences for some of the participants in the exercise.

Later, during the post mortem, Ren and I agreed that the operational liaison should have been at squadron level.

Our liaison meetings with ATC, NSRI and Court Helicopters were casual and pretty much at grass roots level.

Ren was a member of the Atlantic Boat Club, which was based in Hout Bay Harbour, and handled all liaison with them. They had an important role to play as they would convey, on their Tunny Boats, the crews and all the equipment to the site of the ditching.

THE SMALL MISUNDERSTANDING

The scenario that Ren and I envisaged was that shortly after take off on runway 19 at Cape Town the aircraft would be struck by a terrorist heat seeking missile and be forced to fly straight ahead and ditch, a mile or two off the coast, in False Bay. The pilots would have informed ATC of their intentions and broadcast a Mayday call. The stricken aircraft's exact position would have been known, particularly in the light of the fact that the whole drama would have taken place within direct sight of any aircraft in the Cape Town circuit. ATC would have immediately informed Joint Ops at Silvermine, and they would, without delay, have launched a rescue operation simultaneously involving all parties.

Here was where the 'small misunderstanding' previously mentioned came into play. Unbeknown to Ren and myself, the Flag officers of the Airforce had choreographed a sort of 'domino' scenario that, whether by design or accident, pretty much gave the Airforce an exclusive 'bite of the cherry' prior to any civilian rescue organisation's involvement.

They envisaged a scenario whereby, after being informed of the ditching by ATC, they would contact the Airforce base at Ysterplaat who would despatch a DC3 Dakota to search for and determine the position of the ditched aircraft. Once this had been accomplished a flight of Alouette helicopters would be dispatched to the scene and only after they had rescued their capacity of survivors, would the civilian rescue organisations be given the go ahead.

The day chosen for the exercise was December 1st 1988 and early that morning saw great activity on the quay of the Hout Bay harbour where Johannesburg and Cape Town aircrew along with the backup teams were gathered. All the emergency equipment carried on an aircraft to be used during a ditching was piled around us. This kit included two thirty-three person life rafts as used on our B737-200s and an escape slide from an A300 Airbus which doubles as a life raft. The plan was that we would all, with our equipment, be conveyed to the scene of the ditching by four of the Tunny Boats. Once there the boats would come to a stop, and as if it was the aircraft that had come to a stop after a ditching, the exercise would commence with a Mayday call to ATC Cape Town and the launching of the life rafts.

After the rescue Ren had organised a Rock Lobster lunch for all participants at his Atlantic Boat Club clubhouse. Practically all of the Atlantic Boat Club's members had spent the previous day fishing for Rock Lobsters. Poor Ren was so deeply in debt to them that it must have taken years for him to return the favours.

THE 'CAPE DOCTOR' ARRIVES UNEXPECTEDLY

Back then the weather reports were not as accurate as they are today and any plan as complicated as Operation Rescue, that could not be easily postponed or impulsively implemented, was vulnerable to its vagaries. So despite the long-range weather forecast being good and the day being sunny with clear skies, by the time the boats were ready for departure a forty-knot south easter was reported off Cape Point.

Hout Bay where the exercise was planned to have taken place was, due to the wind, patently unsuitable for the exercise so we decided to look for a more sheltered area in the lee of the Cape Peninsula mountains further up the coast.

The topography of the Cape Peninsula at Hout Bay can sometimes amplify the wind strength in the Bay. On one memorable occasion, attempting to make Hout Bay harbour on our yacht, we found ourselves trying to motor into seventy knots of wind off Hout Bay. On that occasion, discretion being the better part of valour we turned and made for Cape Town. On 'bare poles' the wind was so strong we were making over six knots as we ran with it.

We duly found a more sheltered spot opposite Camps Bay, further up the Cape Peninsula and much closer to Cape Town, to launch Operation Rescue. The wind was still fairly strong being between twenty and twenty five knots when ATC were informed that we were ditching and the operation was under way! The life rafts were launched and automatically inflated. I was assigned along with Mike Hayward, a Captain on the Cape Fleet, one of the Cape Fleet First Officers and the chief emergency procedures lecturer, Kenny, to one of the circular thirty-three person B737 rafts. The rest of the complement was made up of cabin crew members.

The second B737 raft was manned by two pilots from the Cape Fleet, an emergency procedures lecturer, the SAA Director of Aviation Medicine, Dr. Eric Peters, and cabin crew members. Both these rafts were launched from Ren's boat while the Airbus slide raft was launched from another boat. It was manned mainly by Johannesburg crew and included the Pilots Association Safety Officer, Captain Sid Bottom.

Ren would not be joining us on the rafts, as he was skippering his boat and coordinating the exercise from the bridge.

The transfer of participants from the Boats to the rafts went surprisingly well with only Sid falling into the water, becoming trapped under the raft, and nearly drowning.

The rafts were detached from the boats and they now stood off, keeping a watching brief. If all went well, they would have no further part to play other than that of emergency back-up. Our first task was, as per standard operating procedures, to attach the two B737 rafts to each other with a line stowed aboard for the purpose. This line was about thirty metres long and was to ensure that their rafts drifting apart would not separate the survivors. This was only accomplished by luck as the two little paddles that we were supposed to utilise to paddle the big, windage prone, inflatable rafts towards each other proved to be a ridiculous concept in twenty five knots of Cape south easter. However, the rafts drifted together and the 'umbilical cord' was attached. This had some unforeseen consequences later and it would have been far better had we not managed to couple the rafts. The rafts were equipped with sea anchors, which we deployed. These could be likened to parachutes for water that created a huge amount of drag, thus ensuring that the wind could not blow us out to sea too rapidly.

A CASCADE OF TECHNICOLOUR YAWNS

Kenny, the Chief emergency procedures instructor, was very assertive, taking charge and insisting that everyone sat flat on the floor away from the opening in the tent-like canopy of the raft. Having an inkling of what was coming, I ignored this and told Mike to do the same, informing Kenny that it was madness not to post a lookout when one was at sea.

Thirty minutes had passed. Surely we should have seen some rescue activity by now! But no, another twenty minutes passed before we heard aero engines and an Airforce Dakota hove into sight, made a few lazy circuits over our position, before disappearing in the direction of Ysterplaat. Again we sat and waited but by now, despite the sea anchors, the wind was drifting us slowly out of the lee and into deeper waters, where not only was the wind strength increasing, but both the swell and chop were becoming increasingly nasty.

I am fortunate in that I do not suffer from seasickness but having sailed for many years I am very familiar with the condition and know that anyone who feels queasy should be on deck in the open air and not down below. Even for people who are not particularly prone to seasickness there are various factors that trigger seasickness such as, the smell of diesel, fish guts, or being downwind of an island inhabited by seals. It may even be as simple as the smell of lighter fluid accompanying the lighting of a cigarette. A very common trigger is, of course, someone else being sick in close proximity.

Now a rather strange phenomenon, that I had not experienced on boats before, manifested itself. Not only were the rafts rapidly rising up on the swells and dropping sickeningly into the troughs, but the chop was running through the thin material that made up the floor of the rafts and making it writhe like a nest of eels. In addition to this the floor of the raft was not inflatable as it should have been, in order to provide an insulating layer between the sea and the occupants of the raft. The Atlantic sea temperatures on the western side of the Cape Peninsula are cold and the poor youngsters sitting on the floor of the raft in their skimpy clothing had only a thin layer of neoprene between themselves and the 10°C ocean.

It was only a matter of time before the inevitable happened! As they had all been forced to sit on the floor of the circular raft facing inwards and each other, the first 'technicolour yawn' shot with great force into the centre of the raft, spraying all and sundry in the process. This was the trigger and pretty soon the interior of the raft began to resemble some weird rainbow-coloured fountain from 'Charlie and the Chocolate Factory'. Only Mike and I, perched high and dry on the walls of the raft and in the open air, were spared.

Unexpectedly the group on the Airbus escape slide raft were far better off. Their canopy was not fixed, but instead a tarpaulin was supposed to be attached to inflatable posts positioned at intervals down the side of the raft. This tarpaulin had long since blown away leaving the occupants of the raft in the fresh air. Also the sides of the raft were very low, having been designed only to prevent people falling off when it was used as an evacuation slide on land.

In addition, being long and narrow, all anyone who felt the need to 'feed the fish' had to do was turn around and lean over the low side, a far more elegant and less messy procedure than that being experienced by the occupants of the life rafts that our B737 were fitted out with. To be fair though, seasickness aside, a long period at sea in low air temperatures would have been far more survivable in our purpose built type of life raft.

Eventually, three air force Alouette helicopters arrived and attempted to airlift some of the survivors from the rafts. It proved rather difficult in the case of our raft as the cone shaped canopy tended to cause the downdraught from the rotors to blow the raft away from the helicopter and it was very difficult to position the harness over the small openings in the canopy. After a struggle they managed between them to airlift two people from the B737 rafts and four from the much easier open slide raft.

As they disappeared in the direction of Hout Bay, the civilian rescuers were unleashed and within a few minutes Court Helicopters' big Sikorsky S62 was hovering over the A300 slide raft. Court specialises in servicing ships such as super tankers too big to dock in Cape Town when passing round the

Cape. They also service offshore drilling rigs and their crews are very experienced in maritime operations. Today their operations manager John Pocock was flying the S62. John and I were friends and a few months earlier I had the good fortune to be invited to fly the last Sikorsky 58 ship's service with him, prior to the 58 being replaced with the S62s.

In a most impressive and efficient operation they hauled up their allocation of twenty survivors within minutes and left for Hout Bay, leaving the rest of us bobbing on the ocean waiting for the arrival of the NSRI boats and rescue.

Despite the jocular tone I have used to describe seasickness, it can easily become very serious, even to the point of life threatening, due to dehydration. Doctor Eric in the other B737 raft felt that two of the hostesses were rapidly approaching this state and called urgently for a medical evacuation. Fortunately I had a hand-held radio transceiver and was in contact with Ren on the Tunny boat who had communications with all the parties involved in the exercise. As Eric had now declared a medical emergency we decided that the most expedient course of action would be to attempt to get Eric's patients onto one of the Tunny boats, and one of these attempted to manoeuvre close enough to perform the medivac.

That was when it became really scary! The height from the waterline to the rail of the rear deck of the Tunny boat was about two metres and the height from the sea to the top of the inflatable tubes that formed the rafts sides was just over half a metre. No problem in a calm sea but frightening when the boat was rolling violently over the raft. But the situation became much worse as, during her manoeuvring to get close to Eric's raft, one of her props picked up the line connecting the two rafts, which in the heat of the moment we had forgotten about. Instantly both rafts were reeled in and came up hard against the hull on either side of the boat. Each time the boat rolled towards us it was as if a cliff was falling upon us. The raft would collapse on that side and the floor area would halve. This had the effect of doubling the depth of the considerable amount of vomit that the survivors were tumbling about in on the floor of the raft. Even Dante would have been hard pressed to imagine a hell like this!

Still perched high and dry on the wall of the raft at the opening in the canopy, I realised that we were in real trouble unless we could free ourselves from the Tunny boat. When the boat rolled away from us I could locate the attachment point of the tethering line but could not undo the 'granny knot' that someone had tied in the line.

What with the tension and sea water this knot might as well have been a weld, my fingers were cold and I only had seconds before the boat rolled back towards us and buried the knot against the hull. Realising that the only way to free us would be to cut the line and for this I needed a knife. I knew that somewhere on the wall of the raft there was a pocket with a knife but had no idea precisely where it was. It is one thing to have its location pointed out to you on a picture in a lecture room, and entirely another to locate it in the chaotic scenario that we were experiencing. But wait! We had the Senior Emergencies Lecturer onboard; surely he would know how to locate the knife?

Sufferers have reliably informed me that three mental states exist during a chronic bout of sea sickness. In the first you hope it will pass, and that you will feel better. In the second you aspire to nothing more then to survive. In the third you hope to die, and soon, anything to stop the suffering! When I screamed at Kenny to find and pass me the knife, he was in the third stage, where survival is not an issue, or even desirable, so all I received from him was a long drawn out groan and a zombie-like stare. Salvation came when one of the boat crew leant over the rail and handed me a bait knife. This made short work of the line and we were free. By a huge stroke of fortune the tethering line on the side attached to the other raft had been severed by the boats prop initially and had thus avoided the jeopardy and anguish our raft's occupants had suffered. The object of the exercise, to evacuate the two very sick girls had not been achieved, and was abandoned as being too dangerous.

By now the air force Alouette helicopters were on their way back from Hout Bay and two were diverted back to our position to attempt the medivac. After a struggle they managed to hoist the girls up and they were flown directly to the Somerset Hospital. Both girls were in a bad way and were kept in the hospital overnight.

The rest of us were left bobbing about in increasingly deteriorating conditions of wind and swell. We had been allocated to the NSRI based at Granger Bay who would be responsible for rescuing us. Being amongst the last to be alerted, their small boats were making slow headway into the teeth of a howling south easter and a heavy swell.

Nicotine addiction is terrible and I was a smoker at the time. The few cigarettes I had taken along had been smoked long ago. Not unexpectedly, no one had any sympathy for my predicament except for Ren's wife Maureen, who was also a smoker. She endeared herself to me for life by somehow hanging off the bow railing of the Tunny boat, like a trapeze artist, and in those inclement conditions, passing me a packet of her cigarettes.

RESCUED AT LAST, BUT NO LOBSTER LUNCH

We were all pretty relieved when the NSRI boats arrived. The transfer into the smaller boats went easily and we were soon on our way with the wind and swell to Granger Bay. The Tunny boat crews were left with the difficult task of salvaging the rafts before making their way back to Hout Bay against the wind.

The Samaritans of the NSRI had thought to load flasks of hot coffee that were much appreciated. Had the exercise taken place where originally intended the Hout Bay-based NSRI would have rescued us and offloaded us there, where our cars were parked and our lobster lunch awaited us.

The NSRI provided transport by car and bus, and it was after three when we arrived at the Atlantic Boat Clubhouse just as the returning Tunny Boats were docking.

It was here that the heaviest blow fell! All that remained of the lobster lunch were a few soggy sandwiches. No doubt the last lobster had been greedily consumed while we were still bobbing about on the rafts, our absence creating a massive lobster windfall for the earlier arrivals - thirty years later, that still smarts!

By then the culprits were long gone but the club bar was operational so, along with the Tunny boat and NSRI crews, we retired there to drown our sorrows.

The SAA Safety office produced a video of the operation. The first scenes were filmed at Ysterplaat Airforce base in a lecture room where the aircrews were undergoing a briefing in a classroom. There were absolutely no discernible signs of urgency and even a refresher course on conducting a square search was on the blackboard. Briefing concluded the crews were shown casually strolling out to their aircraft apparently in no hurry whatsoever.

The rest of the video was filmed from the comfort of a Tunny Boat with no close ups of anything that was going on in the rafts. There was no commentary at all in the video and as a training aid it was worthless. I would have liked to have been able to say that valuable lessons had been learned from the exercise but sadly this was not the case. Too many people in authority had been taken out of their comfort zones and soon the ditching drills just reverted to the way they had always been conducted. Seasickness was never mentioned in the lectures.

The last ditching drill in which I participated prior to my retirement was conducted in an indoor swimming bath and by then even the requirement for cabin crew to be able to swim had been dropped.

Many individuals did, however, take away valuable life lessons from the exercise and I, despite the lobster debacle, would not have missed it for the world.

16

BLOWN AWAY

This is a story about Florida, a Boeing 737 Freighter, a shiny red sports car, a hurricane and a silver South African Airways Corporate Diners Club Card.

In the mid nineties SAA was replacing its ageing domestic fleet of Boeing 737-200s with Airbus A320s and later Boeing 737-800s. A decision had been taken to convert several of the 200s into dedicated freighters for mainly domestic freight use.

These conversions were not simple as they involved the fitting, amongst other modifications, of an enormous freight-loading door in the side of the aircraft.

Passenger doors on modern pressurised aircraft are of the 'plug in' type. This means on closing they swing into the aircraft, turn and then plug the door opening from the inside. Because the sides of the door are tapered to match the taper of the opening, the more the aircraft is pressurised, the harder the door is forced into the opening.

Incidentally, this is why one need have no fear of a deranged individual opening an aircraft door in flight. They would need to have the strength to lift an elephant to make any headway at all!

A cargo door is a different kettle of fish entirely. It must close from the outside and thus the aircraft's pressurisation is a great force trying to push it open. It relies on a multitude of immensely strong hydraulically operated locks and seals to resist this.

These conversions take several months and a specialist company in Brunswick, Georgia were our appointed contractors. Our crews undertook the delivery flights, there and back, voluntarily and they were offered to us in order of seniority.

I was the most senior Captain on the Fluffy fleet at the time but turned down all the delivery flights to Brunswick as I had gone all starry eyed when I realised that if I fetched a completed conversion I would have a visit to the USA, which at that time was pretty much the shopping capital of the world where everything and anything was available. My return to South Africa would be in command of a truly enormous shopping trolley. The possibilities were mind-boggling!

Our little team consisted of myself and three First Officers, Dave, Pine and Mark. Two training Captains, who had been charged with performing the acceptance trials at the factory in Brunswick, joined us for our passenger flight to Miami on the SAA Jumbo. There were also two ground engineers who were licensed on the 737 and would sign off the aircraft at all intermediate stops between Lauderdale and Johannesburg.

It was the first time I had been to Miami and as we moved through the Airport such was the atmosphere that I genuinely thought for a moment that I had missed an in-flight announcement and that we had diverted to Cuba.

We were soon on our way to Fort Lauderdale and a rather spectacularly situated Marriott Hotel. Its decks seemed to merge with walk-on moorings housing so many luxury yachts as almost to rival Monte Carlo during the Grand Prix. We were only supposed to spend two nights there before flying back to South Africa but it soon emerged that the aircraft we had come to collect was so full of faults that the training Captains, rightly, refused to sign the acceptance papers until such time as these issues were resolved. This situation dragged on for days and gave us lots of time to explore our surroundings and, of course, to shop. In order to get around the very spread out Fort Lauderdale we managed to hire a strange little blue car- a model I did not recognise.

I liked Florida. Despite it being flat, it has plenty of charm in the form of its myriad waterways, lush vegetation, interesting history, architecture and laid-back people. In my youth a serious rival to Ian Fleming's James Bond novels were those of John D. McDonald his main character being Travis McGee whose home base was the 'Busted Flush', a houseboat moored in Fort Lauderdale. Most of the novels were set in Florida and it was strangely satisfying to see so many of the places described in his books.

BMP

We soon discovered an enormous mall that went by the unlikely name of Sawgrass Mills, and this became the main destination for all our non-specialised shopping. I recall it took an hour and a quarter to merely walk from one end to the other.

The people we interacted with in shops and restaurants were very friendly, but strange in the fact that they seemed to know nothing about anything beyond their immediate environment. Over drinks, one of us came up with the theory that they all actually lived on the back of the moon, were teleported down to their place of work each morning and straight back to the moon at the end of the working day.

From then on they became 'The Back of the Moon People' or BMPs to us.

To illustrate this, we had been shopping for shoes in Sawgrass Mills, and on completing our purchases we asked the assistants where the nearest tobacconist was. Nobody even knew if there was one, never mind its location. As we exited the shoe shop, there directly in front of us across the narrow walkway, was an enormous flashing red neon sign. It was arched across the entire shop-front in letters a metre high and spelled out *'Tobacconist'*.

Dave and I were both keen yachtsmen and so decided we would like to visit the Lauderdale yacht club so we declined an invitation to join younger members of our team at 'The Pink Pussy', a nearby topless bar/strip club they had discovered.

The yacht club was not marked on the map the hotel had given us, nor did any of the staff know where it was located so we strolled down to the waterfront and asked the Skipper of a charter big game fishing boat. He seemed to have modelled his persona on Captain Quint from the movie 'Jaws'. Naturally he had no idea that there even was a yacht club where people kept "fancy boats".

Eventually, driving around, we stopped at a petrol station from which the tall masts of the yachts could be seen but the staff had no idea how to get there. Of course it is not that simple in Florida as, even if you can see your destination, your way will be barred by numerous channels and waterways. Still, they were locals!

As by trial and error we blundered into the area of the yacht club the houses became more upmarket, giving way to mansions the closer we came. These were very reminiscent of the old southern plantation houses we saw in films such as 'Gone with the Wind'. The gardens had the most amazing big old Swamp Cypress trees festooned with Spanish Moss. When asking people for directions we now received ever more clear, concise and accurate information. Obviously, we had departed the zone of 'The Back of the Moon People'.

The Lauderdale Yacht Club was very impressive. After a very friendly security check we passed through the imposing gateway and up a long tree-lined avenue to the main entrance. Here we entered a world of teak, mahogany, brass, silver, crystal, Persian carpets and rich red leather. The atmosphere was hushed, and I can only liken it to what I have read regarding the best of old London's aristocratic gentlemen's clubs.

At the magnificent reception counter we presented our membership cards of Yacht clubs whose the décor consisted mainly of chipboard, Melamine and Marley Tile. To our great surprise we were welcomed with open arms, shown around the magnificent and comprehensive facilities which they assured us we would be welcome to use for the duration of our stay in Lauderdale. A vastly better call than 'The Pink Pussy', Dave and I thought!

By now more indeterminate delays had come through from Brunswick and we began to run out of things to do. Our combined shopping would almost have filled a single hotel room at that stage. We considered taking a trip through the wonderful Florida Keys down to Key West. One hundred and eighty kilometres on highway connecting the keys by means of forty two bridges, the longest being the eleven kilometre Seven Mile Bridge. Much as it pained me I was forced to veto that idea. It would not have been a good look if the green light for our delivery came through and we were stuck somewhere down on the Keys. This turned out to be a very good decision in the light of what was to come!

So, instead, the 'petrol heads' amongst us, Dave, Pine and I embarked on a tour of car dealerships. Real American makes had disappeared from the South Africa scene back in the seventies so there was much to attract our interest. The most exciting cars were seriously cheap in comparison with what we would have to pay back home. For example an American muscle car, with all the 'bells and whistles' could be had for the price of basic transport in SA.

CAMARO

At the Chevy dealer I fell head over heels in love with a gorgeous 1995 red Camaro Z28 V8 convertible and this led to a rush of blood to the head and a most monumental case of brain-fade. I seriously started plotting as to how I could purchase this beauty and smuggle it into South Africa. After all, I would soon have a freighter at my disposal, more than capable of carrying a Camaro. Our agents, Combs Aviation in Lauderdale, would be happy to load it for me at no extra charge to SAA. There followed a great discussion and think tank involving most of the team and plenty of alcoholic brain stimulant.

There was, however, an obstacle that no amount of devious plotting could overcome. That was the Customs Service at Johannesburg. After an international flight lands, the passengers and crew disembark and file through customs. Less known is the fact that a team from customs then board the aircraft and conduct a thorough search for contraband. This would normally be hidden on board and removed by accomplices amongst the ground staff. But, how does one hide a big, shiny, bright red Camaro in the empty tube of a freighter hull?

As sanity prevailed, I reluctantly dropped the idea. This subsequently proved to be a very good decision, but strangely enough not for the reason above, as will later become clear.

The following morning we awoke to find the notice below, printed on bright green paper, had been shoved under the doors of our hotel rooms and now the fun started in earnest!

Hurricane Erin was on its way!!!!

Hurricane Information
MARRIOT
Fort Lauderdale Marina

Dear Guest:

They have forecast the possibility of a hurricane for our immediate area and a HURRICANE WARNING is presently in effect.

Our hotel is situated in an evacuation area. If an evacuation order is announced for our area, we will evacuate all guests from the hotel. Once the evacuation is announced, time will be limited. Roads, airports and other systems will be heavily strained. We suggest that you begin considering your evacuation options now, in the event they should become necessary.

√ *Tune your television to Channel 4 or Channel 7 for current information.*

√ *Contact your airline or travel agent to confirm flight plans, or arrange a flight out.*

√ *If you have a car, fill the tank now. You may have to endure long lines and waste valuable time if an evacuation order is issued.*

√ *If you do not have a car, or confirmed flight arrangements, you may want to consider renting a car now, in order to be able to leave the area later.*

√ *If you will be unable to leave the area, several shelters will be opened and staffed by the American Red Cross. Stay tuned to Channel 4 or Channel 7 for locations and opening times of these shelters.*

The hotel management will contact you again when the alert status changes. Please refer all enquiries to extension 6744 or 6866.

Again, we must complete a mandatory evacuation of the hotel if an EVACUATION ORDER is given for our area. Please be prepared to check out of the hotel immediately if this becomes a reality.

Thank you for your cooperation.

Sincerely,

John F. Weit

General Manager

THE HURRICANE

As we had not been watching local TV, we had been caught unawares by the tide of events that would follow. The background to these was that three short years before, in August 1992, Hurricane Andrew had come ashore in southern Florida. It was the most destructive hurricane ever to hit the shores of the United States and the damage was catastrophic. In Florida alone 63,000 homes were destroyed and a further 100,000 damaged. 175,000 people were left homeless. 20,000 to 30,000 tourists were in Florida at the time and their attempts at evacuation led to the biggest traffic jam in the history of Florida.

After Andrew, political capital was made amidst accusations of lack of warning, preparation and under-reaction. Well, they were not going to make that mistake again and if they erred this time it was going to be on the side of over-reaction.

Immediately the 'think tank' of the night before was reassembled in my room to gather information and devise and implement a strategy to see us through Hurricane Erin and its aftermath. I considered myself extremely fortunate in being surrounded with a team of very sharp young men with great organisational skills. Few visitors to Florida would have been blessed with such an advantage during the crisis.

Dave and Pine were immediately dispatched to return our little blue bubble of a car to the hire firm and there to replace it with the biggest van they could find, as I had visions of being stuck on the road to Tampa in an enormous evacuation traffic jam. I assured them that cost was no object as from here on in all costs incurred would be for the account of SAA. The rest of the team started gathering information from the TV and contacts amongst the hotel staff and the SAA offices in Miami

It became apparent that it was highly likely an evacuation of the entire seaward side of Highway 1 would be ordered, to avoid any loss of life in the flooding, from the storm surge, that would accompany a hurricane. Highway 1 runs from Georgia all the way along the east coast of the Florida Peninsula, through the Florida Keys, and ends at Key West. Where it passes Fort Lauderdale it runs a few miles inland of the coast. We were told to find new accommodation on the landward side of Highway 1.

It further became obvious that the Lauderdale Marriott was not going to lift a finger to assist us in finding alternative accommodation, despite being SAA's regular crew hotel for our Miami flights. They also made it quite clear that once the evacuation was announced it was mandatory, and anyone reluctant to leave would be forcibly ejected by security and the police. Neither were any possessions to be left in the evacuated rooms. Having witnessed, throughout our careers, the lengths to which SAA would go in order to arrange accommodation for our passengers following a cancellation or diversion we found this behaviour weird and disturbing!

Similarly, no help was forthcoming from the SAA offices in Miami who appeared to have become overloaded with queries. Sinking under the weight of the crisis, they seemingly dug a hole in which they buried themselves. Here again the team came to the rescue with Mark, in an impressive display of seductive charm practised on various female staff at hotels inland of Highway 1, against all odds managed to secure us all rooms at the North Cypress Creek Marriott.

We had just cracked the first beer when Dave and Pine turned up with our new vehicle and we all poured down to the ground floor to see it- a truly enormous Chevy van with a cavernous interior. It was so wide that passing anything between the driver and front seat passenger required a stretch.

We returned to my room, which was operational HQ, to find this urgent bright pink notice had been slipped under the door:

Hurricane Information: Update
MARRIOT
Fort Lauderdale Marina

Dear Guest:

We have received orders to immediately EVACUATE our area.

Please be advised we must evacuate all guests. Time is limited. Roads, airports and other systems will be heavily strained. We suggest that you begin considering your evacuation options now.

√ *Tune your television to Channel 4 or Channel 7 for current information.*

√ *Contact your airline or travel agent to confirm flight plans, or arrange a flight out.*

√ *If you have a car, fill the tank now. You may have to endure long lines and waste valuable time if an evacuation order is issued.*

√ *If you do not have a car, or confirmed flight arrangements, you may want to consider renting a car now, in order to be able to leave the area later.*

√ *If you will be unable to leave the area, several shelters will be opened and staffed by the American Red Cross Stay tuned to channel 4 or Channel 7 for locations and opening times of these shelters.*

Please refer all enquiries to extension 6744 or 6866.

Again, we must complete a MANDATORY EVACUATION of the hotel. Please be prepared to check out of the hotel immediately.

Thank you for your cooperation.

Sincerely,

John F. Weit

General Manager

. . .

Now it was game on. We packed up and started to move a huge amount of 'American shopping' from our rooms to the big Chevy van.

Pine had four enormous wheels and tyres for his 4 X 4. I had, amongst other things, five white-wall tyres for my 1934 Chevy roadster and a marvellous Brinkman Smoker Cooker that I still have. Many Christmas turkeys have been prepared in the Brinkman over the years.

There were enough Harley Davidson bits and pieces to assemble several bikes,

barbecues, smokers, computer gear, cartons of clothing, outboard motors, yacht equipment, and dozens of mysterious packing cases containing heaven only knows what!

All were carted down on borrowed hotel luggage trolleys and hand trucks.

At this stage police and security were all over the place and our activities attracted considerable attention. Once they had satisfied themselves that it was not the hotel's fixtures and fittings that were disappearing into the maw of our huge van, and that we were so obviously complying with the evacuation order, they became quite friendly and helpful.

In our movements between the rooms and our van we did witness some rather nasty scenes where recalcitrant guests were forcefully ejected from the hotel. We felt very sorry for them, particularly those with language difficulties. No assistance whatsoever was offered and it was obvious they had nowhere to go and were in a state of confusion. It was a harsh 'jackboot' approach, completely lacking in empathy.

Having crammed everything into our van we set off to find the Cypress Creek Marriott. It was a far less imposing structure than the Lauderdale Marriott and seemed to be surrounded by suburbia, but at least we had a roof over our heads. The parking was secure so we could leave all our treasures in the van.

Erin was still on its way and the TV announcers were becoming ever more frenetic as it crept closer. We met and decided that some 'siege preparations' would be advisable. We split up into groups of two and scoured the nearby shops for supplies.

Most of the supermarket shelves had been emptied, but by visiting smaller shops we were able to obtain food and alcohol supplies to last us for a few days. We were also able to buy torches, batteries, a camping stove lamp combination, a hunting knife and a first aid kit. As a precaution we filled all the bathtubs in our rooms with cold water.

We then all sat back in front of the TV, enjoyed our sundowners and awaited the imminent arrival of Hurricane Erin!

DAMP SQUIB

Anyone who is now expecting a dramatic tale of hurricane survival will, I am afraid, be disappointed, as hurricane Erin turned out to be a bit of a damp squib. The winds built up overnight to about the speed of those of your average strong Cape South Easter and then died away completely towards morning. It had crossed the coast to the north of us and spent itself soon after.

We did not, however, escape Hurricane Erin unscathed. It had caused a deluge over Brunswick. Some clown at the factory had neglected to close our freighter's doors and it had been flooded. The damage to the electronics eventually added another week to our stay in Lauderdale. We took a vote and decided to remain at the Cypress Creek Marriott. It was not as upmarket as the Lauderdale Marriott but they were friendly and had been very good to us during the crisis.

The longer I stayed in Florida, the more I came to love its uniqueness. The restaurants had Catfish, soft shell crabs, shrimp gumbo, conch chowder, and a wonderful combination of spices used in their Cajun dishes.

Due to the factory always claiming that the aircraft would imminently be airworthy and ready for our departure, we were on permanent standby and thus we never did manage to travel down to the Florida Keys.

Years later, Corleen and I made the trip down to Key West with our friends from Marco Island on the Gulf Coast of Florida. It was a wonderful trip and I can confidently state that Key West is the most vibrant place that I have ever visited.

At this stage another rather serious worry raised its ugly head. Our routing back to Johannesburg was via Bridgetown in Barbados, Belem in Brazil, Isle de Sal in the Cape Verde group, and Libreville in Gabon. It had taken months to obtain clearances and overflying permissions to fly this routeing. There were time limits on some of our clearances that, by now, were in danger of lapsing, due to the accumulated delays. Should these lapse it might take months of renegotiation to have them reinstated.

This would have meant we would have to return to South Africa as passengers and only return after new clearances were received. Considering the van load of freight that we had accumulated it would have been a disaster for us.

Fortunately, and in the nick of time, I received a call from one of the training Captains in Brunswick with the good news that they had signed the acceptance documentation and would be bringing the aircraft through to Lauderdale for us the following day.

And so we began to make arrangements for our departure. On checkout we were presented with a hefty hotel bill, six guests for two weeks at the Marriott Marina and Cypress Creek. In the normal course of events the local SAA office would have handled all the financial arrangements but SAA Miami were apparently still in hiding and not even reacting to frantic telexes from Johannesburg.

At this point it struck me that I had, some time ago as a management pilot, been issued with a, very grand looking, silver SAA Corporate Diners Club Credit Card. I had never previously used this card, probably due to a (very valid) premonition that its use would later involve a mountain of paperwork. Out it came and, to the surprise of all of us, the bill was successfully paid.

THE FLIGHT HOME

Shortly after our arrival at the Lauderdale airfield our Freighter arrived from Brunswick and was taxied to Combs Aviation in a quiet backwater of the airfield.

As we familiarised ourselves with the new systems we found the forward galley had been retained and aft of that two rows of seats were fitted for the off duty crew members. Behind these seats an enormous box had been strapped down, and this contained all the spares and tools that our engineers would conceivably require should we experience mechanical failures en-route. I noted from the loadsheet that this box was extremely heavy. Aft of this box was empty load space until near the back where several rows of seats had been fitted. The whole floor was of the roller ball type so as to enable cargo to be easily pushed around.

We loaded our goods, filed the flight plan and completed the pre-flight checks but there was still one more impediment to our departure. True to form no arrangements had been made to pay Combs Aviation for their services including refuelling the aircraft. This came to over $37,000, a considerable sum in 1995. If this was not paid we could not leave and our clearances would lapse with grave financial implications for SAA.

Once again, and with great trepidation, I passed over the SAA Corporate Dinners Club Card. Surely someone would have been far sighted enough to put limits on unsupervised corporate card spending! Apparently no, as payment went through immediately and we were free to leave at last. By this time it was late afternoon and the sun was low in the west.

The flight down the Caribbean to our first refuelling stop at Barbados took three hours and forty minutes and was uneventful. At all our en-route stops SAA's agents had taken care of financial arrangements so we had no further trouble in this regard.

On take off from Barbados, as we rotated and got airborne, the nose pitched up suddenly and this was accompanied by an almighty crash from the rear of the aircraft. We were able to stabilise the aircraft and continue the climb. When we had regained our composure we found that the huge, heavy box of spares had broken loose and skated right to the back, where it completely demolished three rows of seats, and was eventually stopped by the fourth row. Had a shiny red Camaro been aboard it would have been so positioned as to have stopped the runaway box and no doubt have had the front end demolished in the process.

Dawn broke just in time to show us the most amazing views of the three hundred and thirty kilometre wide Amazon Delta which took us thirty minutes to cross, twenty minutes of which we were on the descent. Belem is situated on the Para River that is the southern edge of the delta and looked interesting. We would have liked to find an excuse to slip there, but as the Atlantic weather for our crossing to Isle de Sal in the Cape Verde group was unusually good, it would not have been prudent to delay our departure.

SMOKE AND MIRRORS

Sal was five and a half hours away across the Atlantic and required ETOPS or Extended Twin range Operational Procedures Standards. This in my humble opinion, and for which I will probably be shot down in flames, was a 'smoke and mirrors' procedure that made twin engine aircraft operations further than sixty minutes away from an emergency landing field legal, if nothing else!

Flying against the sun, we landed in Sal in the late afternoon. Sal was familiar territory to us- for years our crews had slipped there en-route to Europe and New York.

After a few drinks and a good night's sleep we were ready to tackle the final two legs of our delivery. First light saw us airborne and setting heading for Libreville in Gabon, where five and a half hours later we landed for a brief refuelling stop before taking off for Johannesburg. Another uneventful five and a half hours saw us on final approach for Johannesburg.

Upon landing a rather pleasant surprise was in store for us! It would have been normal for us to be cleared to taxi to the freight apron where customs would have awaited us. Instead some Samaritan had pulled strings and ATC cleared us to taxi directly to the SAA technical area. We taxied through the security gates and we were marshalled to park directly in front of a hanger with open doors. As soon as the engines were shut down a waiting tug was connected and we were towed into the hanger and the doors closed behind us. All in all it was a pretty slick stealth operation.

The crew bus then took us, with just our small suitcases, to the air-side customs entrance so we could clear customs. Customs did not take much notice of us, probably assuming we were from one of several regional flights that were landing at about that time. We were then bussed back to the hanger and, after several trips to collect our shopping, were eventually deposited in the Flight Operations car park. It struck me that under the circumstances I could have quite easily sneaked the Camaro into the country. I, however, immediately felt better as I remembered the incident of the runaway crate on take off at Barbados.

A few days later a form arrived with regard to "Expenses incurred on SAA Diners Club Card". Apparently no one had ever spent anywhere near $4,000 never mind $40,000 on one of these cards and the forms only covered items such as food and beverages for entertainment purposes. I sent off the two letters below which fortunately ended the paper work as far as I was concerned.

SAA | SAL:
South African Airways | Suid-Afrikaanse Lugdiens

AIR/PERS: 784628J FLIGHT OPERATIONS

B737 FLEET

CAPE TOWN

7525

22 September 1995

Mr J. Rentsch, Senior Manager

Flight Operations, Johannesburg

Dear Joggie,
On our recent trip to fetch the 737 freighter from Miami various costs were incurred. I was reluctantly forced to cover these costs with my Corporate Diners Card as, despite telexes from Flight Operations to SAA Miami, no arrangements whatsoever were made to meet our requirements.

The costs as follows:
1(a) Hotel accommodation at the Marriott Marina.
(b) Hotel accommodation at the Marriott Cypress Creek North to which we evacuated due to Hurricane Erin.
Please note that all telephone expenses were official being between the factory at Brunswick and Fort Lauderdale.
2(a) To Combs Aviation for handling charges (S80) and
(b) Jet fuel (S8830-08)
Please refer to the accompanying invoices.
Many Thanks,

Captain Paul Liebrecht
Manager Flight Operations Cape Town

SAA | SAL:
South African Airways | Suid-Afrikaanse Lugdiens

AIR/PERS: 784628Ja FLIGHT OPERATIONS

B737 FLEET

CAPE TOWN

7525

22 September 1995

Mr P. de Jager, Senior Manager

Room 16, SAAFIN Centre, Johannesburg

Dear Peet,
RE: EXPENSES INCURRED ON SAA DINERS CLUB CARD
I am forwarding receipts for the expenses recently incurred on the above card.
I enclose a copy of my letter to Mr Joggie Renstch which explains the situation. As the

forms 1 and 2 from your office do not seem to make provision for the type of expenses incurred, I would be forever in your debt if you would be so kind as to fill out the appropriate forms on my behalf.
As I was just the "driver", I am not even sure to which cost centre these expenses must be debited. (Freight, I imagine?)
Many thanks,

Captain Paul Liebrecht
Manager Flight Operations
Cape Town

Sadly my record spend on an SAA Corporate Diners Card did not last long as one of our newly appointed managers took his extended family to London and managed to spend £60,000. You will recall my amazement at Combs Aviation in Lauderdale when I discovered that these cards had no apparent limits.

Shortly after, and as a result of the London incident, the Corporate Diners Cards were withdrawn never to be seen again.

I will always have fond memories of the wonderful camaraderie that existed between the crew, during a most exciting and challenging flight.

17

SECURITY?

To a greater or lesser extent, all of us who have travelled by air in recent times will have enjoyed the attention of security at the airports from which we depart. In fact, depending on your level of tolerance, you will probably have found it an extremely frustrating and dehumanising experience as you are herded like cattle through the system. As a general rule security staff in many countries are arrogant, unfriendly and totally humourless, making no effort to even crack the smile, joke or friendly greeting that would make the experience a little less demeaning.

Not only that, but as time goes by it gets worse and worse with some authorities now demanding that one be at the airport three hours before an international flight due to enhanced security procedures. Not only are our lives made miserable by all these measures but we also pay handsomely for the privilege of being put through them.

As a pilot and, due to the frequency of flying, so much more exposed to the threat of onboard terror then the average traveller, I could reasonably be expected to be a strong supporter of the most stringent security measures. Sadly my experiences with aviation security have made me rather ambivalent on the subject. And just as pilots are so much more exposed to the threat of onboard terror they are equally so much more exposed to the frustrations of passing through security checks.

THE TALL POPPY SYNDROME

To add to this is the security syndrome that pilots are familiar with but which would not even cross the minds of the passengers. This is what Australians call the 'Tall Poppy Syndrome' which affects a small number of security personnel who are on a mission to 'take those arrogant bastards down a peg or two'. The reason this syndrome develops is quite understandable. Here are people doing a repetitive, non-challenging and soul destroying job and never seeing any positive result from their endeavours. Some of the worlds busiest airports have not intercepted a single terrorist, and despite vetting millions of passengers, creating endless queues and hoops to jump through, poking, prodding, searching and sniffing. All of this at great expense.

It may be mid winter, freezing cold, pouring rain that never stops, and there stands Charlie at the security station. He is nearing the end of his shift, his feet hurt and he knows he will be standing in the rain waiting for two buses before he arrives home. At this point the pilots arrive accompanied by several attractive hostesses. He knows that in an hour or so they will be sitting in the sun, having climbed above the dreary weather, and will be on course for some exotic tropical destination. The ground is now ripe for resentment to build and for Charlie to let some of his misery rub off on the pilots.

Equally it is hard for pilots not to feel resentment and frustration at overly finicky procedures that they are often subjected to by security personnel. To become an airline pilot has involved years of study, practice, annual medicals, biannual instrument ratings and route checks all in the interest of safety. Their whole lives are dedicated to avoiding damaging an aircraft or hurting a passenger, which an ill-judged decision or even misreading a graph could so easily do.

And yet I have seen security personnel remove from pilots objects such as tiny nail clippers and standard cans of spray deodorant that contained one hundred and fifty five millilitres, instead of the prescribed limit of one hundred ml of liquid. It should be patently obvious, even to security personnel, how ridiculous it is to remove a tiny nail clipper from a pilot, when mounted on the bulkhead behind his seat is a crash axe and in front of him is a yoke- a flick of which, on landing, could send an aircraft into the airport buildings before the other pilot could react. It is this kind of silliness that leads to antagonism between airport security and pilots where there should be cooperation. After all a pilot has much more at stake should an airborne incident occur then the ground based security personnel.

During the later months of 2002 the relationship between the Cape Fleet and Cape Town airport security had become so toxic that a meeting was called between the acting head of security, the Cape Fleet Pilots Association representative and myself. The acting head of security was extremely 'gung ho' and seemed to be lacking in knowledge regarding onboard practices. At the time the SAA domestic business class cutlery was stainless steel and when we informed him of this he refused to believe us, despite the fact that we were served business class meals on board. Our effort at implementing cooperation was a total waste of time and after the meeting I distributed the following briefing notice to the Cape Fleet:

12 Dec. 02

Gents and Joanne,
Today Gavin Durr and myself had a meeting with two representatives from ACSA security and the head of SAA security in Cape Town in order to try and convince them that the pilots should not be viewed as security risks.
As you can imagine it was not a raving success, as logic does not override blind adherence to various and sundry rules and regulations in the security game. The whole situation will get worse in the run-up to the Cricket World Cup.
A few facts did emerge from the meeting however:

- *The ACSA* Head of Security in Cape Town, that attempted to force us to use the F8 Gate at all times, has been suspended prior to dismissal for 'irregularities'. An acting Head from Durban is relieving until a new one is appointed, so all may change once again.*
- *SAA has not requested ACSA* to search pilots leaving the apron side. If SAA*

requests a spot check than they will have a company representative present. This does not apply to ACSA instigated searches.
- If you utilise F8 to enter the Air-side be aware that 2 out of 5 people will be body searched, regardless of whether or not they trigger the metal detector. <u>If you are searched you have the right to insist that they utilise the hand held scanner and not their fingers.</u>
- If you use F8 to exit the air-side <u>everyone will be searched</u> for the prevention of pilfering that has reached endemic proportions in Cape Town.
- If you utilise the normal pax checkpoints in the departure halls 1 out of 5 people will be body searched and you will be treated like a normal pax. <u>Again, if you are selected to be searched, you can insist on the hand held scanner and that the search be conducted in a private cubicle.</u>
- If you utilise the pax gate at the arrival hall to exit the air-side, like the pax, <u>you will not be searched at all.</u>

Folks these are the fixed parameters at the moment. Please decide on your tolerance levels and select an option accordingly. I personally will never exit through F8, as I refuse to be treated like a common thief. As to entering the air-side I will probably utilise F8 depending on where the a/c is parked. I will, however, insist that the hand held scanner is used and will not tolerate a 'finger search'. The only thing that I can see that will prevent this harassment, at least when entering the security area, is if, and when, we are armed.
I need you to be mature enough to come to terms with this, **as an angry pilot, with raised blood pressure, is a thousand times more dangerous than all the nail files and scissors in the world.**
As a matter of interest, on the domestic, the ban on sharp objects does not extend to catering. The catering trucks are loaded and sealed land-side (obviously by people who are less of a security risk than pilots) and pass to the air-side with no inspection. The anomaly of disarming the pax of sharp objects at checkpoints and then rearming them with steel knives once aboard, completely escapes our security personnel.
All the best,

P. E. Liebrecht.
* Airports Company of South Africa

It was also my experience that any complaints by pilots of inappropriate behaviour by individual security personnel would fall upon deaf ears. None of this was very helpful in engendering a healthy spirit of cooperation between pilots and airport security.

Another factor that comes into play is that aircrew being so close to the operation tend to see so many anomalies in the airport security operation, that they tend to lose faith in how effective the system is and view it as having little more than nuisance value. Unfortunately, during my career at SAA, very little effort was made to explain these anomalies, if indeed there exist rational explanations for them.

THE 3 : 1 : 1 RULE

I think one of the more irritating restrictions to both passengers and aircrew is possibly the 3 : 1 : 1 rule applying to passengers and aircrew carrying liquids from the land-side to the air-side. The exact size of the plastic transparent plastic bag in which these liquids must be carried is even specified.

A pilot may be required to fly six legs on a ten-hour duty cycle, wrestling with the controls through all manner of weather but he may not carry a standard small aerosol deodorant with him because it contains 155ml of liquid. This apparently because he may find some way of extracting explosive liquid from a small pressurised container and manufacturing a bomb with which to blow up his own aircraft.

The obvious fact that people with evil intent could collude in order to pool several 100ml containers of liquid is, apparently, considered 'unlikely' by 'security experts. Reasons given are to my mind rather nebulous, and who amongst us has not experienced 'unlikely' happenings in our daily lives?

It is further interesting to note what happens to the liquids that are confiscated from the passengers. As they are suspected of being liquid explosives, logic would lead one to imagine that they would be immediately conveyed to isolated blast proof containers. Not so! I recently passed through Johannesburg enroute from Cape Town to Perth. Here, after one has passed through normal security, just before the boarding gate one is confronted by the 'liquid squad'. This consists of two tables, each manned by three security staff who 'finger' through ones hand luggage in search of liquids in excess of 100ml.

Should such contraband be discovered, it is conveyed to a bog standard, large wheelie bin of the exact kind we all have for the disposal of household waste. This being conveniently situated near to the 'liquid squad' tables and in close proximity to the stations where the passengers boarding passes are checked. The wheelie bin had been fitted with a hasp and staple and locked with a small padlock. In the lid of the wheelie bin a small hole had been cut through which the suspect liquid was dropped, to fall over a metre before striking the bottom of the bin. Had the bottle of confiscated liquid I witnessed being treated this way contained an unstable liquid explosive, not only would the security staff be 'taken out' but so would the airline staff manning the boarding gates and a few dozen passengers to boot.

Of course, a stable explosive, liquid or solid, requires a detonator to set it off and in the case of the event that triggered the security response to the liquid bomb, the detonator was disguised within the casing of a penlight battery. Think how many batteries are carried onto an aircraft in passengers' electronic paraphernalia and how many are stocked in the duty free shops.

I particularly mentioned that the 3 1 1 rule applies to passengers and aircrew because it certainly does not apply to the thousands of litres of liquid that make their way from the land-side to the air-side of an airport to be placed on the shelves of the duty free liquor shops, air-side restaurants and, of course, in the galleys of the aircraft.

Another source of irritation is the removal of tiny scissors and nail clippers from passengers and aircrew. Why would any villain attempt to take over an aircraft with a nail clipper when the truly scary weapon of a broken wine bottle could so easily be acquired from the drinks trolley?

THE HIJACK THAT ENDED IN A FATAL DITCHING

In November 1996 an Ethiopian Airlines Boeing 767 enroute Addis Ababa to Nairobi, was hijacked by three very stupid, drunk Ethiopian youngsters. Their intention was to seek asylum in Australia. They boarded the aircraft with no weapons, but somehow succeeded in pulling a bluff that there were eleven of them and that they had a bomb. The bomb later turned out to be a wrapped bottle, and in fact the only weapon they acquired was the cockpit crash axe that was part of the aircraft's standard equipment.

Of note was the passengers' extreme reluctance to tackle the hijackers after having been informed by the Captain, on the public address, of the situation, and that they would run out of fuel and end up in the sea. Even after a war journalist who was onboard exhorted them to tackle the hijackers they refused to act.

Due to some extremely clever subterfuges on the part of the Captain after they ran out of fuel, he managed, while still struggling with one of the hijackers, to ditch the aircraft just off a beach on the island of Grande Comore. The death toll was extremely high due to two factors. Having no engine power there was no hydraulic pressure to lower the flaps and thus the aircraft touched down on the water at high speed and broke up. The other factor was that passengers ignored the safety briefings and inflated their life jackets prior to exiting the hull after touchdown. Thus many of them were trapped in the hull by their flotation devices and drowned. One hundred and twenty five of the one hundred and seventy five souls on board died.

In contrast to the reluctance of those passengers to tackle hijackers, I remember an incident from my 707 days. In what had become international fashion, SAA in an attempt to prevent hijackings, decided to place two 'Air Marshals' aboard on international flights. If memory serves me right, these 'Air Marshals' were drawn from the ranks of a long defunct organisation known as the South African Railway Police. One was placed in the economy section and the other in first class. They generally stuck out like a sore thumb and the crew could identify them at fifty paces, one factor being that they invariably wore their Railway Police uniform issue brown shoes. Another give away was that they would never remove their jackets as these concealed the weapons they were carrying.

The 'Air Marshal' stationed in first class was about as far away as one could get from the profile of the average first class passenger back in the seventies. In a deluded attempt to have him blend in, he was permitted all the privileges of the other first class passengers including an unlimited supply of free booze. It was, of course, this largesse that led directly to 'the incident'.

He was consuming copious quantities of cane and coke and this resulted in the usual diminished responsibility syndrome that accompanies such activities. A secondary effect necessitated frequent trips to the toilet, which on the 707 was located forward of the front galley and next to the cockpit. By this time our 'out of place' passenger had attracted the attention of some of the other passengers who were now watching him attentively. Feeling the flush of alcohol, no doubt, he had loosened his jacket and as he made his rather unsteady way to the toilet, his jacket flapped open and revealed the large pistol strapped to his side for all to see.

While he was in the toilet two of the passengers flattened themselves against the bulkheads, on either side of the aisle, at the front of the first class section. As 'our hero' entered the first class section on his return from the toilet, he was hit by two sucker punches in short succession from the left and right. Needless to say, that ended his further participation during the flight and, probably, in any other activity for several days thereafter.

9/11 AND POLITICAL CORRECTNESS

9/11 changed the world and had a huge impact on the airline industry. Suddenly the Captain's discretion and authority to decide whom to allow into the cockpit was removed and no one, not even his wife or children, were permitted a cockpit visit. This even applied to the First Officer's three year old child.

But did I say no one? Well that is not strictly true because the strapping young man, who has just completed his cabin attendant course, and joined SAA three months ago, without any in-depth security clearance, has unlimited access to the cockpit. This even should he fit the classical historic profile of a terrorist.

This brings us solidly into the realms of 'political correctness'. Apparently it is 'politically incorrect' to profile persons and single them out for more thorough security screening. We are told that profiling is used by the security chiefs, but is it? Consider a fairly non-contentious profiling parameter: age.

There are, no doubt, terrorists in the advanced age bracket but to date no geriatrics have been involved in operational terror incidents aboard aircraft, for obvious reasons.

I have been flying out of Perth every year for the last twelve years and only once have I not been singled out for an explosive check. I am seventy-five and it has become a standing family joke.

The irony is that while I stand there, being gone over with the explosive sniffing device, a dozen people that fit several profiling parameters walk through freely. Of course, this is a random check and it would appear that selection is at the whim of the officer doing the checking. Clearly his 'random' selections are not being monitored for rationality, as they should be. Just as it would make no sense to stop and search people for stolen laptops, for the sake of 'political correctness', if they were wearing shorts, a T-shirt and carrying no bags.

PERTH IRONY

I think that the most 'ironic explosive sniffing' that I experienced was at Perth some years ago. Corleen and I had flown up to Perth from Albany on a feeder airline and thus had disembarked at the domestic terminal. Flying out to South Africa that night, we needed to get to the international terminal which was on the other side of the airfield. Against the wall of the domestic arrival terminal, near the exit was a phone with a sign above it indicating that the phone was to be used for information regarding transport to the international terminal.

I duly picked up this phone and was told to exit arrivals, turn right and walk to the end of the building where I would see a bus stop under a large car hire billboard. From there a bus would take us to the international terminal.

A bus duly arrived, and after our luggage was stowed we boarded it and found seats. After a while the driver boarded and walked down the isle requesting 'Qantas vouchers'. When we looked at him blankly he said "You must have arrived on the Skywest flight" from Albany. We nodded and after he had taken $14 off us the bus departed.

Shortly we arrived at a security gate where a guard was seated inside a small hut. The bus driver leaned out of his window and shouted "I've got sixteen", whereupon an arm emerged, from the window of the hut, with a 'thumbs up' sign and the gate swung open. As we drove through a bushy area, that screened us from view, I realised we were now airside and thus inside the airport security area having gone through no checks whatsoever.

A few kilometres later we came upon another gate with a hut and this time the guard asked the driver if he had sixteen and, receiving a 'thumbs up' sign from the driver, opened the gate and we were back outside the airport security area.

My mind boggled as I envisaged scenarios whereby a group of young men with fake Albany Cricket Club blazers could drive to the airport with all manner of weaponry concealed in those long bags that normally contain cricket bats and pads. By informing the driver that they had arrived by air from Albany and paying $7 each would have unhindered access to the security side of Perth airport.

We now, once again, being outside the security area, had to pass through security to get to our flight and as usual I was singled out for an explosives check. It is to be hoped that this ridiculous situation no longer exists at Perth airport.

Since 2018 I have not been 'sniffed', as I became bored, no longer deriving amusement from this inanity, and merely fiddled around recovering my possessions from the tray, in which they pass through the x-ray machine, and placing them in my pockets, until the 'sniffer' selected another victim and I was able to pass unimpeded.

Strangely enough, this 'political correctness' that impacts upon the effectiveness of airport security is conspicuous by its absence when leaving the air-side. Just watch border control and customs profile and pick out for their attentions, passengers they consider suspect.

WHO'S PROTECTION IS PRIORITISED?

A thing for which I will be eternally thankful is that I reached retirement age shortly after the impenetrable cockpit doors were introduced. Prior to this cockpit doors had 'kick out' panels meant to ensure access to the cockpit in the advent of a crash. These impenetrable cockpit doors were introduced in the aftermath of 9/11. At the risk of being accused of cynicism, I believe these are not so much meant to protect passengers and crew, than to prevent terrorists from flying an aircraft into buildings. I am sure that the aircraft that hit the Pentagon caused a wave of fear in certain political quarters.

I often asked myself if I would be able to keep that door locked in the face of threats to murder the passengers one by one, starting with children, until such time as the door was unlocked? My answer was always a resounding 'no'.

In my opinion it is a great irony, that while on the one hand, removing fairly innocuous everyday items such as nail clippers and deodorant sprays from pilots, security has on the other hand, provided a mentally unstable pilot with the perfect weapon to take unassailable control of the aircraft and do with it as he wishes. It is my firm belief that, to date, this 'weapon' has been responsible for the loss of at least three aircraft with all souls aboard.

Pilots would obviously like security to be as foolproof as possible but once they have witnessed too many obvious loopholes, and been the victims of endless finicky nuisance value procedures, they do tend to lose faith in the system. Unfortunately until the intense focus that is applied to pilots and their passengers is widened to include all ground staff and ancillary airside operations, 'political correctness' is binned and the lead of Israel is followed in profiling and anti-terrorism intelligence, I cannot see this changing.

18

LOVE, LUST AND FLOATING TROPHIES

THE LOTHARIOS

Take a few men, some attractive ladies, send them to a fancy hotel at an exotic destination for a week and give them a generous allowance in the local currency. Sounds rather like a new romance reality TV show but this was the reality of airline flying in past decades when many international destination were only serviced weekly. This meant that crews would spend a week in these locations, waiting for the following week's aircraft to arrive, before flying home.

This was, of course, a great situation for the airline Lotharios who, amongst the pilots were a small minority group. Some of these would go to almost ridiculous lengths to satisfy their seemingly obsessive needs to seduce any possibly available woman.

The most notorious of these was a married First Officer who unbelievably got engaged to a very attractive hostess in order to have an affair with her. How he managed to keep his two lives separate was a source of wonder to all who knew of his antics. Needless to say it was inevitable that both his *'fiancée'* and his wife would eventually come to know of each other and when this occurred it resulted in a broken fake engagement and a divorce.

He eventually left the airline over a disagreement with management. As silly as it may seem, he refused to cut his hair to the length required by the airline's uniform code and resigned when he was suspended from duty until such time as he complied. All I can surmise is that his vanity was so great that it totally clouded his reason. He was able to find a job as a First Officer with a Middle Eastern airline and left South Africa.

A few months latter I ran into him in Paris. I was operating the B707 freighter and his airline crew stayed at the same hotel as SAA's. He seemed extremely pleased to see South Africans and immediately invited my Captain and me to his room for a drink. In his enthusiasm he must have forgotten that his room was set up for seduction, in case he happened to come across a suitable target in the hotel.

Despite the fact that he was a First Officer, a Captain's jacket was not hung up in the cupboard, but strategically draped over a chair with the four gold bars in full view. On the writing desk, also in full view, was a Captain's pay sheet in someone else's name. On the sideboard was a silver tray with two champagne flutes and an ice bucket. The Captain and I had a really hard time suppressing our urge to burst into laughter. How true the adage that 'A leopard does not change its spots'.

SENIOR CAPTAINS AND THEIR LATE MIDLIFE CRISES

Equally ridiculous, to my mind were the Captains, on the verge of retirement, who seemed to be going through some form of late midlife crisis. Admittedly the retirement age was early for pilots - when I joined SAA the retirement age was fifty five, later it was pushed to fifty eight, sixty and, after I retired at sixty, to sixty three. Forced retirement is, for some pilots, a very traumatic experience. This is particularly true of those who have no hobbies or life outside of airline flying. An airline Captain has a lot of positional power, gets plenty of respect, is accustomed to being obeyed and of, possibly delusionally, being viewed as a glamorous figure. On retirement all this disappears, your airline Captain becomes just another retired old fossil and this knowledge can lead to late onset midlife crisis.

Now the sensible way to handle this crisis is to buy a sports car, motorbike, boat of your fancy or a light aircraft. But no, some of our near retirement

Captains decided that the way to go was a brand new, young trophy wife. Of course, the only young ladies fitting this description that the Captain socialises with, are the hostesses on his flights. Surprisingly, there are many young hostesses whose ambition seems to be to marry an airline Captain, regardless of age. On several trips I witnessed older Captains acting the age of their young partners and found this rather lacking in dignity and, in fact, often quite 'cringeworthy'. More worrying was that it invariably led to a breakdown in the chain of command and discipline aboard the aircraft.

All too often these retired Captains would soon discover that divorcing their original wife to marry a young trophy wife was a far more costly and often less rewarding exercise than buying a sports car, yacht or light aircraft.

I recall, when on holiday, walking with Corleen down the main street of a small coastal town and seeing a couple coming towards us pushing a pram. Each had a hand on the handle of the pram, one being an attractive young blonde lady while the other was a much older man. I immediately classified them as mother and grandfather out with baby. As we came abeam them I was surprised to be enthusiastically greeted by name and realised that this was one of our retired Captains that I had often flown with as a First Officer. Further I vaguely recognised the young lady as a hostess I had, on the odd occasion, flown with.

As we chatted it became clear they were a married couple and he was the father of the baby. Was his idea of a fulfilling retirement night time drill, nappy changes, crying babies and carting around a ton of baby equipment whenever going anywhere? Having to tolerate a teenager in the house when one is deep into one's seventies can hardly be considered an idyllic retirement. To say nothing of the poor child who would have a father the age of his school mate's grandfathers or the wife who would end up as a carer and thereafter a young widow. Somehow it seemed a 'lose, lose' situation to me.

THE FLOATING TROPHYS

There was a group of cockpit crew in SAA whom we knew as the 'Floating Trophies', a nickname given to the colleagues amongst us who had been married three or more times. To the best of my knowledge, we had several three, the odd four , two five and an unbelievable seven timer. We all wondered how on earth they could afford the alimony and the general consensus seemed to be that, for the ex wives, just getting away from them was sufficient reward and that alimony he could possibly pay when divided between so many ex wives was just not worth bothering about.

19

GLASS COCKPITS AND OTHER DELIGHTS

In July of 2000 and as part of the Coleman Andrews 'Americanisation programme' our first Boeing 737-800 series arrived to replace SAA's Airbus 300s and 320s. They took a while to filter down to the Cape Fleet but in January of the following year I found myself on the conversion course for my first 'glass cockpit' airliner.

A 'glass cockpit' is one in which the old analogue instrument displays are replaced by small screens looking much like those on today's tablets and smart phones. They not only display much more information, they also display it in a format that is readily interpreted at a glance. Many of the instruments are integrated so that the information from various instruments may be reflected on the primary screen right in front of the pilot's eyes. A further advancement was the 'Heads Up Display' or HUD, through which the integrated information from the primary instrument screen was projected onto the windscreen, which allowed a pilot searching for the runway in bad visibility still to monitor his instruments.

Another major change was the requirement for pilots to programme the computers with instructions which these computers would then convey to the auto-pilot and auto-throttles to carry out. All this was pretty much a change in cockpit philosophy and I must say that I rather enjoyed the conversion to 'glass'. In the beginning it could be confusing when the autopilot carried out actions that were unexpected, mainly due to programming misunderstandings, but the B737-800 had the familiar red button on the yoke that dropped out all the automatics and allowed the aircraft to be flown manually.

I still consider instant manual reversion to be an essential feature on an aircraft as it allows pilots to return rapidly to the essential basics expressed in the axiom 'Aviate, Navigate, Communicate'. It means, whatever goes wrong, the first priority is to fly the aeroplane, the second to maintain an awareness of where the aircraft is, which could prevent contact with high ground, the third to ensure each of the crew is aware of the other's intentions and that the monitoring of all critical parameters has been delegated and is being carried out.

It has happened that aircraft and lives have been lost due to crew distraction. A classic example of this was Eastern Airlines 401, in 1972, where the crew became so preoccupied and, in fact, so fixated on a landing gear warning light that they failed to notice the auto-pilot had become disengaged and was slowly descending the aircraft, until it smashed into the darkened waters of the Florida Everglades with the loss of 101 lives. That caused by a simple warning light, but the potential distraction inherent in computers is far greater. We have all seen people who cannot even walk down the street without bumping into others, sign poles, street lights and motor cars and falling over objects and into holes, all due to the distraction of one small smart phone screen upon which they are fixated.

To my great relief, I was never required to fly an aircraft that could override the pilot should its software determine they were exceeding some, or other, design parameter programmed into it. Despite the fact that I am fairly computer orientated, that would have been a 'bridge too far' for me.

In mitigation I would plead that I have never seen a headline to the effect:

> 'Automatic System Overrides Pilots. Saves Aircraft and Lives of All Passengers'.

I have, however, seen headlines along the these lines:

> Automatic System Overrides Pilots. Flies Aircraft into Ground. No Survivors.

20

DANGEROUS TIMES

It is a well-known axiom that airline flying consists of thousands of hours of boredom interrupted by moments of sheer terror.

One would have thought that the most dangerous times in a pilot's life would have been caused by operational parameters such as wild weather and technical factors such as engine, control, hydraulic or electronic failures. Sure, all these things do occur and it is highly unlikely that one could have an aviation career spanning forty years without experiencing several of them.

However, having said that, I can confidently state that, for me, the most frightening times in SAA were not related to these factors, but rather more to external events, some of which were not even related to aviation.

THE DOWNING OF THE AIR RHODESIA VISCOUNTS

SAA, at times, flew into areas that could really only be described as 'war zones'. One of these was Salisbury (now Harare) in Rhodesia at the height of the Rhodesian bush war.

On the 3rd of September 1978 a civilian Air Rhodesia Viscount, RH 825, on a normal scheduled flight from Victoria Falls via Kariba to Salisbury was, shortly after take off from Kariba, hit in the starboard engine by a Strela-2 missile fired by ZIPRA (Zimbabwe Peoples Revolutionary Army).

Badly damaged, an emergency wheels-up landing was attempted in a cotton field but a hidden ditch caused the aircraft to cartwheel and break up. Of the fifty-six passengers and four crew, only eighteen survived the crash. The ZIPRA insurgents arrived on the scene shortly afterwards and found ten survivors, many of whom were injured, including four women and two little girls aged eleven and four. These were rounded up and massacred at the scene of the crash.

Five of the survivors who went to seek help and three that had managed to hide in the bush as the insurgents approached were the only survivors of the attack.

THE DEAFENING SILENCE

The governments of the world, and other bodies including the World Council of Churches somehow managed to maintain a silence over the matter and not a single world leader condemned the action. The world press were also strangely quiet which explains why very few people outside of Southern Africa even knew of this atrocity.

It was left to the Anglican Archbishop of Salisbury, John de Costa, to condemn this 'deafening silence' in his moving sermon at the commemorative service held for the victims at the Anglican Cathedral in Salisbury. Here is a short extract from that speech.

> *"Nobody who holds sacred the dignity of human life can be anything but sickened at the events attending the crash of the Viscount Hunyani. Survivors have the greatest call on the sympathy and assistance of every other human being. The horror of the crash was bad enough, but that this should have been compounded by murder of the most savage and treacherous sort leaves us stunned with disbelief and brings revulsion in the minds of anyone deserving the name "human."*
>
> *This bestiality, worse than anything in recent history, stinks in the nostrils of Heaven. But are we deafened with the voice of protest*

> *from nations which call themselves "civilised"? We are not. Like men in the story of the Good Samaritan, they "pass by, on the other side."*
> *One listens for loud condemnation by Dr. David Owen, himself a medical doctor, trained to extend mercy and help to all in need.*
> *One listens and the silence is deafening.*
> *One listens for loud condemnation by the President of the United States, himself a man from the Bible-Baptist belt, and again the silence is deafening.*
> *One listens for loud condemnation by the Pope, by the Chief Rabbi, by the Archbishop of Canterbury, by all who love the name of God. Again the silence is deafening."*

On the 12th of February 1979 a second civilian Air Rhodesia Viscount, RH 827 was brought down by a Strela-2 missile. This time there were no survivors and fifty-nine people died. In both incidents most of the passengers had been tourists visiting Victoria Falls and Kariba. Some were even from countries whose leaders were silent on the issue.

ANTI MISSILE MANOEUVRES

During this time I was a co-pilot on the 737-200 which we operated into Rhodesia. At the time the South African government was actively supporting Rhodesia both militarily and with supplies denied them by sanctions, so it was assumed that it was not beyond the bounds of probability that an SAA aircraft could be targeted. We were thus briefed to utilise missile avoidance procedures when taking off and landing at Rhodesian airfields. The Strela-2 had an operational altitude of between 50 and 1500 metres and thus an aircraft was vulnerable during these phases of flight.

The basic guidelines were, never to approach or depart an airfield on a predictable track. Spend as little time as possible in the danger zone and where possible climb and descend over areas with no cover which could conceal a missile crew. With these scant instructions we were pretty much free to 'ad lib' as to the procedures we would use.

Of course, the one that the airline did not really want to recommend was the one we all used, and that was flying at treetop level, as it was practically impossible for a Strela operator, in cover, to get a lock on during the time it took a 737 to scream past at low level. Immediately after take off we would initiate a steep turn onto a random heading and allow the speed to build up to 320kts as we skimmed the treetops. When we thought we were far enough from any likely launch site we would commence a max rate climb thus only spending a minimum of time within the reach of a Strela.

A reverse variation of this procedure would be used when coming in to land.

The passengers would always be told what to expect but I can't imagine that these manoeuvres were very pleasant for them, and further, they would serve to heighten their awareness of a possible missile strike.

I know that, for us, a combination of fear and these manoeuvres certainly got the adrenalin pumping and we always breathed a sigh of relief when we climbed beyond Strela range on our homeward leg.

Unlike the passengers, we could not celebrate that moment with a proper drink. It was a well-known fact that passenger alcohol consumption on these flights was way above average.

LUANDA AND THE BRIGADIER

Another dodgy destination for us was Luanda in Angola. In the early sixties SAA became banned from flying over a number of African countries. Where previously we had flown to Europe via Nairobi and Athens it now became necessary to fly up the west coast of Africa mostly remaining seawards of the continent all the way 'around the bulge' and into Europe. Our routing would generally be via Luanda in the then Portuguese controlled Angola, Sal Island in the Cape Verde group, Las Palmas and Lisbon.

In the seventies Angola was very much a conflict zone, with Russian and Cuban backed MPLA at war with the American and South African backed FNLA and UNITA. Final approach to Luanda's main runway was over an enormous sprawling squatters camp that had the potential to provide cover for all sorts of offensive actions. As such the SAA pilots became extremely concerned and contended that operating into Luanda was putting their lives and the lives of their passengers at risk.

As the pressure on management built up, they decided to call a meeting with the pilots in an effort to assure them that their fears were not well founded.

I remember attending this meeting in the auditorium at Flight Operations where the CEO attempted to convince us that extensive due diligence had been carried out and that there was no risk in operating into Luanda. In this regard he introduced his main speaker who was the SAA Head of Security, one Brigadier Kloppers. I will never forget this worthy's final words after his summation of the situation. Puffing out his chest like a pouting pigeon and pulling himself up to his full height, despite all evidence to the contrary, he stated with the utmost confidence that "Luanda is as safe as my back yard".

Despite the concerns of the pilots, it soon became abundantly clear that management had no intention of using alternative routing to avoid Luanda.

However, scarcely were the words out of Brigadier Klopper's mouth when one of our 747s suffered a rocket and small arms attack on final approach into Luanda. The co-pilot was Chris Hickson who later related the experience to me.

"We were on a visual final approach, with the skipper flying, and all was normal until descending through about 800 ft when the first rocket passed over the right wing tip. This was rapidly followed by the second, which passed over the wing just inboard of the number four engine, and the third passing over the wing close to the number three engine. At this stage it flashed through my adrenalin charged brain, the spacing was such that the fourth would hit me right between the eyes.

By the grace of God, the fourth rocket never came but instead there was a sound like a handful of gravel hitting a windowpane. This was caused by bullets from automatic rifle fire hitting the aircraft. We landed normally, but the aircraft was damaged and had to be grounded in Luanda"

Needless to say, Luanda was then dropped as an enroute stopover and not before time as Luanda became increasingly dangerous. I don't recall ever seeing Brigadier Klopper again. Maybe he was just avoiding the pilots or could he have stepped on a landmine in his own backyard?

TRAMP OPERATIONS

A secondary, and far lesser danger, that arose due to our 'around the bulge' routing was the mid-air collision risk caused by what we called 'Tramp Operations', so named after the tramp steamer ships of the world's oceans.

In order to fly legally over a country, an operator needs to apply to that country for clearance to fly in its airspace. In Africa this can involve an operator in reams of red tape and considerable costs including the greasing of palms. There were many shoe string operators who circumvented all this by the simple methodology of not filing flight plans when flying in and out of certain central and west African countries. Thus nobody knew of their routeing or the levels at which they were flying and they were a significant hazard to navigation. Contrary to popular belief, the airborne radar on civilian airliners is weather radar, wonderful for avoiding thunderstorms, but useless for picking up other aircraft.

Of course, this type of operation could only occur in areas where ground radar coverage was non-existent and the tramps could not be detected, far less intercepted. All the legitimate operators would broadcast their position, flight level and estimates for their next position on a radio frequency reserved for this purpose. Thus we looked after our own traffic control over areas where there was none, or where it was ineffective. The tramps were bound by no such convention and kept radio silence thus creating a far from ideal situation where a mid-air collision was always a possibility.

THE HELL RUN

Having spoken about war zones and illicit navigation hazards, these paled into insignificance in comparison to driving to the airport at odd hours of the night during the civil unrest and plain thuggery that South Africa was experiencing in the late nineteen nineties and early two thousands. The N2, which was the main route from Cape Town to the east coast and the Garden Route, had deservedly become known as the 'Hell Run'. Never has the axiom 'The most dangerous part of your flight is the drive to the airport' been more true!

To the east and abeam of the airport, the N2 passed between two squatters camps. Despite the fact that a pedestrian bridge had been built across the N2 joining these areas, there was a constant flow of humanity, on foot and often carrying bulky or lengthy items, dodging the fast moving and busy traffic flow, while attempting to cross the highway. This was bad enough during the day but deadly at night or in reduced visibility. There was a 1.5 metre wall dividing the east and westbound lanes and at intervals all along this were crossing points where crates had been stacked as steps to facilitate climbing over.

The pedestrian death toll on the N2 was never published, but we had all witnessed horrifying accidents involving pedestrians and knew it must have been extremely high. All this could have been avoided by increasing the height of the wall to make crossings impractical. The authorities however decided that the best solution was to fence the camps off from the highway. In their wisdom they decided on tall concrete picket fencing which was built from square reinforced concrete poles resembling lintels. Of course these were a wonderfully versatile material for the construction of shacks and it was not very long before gaping holes appeared in the fences, and the N2 crossing slaughter continued.

Many of our cockpit crew, myself included, lived to the east of the airport in the town of Somerset West. Another danger we faced was caused by the fact that the airport was in the Cape Flats which, being situated on a low-lying narrow strip of land between Table Bay and False Bay, was in a fog belt. Thus travelling on the N2 for early flights in winter was often done in severely reduced visibility. This was extremely hazardous due to so many cars on the road being unroadworthy and often having no lights whatsoever while creeping through the foggy darkness. On one never to be forgotten occasion, I nearly rear ended, of all things, a donkey cart. It was a dark, foggy morning well before sunrise and the donkey cart did not even have reflectors, much less tail lights. This on a major four-lane highway!

Far more frightening were the deliberate acts of violence that erupted on the N2 quite regularly. There were many indiscriminate stonings of cars by gangs of youths on the N2 and many people were injured. Anyone who had the misfortune to break down at a quiet time on the N2 was in very real mortal danger.

During this period SAA had awarded domestic freighter flights to the Cape Fleet. These flights utilised our converted Boeing 737-200 freighters. Our routeing was Cape Town – Johannesburg – Durban – Cape Town. These were overnight flights that returned to Cape Town in the very early hours of the morning, which were the most dangerous times to be on the 'Hell Run'.

This was when criminal gangs emerged to plague the N2. When there was very little traffic a lone car was at its most vulnerable. Their strategy was to attempt either to stop a car, or failing this, to cause it to crash so it could be plundered.

One of the methods used was to lower a brick on fishing line from a bridge, so that it dangled in the middle of a lane at windscreen height. This was very hard to see in time to avoid at night, and resulted in some pretty nasty facial injuries.

The other method was simply to obstruct the road by placing objects across both lanes. The concrete lintels from the fences were ideal for this as the Cape Flats is a sandy area with very few rocks.

We learnt always to swap lanes suddenly just before a bridge and to avoid being in the middle of a lane when actually passing under the bridge. On two occasions I was lucky enough to avoid obstruction ambushes on the N2 when returning from a freighter in the wee hours.

On the first of these it was a gang of six or so who were setting up the ambush. They had not yet managed to obstruct the whole width of the road, so when they saw me coming at speed, stupidly decided to block the gap by standing in it. Full of adrenalin by this time I just aimed the car at the gap and floored the accelerator. This took them by surprise and they rapidly scattered, very narrowly avoiding being hit.

On the second occasion I was driving an all wheel drive vehicle and managed to get around the obstructions by going off road and somehow ploughing through the soft sand and regaining the road past the ambush.

The Hell Run was a lot more frightening then anything I had ever had to face in the air!

DEAF EARS

As the manager of the Cape fleet I was extremely concerned for the safety of the Cape crews and requested that the freighter flights be rescheduled so that they could be operated by either the Johannesburg or Durban Fleets who had no such issues driving to and from their respective airports. It was during the Coleman Andrews era and my plea fell on deaf management ears.

At the time the authority responsible was The Minister for Community Safety, Hennie Bester, and my next strategy was to attempt to get SAA management at the highest level to take up the matter with the Minister. In this regard I sent the following letter to the Vice President of Flight Operations, one Anton Richmond, and a similar letter to the President of SAAPA, the SAA Pilots association.

Captain P.E. Liebrecht B737 Fleet

Cape Town International Airport

7 February 2001

Anton Richman

Vice President Flight Operations

S.A. Airways

AIRWAYS PARK
Dear Anton
You will no doubt be aware of the recent publicity both in the papers and on TV regarding security on the N2 in the vicinity of Cape Town International Airport.

The publicity is unfortunately not 'media-hype' and the dangers of travelling this road are very real.

The Cape Fleet in the near future will, I estimate, have in the region of 200 members per month travelling this road between the hours of midnight and 06h00. I personally have experienced an ambush attempt at 04h30 while returning off a freighter. Following a mechanical breakdown, your chances of survival are definitely doubtful.

There is presently a 'Let's make the N 2 safe' campaign in progress. The responsible person is the Community Safety Minister - Hennie Bester.

I believe that:

SAA should contact the Minister and apprise him of our concerns.

We should publicly be seen to be supporting the above-mentioned campaign.

SAA Security should be drawn in and a strategic meeting held to explore possible ways of ensuring the safety of our crews on this road during the more dangerous hours.

The initiative should come from the highest possible level within SAA.

I will be drafting a similar letter to the SAAPA chairman in order to solicit their joint support in this very serious matter.

Kind regards,

Paul

Anton was a First Officer who had extraordinarily been promoted to Vice President Flight Operations as described in the next chapter, The Slippery Slope.

This 'worthy' did precisely nothing, not even bothering to reply to my letter. Thus it was my lowly position that turned out to be the 'highest possible level within SAA' and I addressed a letter of concern to the Minister on SAA's behalf.

The President of SAAPA, John Harty also wrote a letter to the Minister expressing the association's concern.

There was also great pressure on the Minister from the Chamber of Commerce to address the situation on the N2 as Somerset West was within Cape Town's commuter belt. The situation on the N2 gradually improved and by 2002 the term 'Hell Run' was no longer heard so frequently.

A BRUTAL TRAGEDY

A particularly tragic and brutal incident involving one of our First Officers returning from one of our freighter flights occurred on the 3rd of July in 1998. Andre Viljoen had spent seven years in the South African Air Force prior to joining SAA in 1995, and had been posted to the Cape Fleet in 1997. Andre was to me the epitome of an excellent co-pilot, and was quiet spoken, well mannered, intelligent, efficient, enthusiastic and a good pilot. I often flew with Andre and became quite fond of him.

Andre was driving home after his freighter flight landed in Cape Town when he made the mistake of stopping at 3.30 am, to draw money at an ATM. Having drawn the cash he was shadowed back to his car by four men, one of whom was brandishing a gun. After being forced into the passenger seat of his car he was taken on a terror ride through the streets of various suburbs and, despite offering no resistance, he endured a pistol whipping and a shot fired so close to his ear that he suffered a burst eardrum. He also had to listen for hours to a protracted argument, between two of the thugs, over whether or not to kill him.

Eventually as daylight was approaching the thugs tired of their game of terrorising Andre, stopped at a field in Mitchells Plain and, dragging him out of the car, forced him to lie face down in the grass of a vacant lot where they shot him in the back of the head and left him for dead. By some miracle Andre survived and was able to get to his feet and seek help. It took him fifteen minutes to get to a nearby house where the resident refused him entry but agreed to call the police. Andre sat on the veranda for nearly half an hour, on a freezing winter morning, before the police arrived, only losing consciousness on the way to the hospital.

It was discovered that Andre had managed to protect his head with his hand and the bullet had passed through his hand, causing it to be slightly deflected before penetrating the skull, where without directly penetrating his brain, it ran around the inside of his skull eventually becoming lodged near his temple.

It was sitting in the corridor of the hospital, awaiting news from the operating theatre, that I first met Coleman Andrews who had just arrived from America in order to take up the position of SAA CEO, and who was there to 'show his concern for Andre'. In the light of his management's attitude towards our later N2 safety crises, it would seem his concern was more of a PR exercise than anything else.

That very same day the police found Andre's car parked in the driveway of a house in Mitchells Plain, and, no doubt, a bit of robust persuasion convinced the residents to cough up the names of their friends who had parked it there. Within a short time they were all rounded up and behind bars.

The surgeons determined that it would be too risky to remove the bullet so it was left where it was. Although Andre made an amazing recovery the trauma resulted in headaches, epileptic fits and loss of peripheral vision. As a result of this Andre lost his flying licence and a young pilot's promising career was ruined.

Worse was to come though, as a few months later a letter being smuggled out of prison was intercepted by the authorities. This was from one of the perpetrators awaiting trial, all of whom were members of the Mongrels, a notorious Cape Flats criminal gang, and it effectively placed a price on Andre's head with the aim of preventing him from testifying at the trial.

Now being in mortal danger, Andre and his wife Sandy could not even remain in their home and for the next few weeks spent time with friends, living in a variety of locations until such time as they could make arrangements to move to the UK. Fortunately Sandy had a British passport and was able to obtain a remedial teaching post in England. Andre was later able to obtain work in a company selling pilot supplies. He is further handicapped by his vision not allowing him to drive.

In early 2001 the perpetrators were brought to trial and Andre returned from the UK and gave evidence. The two identified as the ringleaders were found guilty of aggravated robbery, kidnapping and attempted murder. They were sentenced to forty-four years with the judge stipulating a minimum time of twenty-five years to be spent in jail before they could be released. The other two received lesser sentences.

In 2005 the appeal court overturned the sentences of the ringleaders, effectively making them immediately eligible for parole.

Andre and Sandy missed SA and returned regularly to visit. However, their visits became less frequent after Sandy was nearly hijacked in Claremont.

Dangerous times indeed!

21

THE SLIPPERY SLOPE

During my time with SAA I experienced many different management regimes, under a variety of CEOs. From managements that took huge advantage of a pilot body that, due to the policies of the then government, were effectively barred from taking up employment internationally, to the fair and ethical attitude of CEOs such as Mike Myburgh. The statement by CEO Frans Swarts "That's the price you have to pay if you want to live under the South African sun" typifies the prevailing attitude of the former. At the time cabin crew were taking home more pay than domestic co-pilots. Following Swarts we even had a CEO whose aversion to the pilot body was so obvious that conspiracy theories were rife, in the main asking the question whether his wife had possibly had an affair with a pilot?

Throughout all these management changes the South African Airways Pilots Association had always taken a reasonable and responsible attitude, evidenced by the fact that, despite undue provocation, the SAA pilot body had never gone on strike. Often, I thought, too reasonable as the only time the SAA pilot body had made any progress towards parity with their international colleges was when SAAPA was under the chairmanship of highly militant individuals such as Captains Blake Flemington and Clair Fichardt.

THE START OF THE ROT

All the shenanigans of previous CEOs, however, paled into insignificance with the controversial appointment of one Coleman Andrews. The previous CEO, Mike Myburgh had retired after his hands had been tied by the strange appointment of Zukile Numvete as an executive director with shared executive powers. This left Numvete running the airline and was followed by a two year period of 'negative profit' for which Numvete was blamed. Thus the Head of Transnet Saki Macozoma appointed Andrews based on his supposed turnaround of World Airways, a US Company about one fifth the size of SAA and mainly in the charter business.

In a 'Special Staff Announcement' publication of 15th June 1998, Macozoma had this to say

> *"Coleman Andrews will steer SAA through the crucial period leading up to its partial privatisation and beyond. He comes to the job with extensive experience in airline strategic and financial management and I am sure he will add enormous value to SAA."*

Not everyone was so confidently upbeat and soon less encouraging reports began to appear in the press indicating that all was not well with World Airways that the new head of SAA had left in debt. These were denied by the Transnet bosses and Andrews. A cartoon appeared in 'Die Burger', a local newspaper, showing Andrews, battered and bent, limping away from a crashed World Airways plane and towards a cringing and terrified SAA Boeing 747. The caption read *'Let's see if I can keep this one in the air'*.

In the August 1999 copy of Airline magazine a letter from an employee of World Airways appeared:

South African Airways

I can hold my tongue no longer. The interesting article on SAA (Changing Times in Johannesburg March 1999) brought back fond memories of my four years in South Africa and numerous flights on that airline. During those difficult days, SAA flew to Europe around the 'bulge' of Africa with its new Boeing 747 Super Bs, reliably and with great service.

It really galls me that the South African government chose a CEO who comes from an airline – World Airways – that is hardly a success story. This man and his cronies from the consulting world will ruin SAA and loot the national treasury at the same time.

His consulting second-in-command charged my airline an egregious amount of money and and almost ruined us in the process – ie, our worst annual financial performance in the company's 26 year history.

It is not surprising that they would cut off support for the Historic Flight. These guys are like old Bolsheviks who think the past is irrelevant to the future.

When will shareholders and governments figure out that glib, slick presentations are no substitute for experience?

Charles T Cleaver

Bandera, Texas

August 1999 - Airways

Andrews was forty three and an American spin doctor from the bible belt. He arrived in South Africa amongst media hype and fanfare worthy of the second coming. I was one of the first SAA managers to meet Andrews, as he arrived at the hospital where I was awaiting the results of surgery to remove the bullet from Andre's head, and introduced himself to me with his standard 'Call me Coleman' greeting.

Unusually for me, I took an instant dislike to the man, sensing a lack of sincerity, and that the tragic occasion was merely a public relations exercise for him. From then on I viewed the man with suspicion, considering him to be smooth enough to slide uphill.

In Johannesburg he arrived with a big splash, creating publicity and photo opportunities for himself by the score. Every internal staff publication sang his praises to an almost obscene extent. To me, the whole scenario was reminiscent of a old time 'Snake Oil' salesman arriving in a tiny frontier town and grabbing the attention of all the inhabitants through his flamboyant antics.

His team from the American consulting firm Bain Consultants, for whom he had previously worked, practically took over the Flight Operations building as they performed a six week study delving into all that was wrong at SAA. They found plenty wrong, although very little with the flight crews or Technical as evidenced in an extract from the University of Cape Town Business School study titled The Turnaround of South African Airways: 1998 – 2000. (A rather ironic title in the light of hindsight.)

'What was working well at SAA was the performance of the entire flight deck and cockpit crews (sic), who were ranked among the very best in Asia, Europe or the United States. The airline also had a high technical proficiency although costs in this area were too high'.

One would have thought that, in the light of that, Andrews would have left the flight deck and Technical alone, while he fixed the bits of the airline which were truly broken, but this was not to be.

TO HELL WITH SAA'S PROUD HISTORY!

One of the first results of this six week study was the announcement by Andrews that SAA was to withdraw support for the Historic Flight, as it was not the 'core business' of the airline. The SAA Historic Flight was in fact SAA's corporate museum. It was maintained by very dedicated members drawn in the main from the technical and pilot bodies that dedicated thousands of hours of their own time to this end. The Historic Flight had no staff paid by SAA.

Companies of all sizes that are proud of their heritage have museums. One example being the Mercedes Benz museum in Stuttgart, and one can merely imagine the reaction should an incoming CEO attempt to shut it down, as it was not the 'core business' of a motor manufacturer. The fact that Andrews was considered a blow in from America with no appreciation of SAA's proud history did not help either. Thus one of Andrews first actions as head of SAA alienated a large group of staff and won him no friends amongst the technical and pilot groups. The Historic Flight created plenty of good publicity for SAA and, considering the slim savings to be gleaned from shutting it down, the game was scarcely worth the candle.

SAA'S NEW HISTORY AS SEEN BY ANDREWS

To rub salt into the wound after his assault on our history, a little over a year later, he commissioned Denis Beckett to write a book with the rather narcissistic title of, *'JETLAG SA Airways in the Andrews Era'*. Denis Beckett was an author of several books but better known to South Africans for his SABC TV series, 'Beckett's Trek'. This blatant bit of ego stroking that this book represented cost SAA, or effectively the SA taxpayer, R300,000 and was apparently considered by Andrews to be part of the core business of an airline.

THE AMERICAN INVASION

After six weeks the Bain consultants did not return to America, and what came to be known as 'The American Invasion' had begun. The consultants were mostly very young, cool, hip, recently graduated, long on theory, short on practical experience, reminiscent of escapees from the Ally McBeal television series and always underfoot in the corridors of Flight Operations.

They spoke in corporate buzzwords and terms such as 'corporate synergy, cascading down, deep dive, ideate, wheelhouse, low hanging fruit, bandwidth, ping' and the like flew around like flies at an Australian picnic. To raise even more resentment, for each so called consultant SAA was billed at an hourly rate that would have hired more than a dozen bright young graduates from our own universities.

Of course, I was in no position to judge the expertise of these consultants until the day I was asked to attend a rostering lecture by one of them, this being a field I knew a little about, as for years we had been designing pairings and doing our own rosters on the Cape Fleet. It was probably the reason I was asked to attend as no other pilots were amongst the attending roster clerks.

Pairings are how flights are put together, to be operated by a crew in the most efficient manner. For example a pairing may be to operate Cape Town

– Johannesburg – Durban – Johannesburg – Cape Town on the same day. To design efficient pairings it is necessary to take into account, aircraft availability, positioning, maintenance requirements, connecting flights, crew flight and duty regimes and many other complicating factors.

A roster is a programme consisting of pairings that a pilot will operate over a month. It will also indicate standby or flight watch days, any training days and days that he or she are not rostered for duties but are available with the required notice for duty should the need arise.

They are, in fact, a monthly 'map' of a pilots life. They must comply with complicated Flight and Duty Regulations designed to avoid fatigue and ensure a safe operation. They should be flexible enough to cater for personal emergences and they should also be empathetic. For instance to roster a pilot for an off day returning him from a flight the day before at 23.00 and sending him out at 05.00 the day after, although legal in terms of Flight and Duty, would not be considered empathetic rostering.

The 'lecturer" was one of Bain's young 'yuppies' and after ten minutes I came to the conclusion that she had no inkling of what she was talking about and had obviously never compiled a block of pairings or drawn up a roster, yet here she was supposedly giving a lecture on the subject to people who had for years been doing just that. For this we were being billed an hourly rate that would have made a Senior Counsel blush.

THE ANDREWS'S WILD WEST SHOW

During all this the Andrews show rolled on, very reminiscent of Buffalo Bill Cody's Wild West Circus, with Andrews very much the ringmaster and bathing in the light of publicity and photo opportunities. The 'Laduma car' scheme was introduced whereby if on-time departure targets were exceeded staff would be given the chance to win one of the two cars that would be raffled at a ceremony held every few months in a huge maintenance hanger. Entertainers, dance troupes and singers would be hired for the occasion. These raffles raised a certain amount of resentment when, on two occasions, the cars were won by Senior Captains.

Andrews further alienated a section of the airline and in fact the South African public by decreeing that Afrikaans was no longer to be utilised in cabin PA announcements and that it would be optional for cockpit PA announcements. I recall having to go back to the cabin in order to calm a rapidly escalating incident as a result of this edict. There I found a nineteen year old hostess in tears as a result of three hulking great men taking out their frustrations upon her.

Understanding that they felt their language was under attack and having a certain amount of sympathy for their point of view, their reaction was misdirected and intolerable. Very calmly, I asked them if they genuinely believed that the lovely young lady, who was now in floods of tears, was responsible for SAA's new policy? To their credit, when that realisation struck home, they immediately apologised profusely to her. Having been saved the paperwork storm that would have resulted from having them arrested after landing, I took a great delight in providing them with the name of the person responsible for the new policy and giving them Andrews' contact details.

Many flight delays were caused by cabin crew members booking off sick in unacceptable numbers and particularly over weekends. To combat this Andrews had, what he thought, was a clever idea. He would send drivers into the townships and to the homes of the 'off sick' cabin crew members in order to deliver fruit baskets with get well cards. Of course, should the sick ones not be home to receive their fruit baskets they would be for the high jump on returning to work.

This ploy was not well received by the union and they distributed a notice to their members. This notice addressed the members as 'Comrades' and read as published:

'BOOKING OFF SICK.

It is a right in the 1st main agreement to book-off sick. A right we are prepared to reserve and uphold. Anyone who questions that right, is merely overlooking or undermining our agreement. Under no circumstances shall any employee come to work if he/she is booked off-sick by;

A) A certified medical doctor.

B) A traditional healer recognised by the Medical Association of S.A.

Any ploy from management's part to question the credibility of the above metioned, will be undermining humanitarian principles (Ubuntu), the rights of human rights of the employees.

You should also note that it is ethically wrong to perform your duties as a Safety Officer whislt you endanger the safety of the aircraft and the passengers as well.

We would appreciate management's to look after the sick rather than investigation. I would recommend to management that they firstly consult, with your union, on issuses that concern your wellbeing.

We however reprimand them for prying into your private enviroment of the employees shall not be held liable for anything that happens to the messenger's vehicle which ferries the "fruit-baskets" especially in the townships and other "unsafe" havens (Katlehong, Alexander, Tembisa, Hillbrow and Eldorado Park) to name but a few'. (sic)

As it then required a very brave driver to carry out these missions, the clever scheme collapsed.

Andrews also appointed several Americans from his 'old boys club' to top positions in SAA after changing his title from CEO to President and changing the heads of departments titles from Executive Officers to Vice Presidents. Don Garvett to Executive VP Strategy and Planning, Bill Meaney to EVP Alliances and Network Strategy, Kevin Wilson EVP Technical and Cargo and Marilyn Hoppe in charge of Revenue Management. It is little wonder that the rank and file coined the phrase 'The American Invasion'. It was not long before Andrews had seventeen Vice Presidents reporting to him.

ANDREWS AND THE PILOTS

At the time of Andrews arrival the CEO of Flight Operations was the well liked and respected Peter Cooke. Andrews made poor Peter his 'hatchet man' and letters flew from Peter's office informing a variety of people that 'due to the redesign of management and leadership functions', their jobs were being made redundant and that they were free to apply for the same posts, with newly created titles, along with the other identified candidates. These redundancies applied not only to managers but to all levels of Flight Operations Staff.

A second major friction, involving the pilot group, came with Andrews refusing a salary increase as defined in the Maintenance of Parity agreement that the previous management and SAAPA had signed. This, as the name suggests, was to keep SAA pilot salaries vaguely in line with those of a spread of overseas and domestic carriers. We had fallen behind to the point where the agreement allowed a 25.7% increase. SAAPA was, however willing to accept 17% so as not to place too much of a burden on SAA's finances. Andrews idea of negotiation was to offer **minus** 15%.

Andrews, being so confident of his case, then agreed to a 'final and binding arbitration' where he hoped to persuade the arbitrator to award zero. To his great shock, the arbitration court awarded 17%. The true ethics of the man then became obvious when the following letter, signed by both Andrews and Peter Cooke and, which I copied from a faded fax, was distributed.

JOINT COMMUNIQUÉ

TO: *ALL FLIGHT DECK CREW*
SUBJECT: *MAINTENANCE OF PARITY ARBITRATION AWARD*
DATE: *30 JUNE 1998*

Today the arbitrator in the above arbitration presented the findings and award. The quantum of the award is 17%.

The Company has every intention of honouring agreements. But, obviously an award of this magnitude with its full implications would be entirely destructive of our efforts to revitalize South African Airways.

In representing the interests of the Company, we do have the right to take the arbitration award under review. Considering the present financial plight of our airline and the need to turn it around decisively, we will in all likelihood take the award under review.

Your understanding, patience and continued professional approach will be appreciated whilst we consider our options. You will be kept informed.

COLEMAN ANDREWS
CHIEF EXECUTIVE
SOUTH AFRICAN AIRWAYS

PETER COOKE
EXECUTIVE MANAGER
FLIGHT OPERATIONS

It was signed by both Andrews and Peter Cooke but the give away as to who had written it was in the spelling of 'revitalize'. It was the only 'Joint Communiqué' I ever saw that came from Andrews's office. I think that it was an attempt to draw Cooke into the unethical mess and was, in all probability, a 'bridge too far' for Peter who resigned soon thereafter.

Of course, the company had no legal grounds to review the arbitration proceedings, and when SAAPA threatened to take them to court, they reluctantly honoured the award but not before creating a great deal of unnecessary conflict and unhappiness within the pilot body.

FROM FIRST OFFICER TO VICE PRESIDENT IN ONE GIANT LEAP

Peter Cooke's resignation afforded Andrews the opportunity of making another of his controversial appointments that, all too often, followed along the lines of the 'Peter Principle' or were true to the axiom of being a little too clever for one's own good. This one, which impacted heavily on the pilots, was the appointment of Anton Richman to Vice President Flight Operations. This folly was described in Denis Beckett's book as a 'brainwave'. Most of the pilots described it as a 'brain fade'.

Anton was a junior First Officer who had obtained a law degree prior to forging a career in aviation. There was nothing particularly surprising about this, as many pilots had degrees, diplomas or tertiary qualifications in a wide variety of fields. Like nearly all of us, when Anton started as a pilot at SAA, he joined the South African Airways Pilots Association (SAAPA). Because he liked the law and to keep his legal mind sharp he volunteered his services to SAAPA's legal committee, where he made his mark as a valuable member and negotiator. He soon became a thorn in management's side with his sharp mind and legal skills, helping to negotiate several outcomes advantageous to the pilots.

Andrews thought that, with one fell swoop, he would remove access to Anton's skills from SAAPA and place them at management's disposal. He offered Anton the position of VP Flight Operations and gave him a day to decide. Previous heads of Flight Operations had been drawn from the ranks of Senior Captains. They had been with SAA a long time, had earned the respect of the pilot body, had huge presence and knew all aspects of the airline well.

Captains are, in effect, managers in their own right, as are their First Officers. A Boeing 747 400 may cost in excess of $200 million US and, depending on the seating configuration, more than 500 passengers and 16 plus crew. The Captain may be called upon to make decisions upon which lives and property, both in the air and on the ground depend, without the assistance of board meetings, management meetings or think tanks. Nor do they have the option to make use of consultants or even to go home and 'sleep on the problem'. In an airborne emergency they will not have a quiet office in which to think and their decisions may have to be made very quickly in a chaotic environment. When things do go horribly wrong halfway across an ocean they and their crew will be on their own and the only really useful resources will be within the confines of the aircraft.

Pilots did not fit into any management grading system within SAA and were of necessity, strong personalities with little patience for bureaucracy or company politics. As such they are not easy to manage particularly by anyone who has not earned their respect.

In the eyes of the pilot body, Anton did not have the seniority, maturity or the leadership strength to be in charge. To make matters worse, his defection to the other side was widely viewed as bordering on treason. This view was reinforced by what they suspected was his use of insider knowledge in attempts to nullify previously negotiated settlements between management and SAAPA. To further cloud the issue, Anton, in an effort to keep his flying licence current, was still flying as a junior First Officer and thus the Vice President and boss of Flight Operations was subservient to the fellow in the left seat whenever he was flight crew. Hardly a desirable recipe for a safe and sound operation.

Anton's promotion was a 'leap frogging' example of the 'Peter Principle' on steroids. For those unfamiliar with it, the 'Peter Principle' is a concept in management developed by Laurence J Peter which observes that people in a hierarchy tend to rise to their 'level of incompetence'. In other words, an employee is promoted based on their success in previous jobs until they reach a level at which they are no longer competent, as skills in one job do not necessarily translate to another. The concept was elucidated in the 1969 book 'The Peter Principle' by Peter and Raymond Hull.

The undoubted legal and negotiating skills that Anton had did not translate to his being in charge of seven hundred pilots. For a so called 'turn around expert' being paid a fortune, Andrews could have been expected to know that. Perhaps his judgement was clouded by his own cleverness in trying to deny SAAPA Anton's legal skills. So much for Beckett's 'brainwave'.

THE HAMBURGER MAN, THE GAMBLER AND THE SCHOOLMARM

Anton decided that, as in the past, the CEO Flight operations, negotiating with SAAPA contained the seeds of a conflict of interest. His reasoning was that, because the CEO was also a pilot, any benefits that accrued to the pilots in these negotiations would also accrue to the CEO, now Vice President. To obviate this he decided to assemble his own negotiating team.

This 'Dream Team' consisted of a recently appointed Human Resources Manager, Themba Sidaki who had previously been employed by MacDonalds, Peter Salemink an also recently appointed friend of Anton's who had previously been employed by a casino and Patricia Pargiter. I had been responsible for Patricia's appointment and induction into SAA, as my secretary and the first administrative support person on the Cape B737 Fleet. Previously she had been a domestic science teacher.

This 'Dream Team' was considered by most to be an insult to the pilot body and they were soon dubbed 'The Hamburger Man, The Gambler and The Schoolmarm'. They were soon to face an incredulous SAAPA negotiating team that was having great difficulty in believing that they actually had a mandate to negotiate anything. After much assurance from Sidaki that they had, negotiations went ahead and the successful outcome thereof was reported to the pilot body. A few days later everything they had negotiated was dishonoured by senior management and the whole negotiation had turned out to be a monumental waste of time. The relationship between management and the pilots reached a new low!

Another negotiation was arranged but this time Anton and the whole of Flight Operations management, would be in attendance. Managements objective was to attempt to change the priority status of the pilots in regard to on and off duty travel. This included an attempt to restrict pilots using the SAA lounges. A counter productive move, in my opinion, as when delays resulted in anger and frustration, passengers would gather around the Captain of their flights in the lounge, and so often the situation would be defused. The passengers using the lounges are often executives and prefer not to be dealt with by, all too often, junior ground staff who, unlike the flight crew, are not sharing the frustrations of the delay.

In an attempt to facilitate this downgrading of flight deck crew status, a document was produced by Sidaki titled 'Differentiation between Management and Flight Deck Crew'. I was not able to determine precisely who penned this document. It came from Human Resources and judging by letters from Sidaki' that I have seen, it fitted with his arrogant, bullying and pompous style of communication. I cannot however, due to the phraseology, rule out input from the other two suspects. It was a ridiculously divisive document that, under twelve headings, attempted to make the case that pilots were inferior to, and worth less then managers.

This document was read out and when the heading 'Freedom to Think' was reached and the meeting was informed that pilots think 'Within set procedures and parameters' while managers 'Design of own parameters and without clear precedent', the SAAPA President, John Harty stood, and furiously pointing a finger at Anton, loudly informed him that "If I take this shit to the members, they will hang you". The fat was now in the fire and amazingly both Anton and later Andrews, who did not attend the meeting, claimed that they had never read the document as incredible as that may seem. Needless to say, they were not believed and a new all time low was reached between the pilots and management. Below is an extract from a letter I wrote to John Harty at the time which summed up the way the pilots that I spoke to felt at the time.

I, as do my colleges on the Cape Fleet, find their little exercise of pumping up their own egos at the expense of the Flight Deck Crew, to be tasteless and tacky in the extreme. I can however not pretend to be surprised, having an intimate knowledge of the calibre, competence, track record and morality of certain of the individuals involved in our present so called management.
I am sure that any Pilot with half a brain could come up with an even longer FDC 'Full impact' and Management 'None' list, if we wanted to stoop to their level.
I was amused to note that they had the unmitigated gall to mention the word 'responsibility' six times in their comparison. To their credit however they did not mention the word 'accountability' even once.

As a result of this debacle, SAAPA called a Special General Meeting, to be held on the afternoon of 23rd January 2001, upon which the main item on the agenda was a vote of no confidence in management. In an attempt at a 'pre-emptive strike', management scheduled a meeting, at which Anton would explain management's position to any of the pilots who wished to attend. I attended the meeting and estimated that about sixty pilots were present. In my opinion, the cause of the low attendance was that morale was at an all time low, as was management's credibility, and most of the pilots saw no point in listening to anything management had to say.

Beckett claimed in his book that intimidation took place to encourage pilots not to attend. I neither saw nor heard any evidence of that. In fact, SAAPA published a letter advising against boycotting the meeting . In my experience, attempts to intimidate pilots into following a course of action, would invariably have the opposite effect and who would know this better than SAAPA? Beckett further quoted a pilot, apparently very impressed with Anton, as saying, after the meeting "We are in a big quest here, a noble quest". That does not sound like anything any SAA pilot I have ever known would say and I have to wonder about the source of this and other of Beckett's anonymous pilot quotes.

In contrast the later SAAPA meeting, at their offices in the nearby Kempton Park, was attended by over three hundred holding proxies for another four hundred pilots, who were flying or otherwise unable to attend. For the first time, the venue was too small to cater for the numbers that attended and many had to stand outside the hall. It was obvious, to anyone there, that the pilot body had reached the point of total disenchantment with management and a vote of no confidence was passed by a huge majority. A press release was prepared and articles about low pilot morale and its effect on flight safety appeared in the media.

At last Andrews stopped hiding behind Richman and was jolted into action. In the ensuing meetings he apologised profusely for management's part in the events that led up to the vote of no confidence, including the infamous insulting Differentiation between Management and Flight Deck Crew document.

R232,000,000 DOWN JACKSON HOLE

Andrews had, however, upset not only the pilot body, but many others in positions of power, particularly over predatory practices that had resulted in the demise of Sun Air. He departed SAA two weeks later to return, despite the name, to the very upmarket town of Jackson Hole in Wyoming. He did not return with empty pockets but with R232,000,000 of South African taxpayers money. This followed the R243,000,000 paid to Bain Consultants and the R119,000,000 paid to American expatriate VPs . It seemed that Charles T Cleaver's letter had been quite prophetic!

The VP Finances then took over as CEO and shortly admitted that the Andrews turnaround was "a nice story based on fragile issues" and not as rosy as South Africans had been led to believe. He stated that the seventeen Vice Presidents that reported to Andrews would be reduced to four CEOs. He intended moving Anton Richmond to a legal position within SAA but Richmond pre-empted this by resigning. As only two weeks previously, Richmond had informed me that I would need to reapply for my position as Flight Operations Manager of the Cape Fleet, I could not find it in my heart, at the time, to feel any sympathy for him. With the demise of the Andrews's regime all this went away and I remained in the position until my retirement in 2004.

Denis Beckett was also left floundering after Andrews departure and had great difficulty in finding anyone in SAA management who would talk to him. He did, nevertheless, manage to finish his book which is humorously written and a good read. I must, however take issue with some of his rather sweeping and sensation evoking statements regarding pilots.

His chapter titled 'In the Cockpit' opens with: *'An airline pilot is the most pampered animal in the industrial zoo. He works as many hours per month as your average yuppie puts in per week. His income is stratospheric. Most of his time on duty consists of sitting in a leather armchair with little on his mind and a spectacular view before his eyes. For ninety-eight percent of his working life his conditions are the epitome of restfulness'.*

Firstly Denis falls into the all too common delusion, possibly through superficial research, of assuming flying hours are the sum of working hours to which, in fact, they bear no resemblance. Flying hours are sector chock to chock times that a pilot enters into his logbook.

Working hours are from sign on to sign off and include the mandatory hour before departure that a domestic pilot is required to sign on. They also include the hours hanging around airports between turn arounds and the mandatory half hour debriefing at Flight Operations when his flight pairing terminates. A pilot's logbook does not reflect the hours he spends sitting in a classroom during courses and endless refreshers or the hours spent with his nose in the books. Nor does it reflect standbys, flight watches, reserve duties, positioning or dead heading flights. His hours as collated by the airline for statistical purposes do not even include the many hours spent sweating in simulators.

From personal experience, one could roughly double flying hours to reflect working hours as a reasonable ball park figure. Thus a pilot writing twenty hours a week in his logbook is generally working forty hours or possibly more. Show me the yuppie working four times that at one hundred and sixty hours a week.

Secondly, 'astronomical incomes'? Not really Denis, not when the fellow that commissioned you to write the book was making over one hundred times the salary of a senior Captain at the time. When you use the word 'astronomical' to describe salaries, you are in the world of the corporation big wigs, and there are plenty of them around airlines. In 2018 Alan Joyce of Qantas took home 23.88 million Australian dollars, roughly 240 million rand.

Thirdly, 'ninety eight percent of a pilot's working life the epitome of restfulness'? No doubt the source of this nonsense was the same management clowns that came up with the Differentiation document. An airline pilot is the most rigorously poked, prodded, checked, tested, examined, refreshed, retrained and monitored individual on the planet. Every six months a mandatory comprehensive medical which may include stress cardiograph and lung function testing.

Also at six monthly intervals a simulator test where multiple compound failures and emergences will have to be successfully handled. These tests may last for up to five hours and are exhausting. Failing either of these could lead to the loss of ones licence to fly and termination of employment. Failing the additional regular route checks in the aircraft could result in a similar outcome.

In addition to all this there are the annual refreshers and exams in Emergency Procedures which include fire fighting, ditching in the ocean, evacuations and the like. There are also the refreshers in Cockpit Management Training, Weight and Balance, Aircraft Technical and Extended Range Operations. Pilots are also expected to be up to date on all changes to aviation law, updates to navigation and procedural charts, Standard Operating Procedures, amendments to aircraft manuals, of which there are dozens each year, and company policy. In fact a pilot spends a good deal of his working life with his nose in the books and rightly so. I have often wondered, by how much the ranks of other professions would be thinned if they were subjected to a similarly rigorous and continuous regime in order to be able to practice their professions.

All of these factors add up to far more than two percent of a pilot's working life and could hardly be described as the 'epitome of restfulness' despite the fact that up to this point no in-flight stresses have been involved. Denis goes on to say 'The unrestful portion may amount to twenty hours in his year'. Really? I have had more than twenty 'unrestful' hours during three weeks of, mainly five leg, double coastal flights during periods of howling winds, rain and fog.

Denis also goes on to describe Cockpit Management Training as 'a total revolution in aviation, a radical swing'. In referring to the pre CMT Captain he uses phrases such as, a god, a sole arbitrator and a dictator. As far as SAA was concerned, as both a copilot and a Captain, I found that a great majority of Captains I flew with operated within CMT principles, which were really nothing more than common sense, long before anyone formalised and labelled them as CMT. Sure, we had a small minority of one man bands but in all honesty no amount of classroom CMT was going to make a leopard change its spots when unobserved in the privacy of the cockpit.

THE EVER STEEPENING SLIPPERY SLOPE

Six months after Andrews' departure at the end of March, Viljoen announced that up until March SAA made a net profit of R408,000,000 but after subtracting property and aircraft that had been sold, a loss of R735,000,000 was revealed. Viljoen's appointment surprised many people. He had presided over SAA finances during Andrews stint with the airline and hardly distinguished himself as the CEO. The least rude thing Robert Kirby, of the Daily Mail and Guardian, called him was 'that famous corpse impersonator'.

Andrews did not only fail to turn SAA around but also presided over many failed projects. Amongst these was the 'All Africa Hub', the 'saa.com' and the 'Veer' website fiascos.

SAA is still feeling financial repercussions from the Andrews's and Viljoen era as in 2017 the courts awarded Comair R1.16 billion for SAA's anti-competitive behaviour in a scheme that ran from 2000 to 2005.

Andrews had also negatively impacted heavily on the lives and flying careers of two pilots. Peter Cooke was a very well respected and popular CEO, he was young, personable and had modern management ideas. In the normal course of events he would have had a long and fruitful career in SAA.

As for Anton, an enormous carrot was, for dubious reasons, dangled in front of a very young man who was forced into making a life changing decision, with unseemly haste, by a smart operator, with ulterior motives. One who would have no trouble selling 'snake oil'. Thus Anton became one of Andrews' victims and lost his flying career in the process.

Viljoen's departure was followed by a long line of political appointees none of which were appointed for their track records in the airline industry. Possibly the worst and most notable being a cohort of President Jacob Zuma, Dudu Myeni who the courts have recently declared a 'Delinquent Director'.

SAA started life as Union Airways in 1929, was taken over by the government and became SAA in 1934. The sixties saw a great deal of expansion and the orange tails were introduced with the arrival of the Boeing 707s. These orange tails were familiar sights at at airports all over the world and the 'springbok' call sign well known in aviation circles everywhere.

In its rich history SAA has faced and overcome many challenges including years of sanctions, that forced the uneconomic routeing around the bulge to be flown, with its penalties in fuel and time. Despite this SAA was able to remain competitive and viable.

What SAA was not able to survive was the last twenty odd years of corruption, nepotism, cronyism, greed, incompetence, ineptitude and social engineering. Had not great taxpayer funded bailouts been regularly injected into its coffers, the demise of a once great airline would have come much sooner, and long before the Covid crisis which merely slightly speeded up the inevitable outcome.

It was very sad for me, from retirement, to have witnessed the destruction of an airline I loved and gave thirty eight years of my life to. How much more tragic for all the loyal staff who no longer have an income and very little chance of reemployment in an industry they love!

I, personally, have always felt that the slippery slope commenced with the resignation of Mike Myburgh, but steepened considerably with Saki Macozoma's appointment of Coleman Andrews who, in my opinion, had little understanding of Africa and whose confidence far exceeded his ability to turn SAA around.

Having said that, in all fairness, I do believe that, had Andrews never been appointed, the eventual outcome would have been the same.

22

CAREER'S END

I nevitably, and all too soon my sixtieth birthday approached and on the 26th of July 2003 I was rostered for my last flight with SAA. It was on a Boeing 737-800 and was to Johannesburg and back.

My co-pilot, Joanne, was the first lady pilot that I had ever flown with, and of whom I was very fond. I guess she felt the same way about me as she had been the first co-pilot to put in a special request to fly with me on my last flight. Corleen also accompanied us as a passenger.

I had always loved the beautiful scenic descent and approach into Cape Town and a great sadness swept over me as the realisation hit me that this would be the last time I would do this in command of an airliner. I had hoped to treat my last passengers to a panoramic flight around the Cape Peninsula but unfortunately the weather did not play along and a layer of low cloud obscured it.

As we taxied in my mood lifted as fire engines on either side of the taxiway used their water cannons to create a great sparkling arch for us to pass under as we entered the hardstand where I saw practically the whole Cape Fleet in, uniform, lined up and waiting to welcome and conduct us to a little informal party that they had organised at the airport.

A week later my official retirement party was held at a restaurant near the Stellenbosch Flying Club. It was a grand affair and I was presented with a beautiful oil painting of a rural scene at the foot of the Swartberg Mountains in the Little Karoo, an area that everyone knew was close to my heart.

One of our Captains, Chris, who had flown many hours as my co-pilot and who owned a much loved Tiger Moth, decided that the last entry in my logbook should reflect the same aircraft type as the first, a very touching gesture.

A few days later I entered:

> 'De Havilland Tiger Moth DH82A ---ZS-DNP--- 1 hour'

into my logbook and with great sadness closed it for the last time.

www.ingramcontent.com/pod-product-compliance
Lightning Source LLC
Chambersburg PA
CBHW021943290426
44108CB00012B/950